HISTORY

of

YORK COUNTY

FROM ITS ERECTION TO THE PRESENT TIME;
[1729-1834]

BY

W. C. CARTER & A. J. GLOSSBRENNER.

NEW EDITION; WITH ADDITIONS
Edited by
A. MONROE AURAND, JR.

Privately Printed:
THE AURAND PRESS: HARRISBURG, PA.
NINETEEN HUNDRED THIRTY

Notice

In many older books, foxing (or discoloration) occurs and, in some instances, print lightens with wear and age. Reprinted books, such as this, often duplicate these flaws, notwithstanding efforts to reduce or eliminate them. The pages of this reprint have been digitally enhanced and, where possible, the flaws eliminated in order to provide clarity of content and a pleasant reading experience.

HISTORY OF YORK COUNTY, PENNSYLVANIA,
FROM ITS ERECTION TO THE PRESENT TIME;
[1729-1834]

Originally published
Harrisburg, Pennsylvania
1930

Reprinted by:

Janaway Publishing, Inc.
2412 Nicklaus Dr.
Santa Maria, California 93455
(805) 925-1038
www.janawaygenealogy.com

2009

ISBN 10: 1-59641-179-1
ISBN 13: 978-1-59641-179-1

Made in the United States of America

YORK COUNTY

Limited Edition

This edition is limited to One Thousand copies;
numbered and signed.

Number

COURT-HOUSE,

YORK, PA.

The Building in which the American Congress sat during the gloomiest period of the Revolution.

INTRODUCTION TO THIS EDITION.

YORK COUNTY, PENNSYLVANIA, established by Legislative procedure on August 19, 1749, from part of Lancaster county, marks the birthday of a great political and civil division in Pennsylvania. This county was the scene of many early conflicts with nature; yet its subsequent triumph and final emergence among the uppermsot of all counties in importance to any and all worth-whole achievements, is now a matter of history. Handicapped with poor soil, unwelcome guests, land titles hard to acquire, and many other incidents quite disturbing to a struggling pioneer people, we now see how they cheerfully made the best of their many, many problems.

The present day populace of York county is very much the same type of honest, steady-going, industrious, home-loving, thrifty, intelligent, religious and genuinely patriotic people as those who commenced its first and continued settlements just two hundred years ago (1729).

Dividing the county into smaller divisions, one notes the generous distribution of German, English and Irish towns and townships. This admixture and commingling of the races just mentioned has made York county signally fortunate and rich in her industry, wealth and history. To write a complete history of the past two hundred years of York county would require the life-time efforts of several scholars, to say the least; not to mention the costs in dollars and cents. So an enlarged history is not our subject at all.

Only too true is it, that every single day, every week, month, year, etc., is making new history. Newspapers, doctors, lawyers, ministers, teachers, businessmen and farmers are the mediums through which the process operates. It is only too true that America, of all important nations in the world, can say with a degree of accuracy that she knows most of her history from the beginning. It is good for us that our active history—American history—does not go back too far. Much that we would like to know of America's early years, however, is buried with the past, and there are but few living today who can read the "signs" which the passing decades are more and more successfully obliterating.

To most persons historically inclined, the 1700's are the years wherein history was made—and of these years we love to read about. So many wars, and other privations were borne by the pioneers in the New Land that all of the 18th Century may be said to have been the "nebular" years, or period when the pioneers were to adjust and adapt themselves to soil, new associations, mode of living and environment generally. Out of those years of struggling for existence have come the men most famous in America's early history.

It was but natural that the continued healthy growth of the New Nation would induce the publishing of innumerable books and pamphlets dealing with every sort of subject conceivable, running the gamut of the alphabet. Historical treatises, quite extensive, were plentiful even before the close of the 1700's. These were, however, usually general in their scope, and included such as Proud's *History of Pennsylvania*, Philadelphia, 1797, (2 vols.); Franklin's *Historical Review of the Constitution and Government of Pennsylvania*, published in London, 1759; various titles by William Penn on the New Province; Loskiel's *History of the Indians of North America*," London, 1794; Smith's *History of Pennsylvania*," &c., and other titles, quite numerous.

The 1800's, following closely after the adoption of a permanent constitution for the government of the United States, saw a great deal of activity in the New World, and the publishing of books, magazines, newspapers and tracts was on in earnest. Many missionaries and travellers had gone up and down through the land and their records and diaries commenced to appear as if by magic. Choice lands, tendered patriotic leaders and officers of the Revolution, now made more safe for the whites, were taken up quite rapidly. Industry flourished; frontier towns not long since, were becoming more or less aged, and settled; canals were built; roads rebuilt and others laid out.

About a hundred years after the first settler had come in to what is now York county, and canals were now proving their value as a means of transportation, the proponents of the steam railroad had triumphed—the steam engine for railroad purposes had proven a success. (In after years the city of York had a large part in the development of the locomotive). Simultaneously with the first demonstration of the value of the railroad, there appeared in Philadelphia, one of the most interesting and valuable periodicals published during the second and third decades of the last century—Samuel Hazard's *Weekly Register of Pennsylvania*. Containing as it did, information of almost every sort from over the entire State, it is outstanding to this day, as a source periodical for the student. It must have been a source of inspiration to many readers of a century ago, and at this day and age, from a rather professional point of view, it appears to have been a "work of love," for it was rather short-lived, having been issued from 1828 to 1836, when it passed away from a lack of nourishment.

This is a mere pencil point picture of general conditions as they were up to the time of the close of the first hundred years of the history of York, looking toward the time when Mr. W. C. Carter, a student of history, made a number of notes gathered in various parts of the county, and which were, after his death, the basis for publishing the first county history of any county in the Commonwealth of Pennsylvania. Mr. Carter may or may not have had an inspiration from such periodicals as Hazard's *Register*, or his interests may have been developed locally and naturally. Left, as they were, in a skeleton form on Mr. Carter's death, Mr. A. J. Glossbrenner, a comparative newcomer in York at that time (1831-34), acquired these "notes" and expanded and enlarged on them until they all came into print and subsequently became the *History of York County*.

As an initial venture let it be said here to the credit of these early writers, that those who followed in their footsteps in writing local York county history, have had nothing but praise for the interesting, concise, accurate, admirable and scholarly accounts. George R. Prowell, the eminent historian of York county, in Gibson and Prowell's *History of York County,* (1886) says: "The *History of York County* (1834) contains facts concerning the early history of the press of York county. It was evidently prepared with great care, and, like other parts of the same work, has much valuable information, which, if the book had not been published, would now be lost to history."

The Carter and Glossbrenner *History* is credited as being "quite good," etc., by any number of others who have had occasion to use it for reference and source purposes.

In setting the type for this edition, the first complete reprint, coming, as it does, ninety-six years after the original edition, the undersigned was greatly surprised to note the uniform regularity of its general make-up, and the almost total absence of errors in the spelling of proper names, as well as those we commonly term "typographical errors." A few notable minor exceptions are that some words are divided in the original edition, different from the accepted way of today. Some few transpositions may be noted in the original edition, which would not necessarily be noticeable to the average student, and in this reprint we have followed closely, word for word, the entire text of the original edition.

In less than half a dozen instances have we added brackets [ ] where clarification was desired. Short "and" (&) was used where it appears in the original, which sometimes, it appears to us, was used by the original compositor to save time in filling out a line, rather than that the "&" was "style" and "proper."

While the names of attorneys, and the various State and county officers, etc., appeared in quite large type in the original edition, we deemed it a desirable and justifiable departure from the old arrangement to place these names in smaller type and in two columns to a page, instead of one column. This enables us to produce a more attractive page, and robs no one, at this time, of any "publicity." In the furtherance of our plan to produce a creditable reprint of this pioneer county history, we have employed the use of an old style type, which, we believe you will agree, lends much toward its attractiveness.

The *frontispiece* of the original edition is herewith reproduced, exactly as it was known to the residents of York in the early 1800's. It was engraved as the artist knew it best, which (since it was engraved in 1833-34) included several notable changes that had been made after Congress held its sessions therein in 1777-78. When Congress met in York the court house had gables at two ends only, none appearing at the front of the structure, such as that part containing the "rainbow" window; nor was all the superstructure, or cupola as depicted in our edition, on the building when Congress met therein—half of it being added some years after Congress returned to Philadelphia. Reference to these facts are made at this time because of some confusion that arises when persons inadvertently are led to believe that Congress met in the court house as pictured in the original edition of 1834, and now again reproduced. Congress met in this building, without question, but some years after that the building was remodeled, probably twice, or so, as we now show. An artist's reconstruction of the original court house, with floor plans, etc., complete in every detail, has been made within the past five years, based on old documents in York and Lancaster, the previous county seat. These reconstructed views have recently appeared in the York directory, and several other reports issued at celebrations in that city.

Springettsbury Manor is sometimes spelled with one "t," and sometimes with two. The Penn for whom the Manor was named was known as "Springett" Penn, and the 1834 history spells it "Springettsbury." We have followed that spelling in this reprint. This spelling is at variance with that of the Surveyor, Jno. Lukens, who resurveyed the Manor "In pursuance of a warrant of resurvey under the hand of James Hamilton Esqr" etc., "dated 21st day of May 1762." The re-survey was "returned into the Secretary's office," as of "12th day of July Anno Dom: 1768." The original return of this resurvey, which may be seen on file at Harrisburg, bears but one "t." A copy of this resurvey is included in Vol. IV, Third Series, *Pennsylvania Archives*, part 63. It is therefore fairly safe to assume that the ancient spelling would be "Springetsbury."

Another of the Proprietary Manors laid out by William Penn, was that sometimes spelled "Springgetsbury Manor," of 1840 acres; granted in 1703, at Philadelphia.

Volume III, *Colonial Records*, pages 184-5, we read under "Copy of Warrant for Surveying the 'Mannor of Springetsbury'," (1722) the return of Messrs. "Colo. John French, Francis Worley, & James Mitchell, Esqrs.," that they completed the survey of the "Mannor of Springets-Bury, upon the River Sasquahannah," etc.

Ancient spellings are bound to vary from generation to generation, and while these variations ought to be guarded against, they cannot well be avoided or ignored, since they are ever-present. In other words, the crossing of a "t," or dotting of an "i," are not nearly so important as getting at the meat of the nuts! Facts should not be set aside because of mere fancy!

The reader will note in the present edition the reproduction of an early map of the county of York, which then also included what is now Adams county. This map is copied from one made for the Proprietaries, by William Scull, in 1770. The map appears as it has come to the undersigned, and there can be no doubt but that its reproduction in this edition will be appreciated by many who have never seen its counterpart before. It details many roads, towns and ferries, which may or may not be exactly as the historians of today think they ought to be. So far as we can learn, it has been a faithful reproduction of the county and surrounding counties, as nearly so as the cartographer knew how to make it.

York county is rich in historical material—much of it lying dormant. Almost without exception, those who have published any histories about the county have always referred to its first history. Thus we note such as Prof. I. D. Rupp, Sherman Day, John Gibson, George R. Prowell, etc.

John Gibson, in his "Introductory" to the *History of York County*, (1886) has this to say regarding the edition of 1834: "A complete history to its time, was written by Glossbrenner and Carter—a work well known to the citizens of the borough of York, but copies of which are now scarce (1886).

The great amount of information contained in it, the accuracy of its details of facts, and the pleasing style of its composition, as well as the curious nature of its contents, have made it a literary production." Gibson further states: "The work, therefore, ought to be perpetuated for the benefit of our people."

The preceding statement was made in 1886, by one of York county stock, who was prompted by the most sincere regards and motives, and forty-four years have elapsed since his petition was made, and which, with the publication of this edition, is now come to fruition.

History, being the true account of the lives and accomplishments of a people over a period of years, such as have passed since the first settlement of York county, ought not be left unlearned and unloved. The heritage of a people is that which our forebears have made and left at their going. Without any mental reservation or evasion whatever, it seems but right and proper that there is not a single thing in the world that ought to interest the people of York county more than * * *the people of York county!*

If the achievements of those of the pioneer days are not worthy of mention and study at this day and age, of how much less value and appreciation will our labors appear to those of a not-far-off-tomorrow?

The men in the shops, in the fields, in the offices; the professional men and the tots in school ought to and must be made more fully acquainted with their coming into the community through a generous and right-thinking ancestry; and there is no more profitable, agreeable and consistent way in which this education of the people can be accomplished, than through an applied study and reading of just such books as local history, in all the schools and homes of the county.

It is because of a firm belief that York county's traditions have always been of an ideal nature, and that Messrs. Carter and Glossbrenner have given to them a type of book second to none for the home, school and office, that this edition of a very scarce book, is again made available to all.

A. MONROE AURAND, JR.

HARRISBURG, PA., *May* 1930.

PREFACE.

In presenting to the public a "History of York County," I deem it not improper to state, that of the two persons named on the title page as joint authors of the "History," the first named was the originator of the work.

Mr. Carter labored assiduously, for several years, in collecting matter for a "History of York County." He spent many a day in wandering over remote parts of the county in search of such facts as had no record but in the memory of the silver haired representatives of a generation long passed away. Many a weary hour he spent in examining, page by page, the old records in our public offices. In short, no pains were spared by him in the effort to gather all the materials requisite to the accomplishment of the object he had in view. From some cause which I have been unable to learn, Mr. Carter, when he had nearly completed the work, laid aside his manuscripts in a crude and unfinished state, in which condition I found them when, several years after his death, they came into my possession.

Having hurriedly thown together such of the notes as I found completed, I commenced printing the work. In doing so I erred. For it has led to the necessity of here apologizing for slight deviation from *order* in presenting the matter of the volume.

In the hurry of printing, I was often compelled, while one sheet was in the press, to prepare matter for the next; and as Mr. Carter's notes on some subjects were mere *skeletons*, and on others nearly ready for the hands of the compositor, I was sometimes induced to silence the call for "more copy," by handing to the workmen such matter as could most readily be prepared. This was sometimes done without a very strict enquiry as to *the right of immediate succession* of the article thus prepared. It is hoped, however, that, as the reader loses nothing in quantity of matter, he will pardon the slight deviation from correctness in the *order* in which that matter is given. The dishes announced in the bill of fare will all be found—but they are not arranged on the table exactly in the order in which a regular *professor de cuisine* would have desired.

I cannot close this preface without tendering my thanks to many gentlemen in the county for their kind aid during the progress of the work—to the Register and Recorder for their courtesy in allowing me freely to examine the records in their respective offices—and to Calvin Mason, Esq., for a geological sketch of the county.

Confident that all the promises in the prospectus have been more than redeemed—that they have been exceeded in the fulfilment, I hope that the work, as it is now respectfully presented to the public, will meet a kind and general reception.

The Public's very obedient servant,

A. J. GLOSSBRENNER.

History of York County.

CHAPTER I.

INDIAN PURCHASE.

SOON after the first arrival of William Penn in the province of Pennsylvania, which was in the year 1682, he took measures to have the river Susquehanna and all the lands lying on both sides of it, purchased of the Indians for the use of him and his heirs. The lands were not then the property of the Indians who dwelt on them: for in a war some years preceding that time, the original inhabitants along the banks of the Susquehanna had been conquered by their more powerful though not more warlike enemies. The Indians of the Five Nations, who dwelt principally in what is now the state of New-York, were conquerors in the savage war; and in right of such their victory, they had or claimed a right to all the lands possessed by their southern neighbors. It was to them, therefore, that Penn was to apply in making a purchase of the lands on both sides of the river Susquehanna.

As Penn's time was wholly occupied by affairs immediately within the limits of his infant province, he had not leisure to visit New-York and there make a purchase of the Indians in person. Being so circumstanced, he employed as an agent, upon this occasion, Colonel Thomas Dongan, who had been governor of New-York, and was, afterwards, earl of Limerick, in Ireland.

Dongan held a number of councils with the Indians, and at last purchased, or had given him, "all that tract of land lying on both sides of the river Susquehanna, and the lakes, adjacent, in or near the province of Pennsylvania," "beginning at the mountains or head of said river, and running as far as and into the bay of Chesapeak." What Dongan gave the Indians for this land, we do not know; but, having purchased it, he conveyed it to Penn on the 13th day of January, 1696, "in consideration of one hundred pounds sterling."

Dongan's deed was confirmed on the 13th day of September, 1700, by a deed given to Penn by "*WIDAGH & ADDAGYJUNKQUAGH, Kings or Sachems of the Susquehanna Indians.*" This deed is "for all the river Susquehanna and all the islands therein, and all the lands lying on both sides of the said river, and *next adjoining to the same,* to the utmost confines of the lands which are, or formerly were, the right of the people or nation called the *Susquehanna Indians.*"

The Conestogoe Indians were displeased with the sale made by the Five Nations, believing that the latter tribe had no right to make it. They accordingly complained to Penn; and he, in their presence, took out the deed of parchment, and, laying it on the ground, told them that the lands should still be in common between his people and them. The Conestogoes again made complaints concerning this purchase at their treaty with Sir William Keith in 1722.

As yet the lands on the west side of the Susquehanna were not considered as purchased of the Indians; for the words in the deed of 1700, "*next adjoining to the same,*" were inconsistent with an extensive westward purchase; and the Indians of the Five Nations still continued, notwithstanding their deeds, to claim a right to the river and the adjoining lands. The sachems or chiefs, with all the others of the Five Nations, met in the summer of 1736, at a great council held in the country of the Onondagoes; and as the old claims had not as yet been adjusted, they resolved, that a conclusion should be put to all disputes connected therewith. They accordingly appointed their sachems or chiefs as plenipotentiaries to repair to Philadelphia, and there, among other things, settle and adjust all demands and claims connected with the Susquehanna and the adjoining lands. After their arrival at Philadelphia, they renewed old treaties of friendship, and on the 11th of October made a deed to John, Thomas and Richard Penn. The deed, which was signed by twenty-three Indian chiefs of the *Onondagoe, Seneca, Oneida* and *Tuscurora* nations, granted "all the river Susquehanna, and all the lands lying on the west side of the said river to the setting of the sun, and to extend northward up the same to the hills or mountains called, in the language of the Five Nations, *Tayamentesachta,* and by the Delaware Indians, the *Kekachtanamin* hills." On that day, (the 11th of October, 1736,) and not before, do we find the lands of this part of Pennsylvania clearly the property of the Penns, and freed from all Indian claims.

It is a thing which may well excite wonder that a hundred years ago the Indians possessed the fields and the valleys which we not cultivate, and that at present there is hardly a trace or a mark of such beings ever having existed. They seem to have passed away like the beasts that then inhabited the wilderness, leaving no monument of a former existence.

When Springettsbury Manor was laid out in 1722, this part of Pennsylvania was (with the exception of the Maryland intruders) inhabited by none but Indians. In the year 1736, when the lands west of the Susquehanna were purchased of the Indians, the only white settlements in the county, were *firstly,* under Pennsylvania rights, within the limits of Springettsbury Manor, and *secondly,* under Maryland rights, in the southern part of this county, and of what is now Adams county, including the region round about Hanover. The rest of the lands was in the undisturbed possession of the Indians. Even in the white settlements the Indians still had huts.

CHAPTER II.

SPRINGETTSBURY MANOR.

ABOUT the year 1684, a violent dispute arose between William Penn and Lord Baltimore, concerning the boundary line between Pennsylvania and Maryland. The dispute continued until the death of Penn, in the year 1718, when it assumed, on the part of the Marylanders, a character of violence and aggression hitherto unknown to it. Their object was to make settlements many miles up into the present state of Pennsylvania; and having thus taken possession of the lands, to hold them by the strong arm of power. With these views they pushed their settlement with great rapidity along the Susquehanna: even in 1722, many of them were within a short distance of the present borough of York.

Such quick work, and energetic proceedings on the part of the Marylanders frightened Sir William Keith, who was then Lieutenant Governor of the province of Pennsylvania. Keith being zealous for the proprietary interest, was anxious to hinder these encroachments on what he believed to be the property of the heirs of Penn; but affairs were so circumstanced, that he hardly knew how to attempt the fulfilment of his strong wish.

The lands had not, as yet, been purchased from the Indians by the proprietor of Pennsylvania, and much less by that of Maryland. The adherents of Lord Baltimore, little caring whether the land was purchased or not, were pressing onward with great eagerness, and were threatening to settle the whole country. The policy of Penn ever had been to grant no rights to lands, and to permit no settlements on them, until purchased of the Indians. Sir William Keith wished to keep off the Marylanders, and yet, by the usage and laws of the province, was unable to grant rights to Pennsylvanians. To extricate himself from this difficulty, he bethought himself of a plan, which in its consequences has been the source of great trouble to the landholders of this county: it was immediately to consult the Indians in the neighborhood of the Susquehanna, and obtain their consent to the making of a large survey west of the river.

Accordingly, Governor Keith consulted or held a treaty with the Indians at Conestogoe, on the 15th and 16th of June, 1722, when they counselled together concerning the making of a survey for the use of Springett Penn, the grandson, and, as then believed, the heir of William Penn.

The following is a copy of the minutes of the council or treaty between Governor Keith and the Indians:

At a Council held with the Indians at Conestogoe, on the 15th of June, 1722—present

SIR WILLIAM KEITH, Bart., Governor,
COL. JOHN FRENCH,
FRANCIS WORLEY, Esquire,
The Chiefs of the Conestogoes, Shawanas & Ganaways,
SMITH, the Ganaway Indian, and
JAMES LE TORT, Interpreter.

The Governor spoke as follows:

Friends and Brothers!

The belts which I lately received from the Five Nations, signify that they are one people with the English, and our very kind neighbors and friends. They invite me to come to them, and I purpose in a short time to go and meet them at Albany, and to make the chain between us as bright as the sun. When they see me, they will remember their great friend, William Penn; and then our hearts will be filled with love, and our councils with peace.

Friends and Brothers!

You say you love me because I come from your father, William Penn, to follow his ways, and to fulfil all his kind promises to the Indians. You call me William Penn, and I am proud of the name you give me. But if we have a true love for the memory of William Penn, we must shew it to his family and his children, that are grown up to be men in England, and will soon come over to represent him here. The last time I was with you at Conestogoe, you shewed me a parchment which you had received from William Penn, containing many articles of friendship between him and you, and between his children and your children. You then told me, he desired you to remember it well for three generations; but I hope you and your children will never forget it.—That parchment fully declared your consent to William Penn's purchase and right to the lands on both sides of the Susquehanna. But I find both you and we are like to be disturbed by idle people from Maryland, and also by others who have presumed to survey lands on the banks of Susquehanna without any powers from William Penn or his children, to whom they belong, and without so much as asking your consent. I am therefore now come to hold a council and consult with you how to prevent such unjust practices for the future. And hereby we will shew our love and respect for the great William Penn's children, who inherit their father's estate in this country, and have a just right to the hearty love and friendship of all the Indians, promised to them in many treaties. I have fully considered this thing; and if you approve my thoughts, I will immediately cause to be taken up a large tract of land on the other side of Susquehanna, for the grandson of William Penn, who is now a man as tall as I am. For when the land is marked with his name upon the trees, it will keep off the Marylanders, and every other person whatsoever, from coming to settle near you to disturb you. And he bearing the same kind heart to the Indians which his grandfather did, will be glad to give you any part of his land for your own use and convenience; but if other people take it up, they will make settlements upon it, and then it will not be in his power to give it you as you want it.

My dear Friends and Brothers!

Those who have any wisdom amongst you, must see and be convinced, that what I now say is entirely for your good; for this will effectually hinder and prevent any persons from settling lands on the other side of Susquehanna, according to your desire; and consequently, you will be secure from being disturbed by ill neighbors, and will have all that land at the same time in your own power to make use of. This will also beget a true hearty love and friendship between you, your children, and the great William Penn's grandson, who is now lord of all this country in the room of his grandfather. It is therefore fit and necessary for you to begin as soon as you can to express your respect and love to him. He expects it from you according to your promises in many treaties, and he will take it very kindly.

Consider then, my brothers, that I am now giving you an opportunity to speak your thoughts lovingly and freely unto this brave young man, William Penn's grandson; and I, whom you know to be your true friend, will take care to write down your words, and to send them to England to this gentleman, who will return you a kind answer; and so many hearts will be made glad to see that the great William Penn still lives in his children to love and serve the Indians.

* * * * * *

At a council held on the following day, TAWENA, a chief, replied as follows, in behalf of the Indians:

They have considered of what the governor proposed to them yesterday, and think it a matter of very great importance to them to hinder the Marylanders from settling or taking up lands so near them upon Susquehanna. They very much approve what the governor spoke, and like his counsel to them very well; but they are not willing to discourse particularly on the business of land, lest the Five Nations may reproach or blame them.

They declare again their satisfaction with all the governor said yesterday to them in council; and although they know that the Five Nations have not any right to their lands, and that four of the towns do not pretend to any, yet the fifth town, viz., the Cayugoes, are always claiming some right to the lands on the Susquehanna, even where they themselves now live: wherefore they think it will be a very proper time, when the governor goes to Albany, to settle that matter with the Cayugoes, and then all parties will be satisfied.

They asked the governor whereabouts, and what quantity of land, does he propose to survey for Mr. Penn? It is answered, from over against the mouth of Conestogoe creek, up to the governor's new settlement, and so far back from the river, as that no person can come to annoy or disturb them in their towns on this side.

They proceed and say, that they are at this time very apprehensive that people will come when the governor is gone to Albany, and survey this land; wherefore they earnestly desire that the governor will immediately cause the surveyor to come and lay out the land for William Penn's grandson, to secure them: And they doubt not but the governor's appearance and conduct afterwards at Albany, will make all things easy there.

Having obtained the consent and approbation, of the Indians, the governor delayed not; but on the 18th of the same month, while yet at Conestogoe, issued the warrant for the survey under his private seal. On the same day with the issuing of the warrant, he wrote a letter, which he sent by express, to the Gentlemen of the council, giving them information of the whole transaction. On the 19th and 20th of that month (June 1722) the first survey of Springettsbury manor* (now called "Keith's Survey," or "the survey of '22,") was made. On the 23d, governor Keith wrote a letter to the governor of Maryland, giving him an account of all the proceedings concerning the manor of Springettsbury, and sending him likewise a copy of the warrant, survey, &c.: this letter was sent by express.

Not long after the survey, settlements were made under Pennsylvania rights: but as the lands were not fully purchased of the Indians until 1736, licenses to settle and take them up were in the mean time granted by Samuel Bluntson,† who had been commissioned by the proprietaries, and in some cases too by Thomas Penn himself.

A warrant to re-survey the manor of Springettsbury was issued on the 21st of May, 1762, by James Hamilton, then lieutenant governor of the province. The re-survey however on account of the uncertainty of the boundary between Pennsylvania and Maryland was delayed about six years. But the line run by Mason & Dixon being completed in the

---

* The manor received the name it now bears from its being originally laid out for the use of Springett Penn, son of William Penn, Junior, and grandson of the William Penn who was first proprietor of the province. William the "father" died in 1718, and William the "son" died about 1720, it was thence supposed in 1722, when the survey was made, that Springett Penn was of right the proprietor of the province.

† In order to counteract the Maryland encroachments, it was the policy of the proprietory agents, to invite and encourage settlements on the borders. Such settlements were made within the manor of Springettsbury. There was a contract that titles should be made to the settlers whenever the

year 1769, and the boundary between the two provinces being thereby first determined, James Tilghman, Secretary of the land office, afterwards (on the 13th of May, 1768) wrote to John Lukens, surveyor general, requesting him to proceed with all expedition on the re-survey. Lukens accordingly re-surveyed the manor of Springettsbury on the several days from the 12th to the 30th of June 1768. This re-survey is known by the name of "Hamilton's survey," or "the survey of '68."

On the 27th of November 1779, the legislature passed an act for vesting the estates of the late proprietaries of Pennsylvania in the commonwealth. But there was an exception of all proprietary tenths or manors which had been duly surveyed and returned into the land office before the 4th of July 1776. The consequence was that Springettsbury manor remained the private property of the Penns; and as such it has been held, for the most part, down to our times.

Of the warm and tedious disputes which have existed during the last twenty-five years between the landholders in Springettsbury Manor, and the agents of the Penns, we speak not here:—the best account of them is to be found in the books of reports which furnish the lawyer's library. The disputes, however, may well be likened to the border wars connected with the Maryland encroachments on the territory of Pennsylvania previous to the year 1768.

---

lands should be purchased of the Indians. Certificates or licences were accordingly issued, promising patents upon the usual terms for which other lands in the county were sold. A commission was issued to Samuel Bluntson on the 11th of January 1733-4, to grant licences to settle and take up land on the west side of the Susquehanna. The first licence issued by Bluntson is dated on 24th January 1733-4 and the last on 31st October 1737. All of the numerous licences prior to the 11th of October 1736 were for lands out of the Indian purchases; yet these grants, though at first rather irregular, were of right to be confirmed by the proprietors as soon as the lands were purchased of the Natives. The early settlement in York county commenced in quarrels, and the effects of those quarrels have descended unto our days.

CHAPTER III.

EARLY SETTLEMENTS.

Kreutz Creek, &c.

THE first settlements in this county were made on Kreutz creek* and in the neighborhood where Hanover now stands. Before the erection of the county of Lancaster in 1729, a number of persons resided on tracts of land lying on the west side of the Susquehanna, within the bounds of what is now York county. These persons, however, remained but a short time on the lands they occupied—were not allowed time to warm in the nests on which they had *squatted*—and may not be looked upon as the progenitors of the present possessors of the soil of York county. They were known only as "Maryland intruders," and were removed in the latter end of the year 1728, by order of the deputy governor and council, at the request of the Indians, and in conformity with their existing treaties.

In the spring of 1729, John and James Hendricks, under the authority of government, made the first authorized settlements in what is now called York county. They occupied the ground from which some families of *squatters* had been removed, somewhere about the bank of Kreutz creek. They were soon followed by other families, who settled at a dis-

---

* Note.—Some persons say that the proper name of this creek is Kreis' creek from an early settler near its mouth, whose name was George Kreis. But others, with greater appearance of truth, say that the common name is the correct one. It is called Kreutz creek, not from a man of the same name as some assert; but on account of the union of two streams, and thereby the formation of what the Germans call a "Kreutz," (i. e. a "cross".) In the return of a survey made in 1722, it is called the "White oak branch." It had however, no certain name until about the year 1736, when numerous German settlements were made on its banks.

tance of about ten or twelve miles west and south west of them.

Sometime in the year 1732, Thomas Cressap came from Maryland, and forcibly seized and settled on the lands from which the before-mentioned *squatters* had been removed. With him originated the violent measures, sometimes issuing in murdering affrays, which attended the disputes between the proprietaries of Pennsylvania and Maryland, respecting the proper boundary of the two provinces. On the 24th of November 1736, this restless and quarrelsome individual was apprehended by the Sheriff of Lancaster county, and committed to prison on the warrant of the two provincial judges. —Thereupon the President of the province called the council and assembly, who detailed the facts connected with the outrage committed, and referred the matters, in a memorial to the King; which led ultimately to an amicable adjustment of the disputes concerning the boundary. At that period, it is believed, there were between three and four hundred inhabitants within the present limits of this county.

The earliest settlers were English—these were, however, soon succeeded by vast numbers of German emigrants. It is a remarkable fact, that, when the first settlements were made in this county, the great portion of the lands in the eastern and southeastern part of it were destitute of large timber—in sections where now the finest forests of large timber stand, miles might have been traversed without the discovery of any vegetable production of greater magnitude than scrub-oak; and in many places even that diminutive representative of the mighty monarch of the forest was not to be found. This nakedness of the country was generally, and we have no doubt, correctly, attributed to a custom which prevailed among the aboriginal owners of the soil, of annually or biennially destroying by fire all vegetation in particular sections of country for the purpose of increasing the facilities of hunting.

Most of the German Emigrants settled in the neighborhood of Kreutz-Creek, while the English located themselves in the neighborhood of the *Pigeon Hills*. In the whole of what was called the "Kreutz Creek Settlement," (if we except Wrightsville,) there was but one English family, that of *William Morgan*.

The early inhabitants of the Kreutz creek region were clothed, for some years, altogether in tow cloth, as wool was an article not to be obtained. Their dress was simple, consisting of a shirt, trowsers, and a frock. During the heat of summer, a shirt and trowsers of tow formed the only raiment of the inhabitants. In the fall, the tow frock was superadded. When the cold of winter was before the door, and Boreas came rushing from the north, the dress was adapted to the season by increasing the number of frocks, so that in the coldest part of the winter some of the sturdy settlers were wrapt in four, five and even more frocks, which were bound closely about their loins, usually with a string of the same material as the garments.

But man ever progresses; and when sheep were introduced, a mixture of tow and wool was considered an article of luxury. But tow was shortly afterward succeeded by cotton, and then *linsey woolsey* was a piece of wildest extravagance. If these simple, plain and honest worthies could look down upon their descendants of the present day, they would wonder and weep at the changes of men and things. If a party of them could be spectators at a ball of these times, in the borough of York, and see silks and crapes, and jewels, and gold, in lieu of tow frocks and linsey woolsey finery, they would scarcely recognize their descendants in the costly and splendid dresses before them; but would no doubt be ready to imagine that the nobles and princes of the earth were assembled at a royal bridal. But these honest progenitors of ours have passed away, and have left many of us, we fear, nothing but the names they bore, to mark us their descendants.

But all of good did not die with them. If they would find cause of regret at our departure from their simplicity and frugality, they would find much to admire in the improved aspect of the country—the rapid march of improvement in the soil of their adoption. Where they left unoccupied land, they would find valuable plantations, and thriving villages, and temples dedicated to the worship of the God of christians.

Where they left a field covered with brush wood, they would find a flourishing and populous town. The Codorus, whose power was scantily used to propel a few inconsiderable mills they would see with its banks lined with large and valuable grist mills, saw mills and fulling mills—they would find the power of its water used in the manufactory of paper and wire—and they would find immense arks of lumber and coal floating on its bosom from the Susquehanna to the very doors of the citizens of a town whose existence commenced after their departure from toil and from the earth.

But, to return to the situation of the early settlers—For some time after these early settlements were made there was neither a shoemaker nor tanner in any part of what is now York county. A supply of shoes for family use was annually obtained from Philadelphia; itinerant cobblers, travelling from one farm house to another, earned a livelihood by mending shoes. These cobblers carried with them such a quantity of leather, as they thought would be wanted in the district of their temporary visit. The first settled and established shoemaker in the county, was Samuel Landys, who had his shop some where on Kreutz creek. The first, and for a long time the only tailor, was Valentine Heyer, who made clothes for men and women. The first blacksmith was Peter Gardner. The first schoolmaster was known by no other name than that of "Der Dicke Schulmeister."

The first dwelling houses of the earliest settlers were of wood; and for some years no other material was used in the construction. But about the year 1735, John and Martin Shultz each built a stone dwelling house on Kreutz creek and in a few years the example was numerously followed.

Of the settlements in the neighborhood of the *Pigeon Hills*, we shall speak more particularly when we come to that part of our history embracing the borough of Hanover.

SETTLEMENT OF "THE BARRENS."

For several years after the settlements were made in the neighborhood of the Pigeon Hills and on Kreutz creek, the inhabitants of those regions were the only whites in the county. But about the years 1734, 1735 and 1736, a number of families from Ireland and Scotland settled in the south-eastern part of the county, in what is now known as the "*York Barrens.*" These families consisted principally of the better order of peasantry—were a sober, industrious moral and intelligent people—and were for the most part rigid presbyterians. Their manners partook of that simplicity, kindness and hospitality which is so characteristic of the class to which they belonged in their native countries.

The descendants of these people still retain the lands which their respectable progenitors chose upon their arrival in York county. And we are happy to add, that the present inhabitants of the inappropriately named "Barrens" inherited, with the lands of their forefathers, the sobriety, industry, intelligence, morality and hospitable kindness of their predecessors.

The townships comprised in the "Barrens," are Chanceford, Fawn, Peachbottom, Hopewell and part of Windsor, and from the improvements which have of late years, been made in the agriculture of these townships, the soil is beginning to present an appearance which is entirely at variance with the idea a stranger would be induced to form of a section of country bearing the unpromising name of "Barrens."

Before the commencement of the improvements in farming recently introduced, the mode of tilling which generally prevailed was ruinous. Having abundance of woodland, the practice was to clear a field every season. Wheat was uniformly the first crop, of which the yield was from 18 to 20 bushels per acre. The second crop was rye, then corn, then oats. After going through this course, it was left for a year or two, and then the course began again; this was continued until the soil would produce nothing. But most of the farmers have, as we have said, much ameliorated the condition of their lands, by the adoption of a better system of culture.

Having introduced the first settlers of the "Barrens," we shall defer further remark upon this section of country—while we return to "olden time," and look after the early settlers of other parts of the county. We have now settled the eastern, south-eastern and south-western part of the county, and leave the settlers "hard at it," while we take a view of the north and north-west.

SETTLEMENT OF NEWBERRY AND THE ADJOINING TOWNSHIPS.

About the same time that the "Barrens" were settled by Irish and Scottish emigrants, Newberry township and the circumjacent region was settled by a number of families from Chester county, who, under the auspicious influence of that spirit of peace and amity which had been spread abroad, by the wise and excellent proprietary of Pennsylvania, sat themselves down here and there in a few rudely constructed cabins, surrounded on all sides by the still more rude wigwams of their aboriginal neighbors. Thomas Hall, John McFesson, Joseph Bennet, John Rankin and Ellis Lewis were the first persons to visit this section of the country; and having selected the valley in which the borough of Lewisberry is situated, they gave it the name of the "Red Lands," from the color of the soil and "red rock" on which it is based. By this name it was principally known to them and their eastern friends for many years. It was by a descendant of Ellis Lewis that Lewisberry was laid out—and it is from Joseph Bennet that the main stream which winds its devious way through the valley, derives its name of "Bennet's Run."

An anecdote is related of Bennet, Rankin and Lewis, connected with their first visit to the "Redlands." Having arrived at the eastern bank of the Susquehanna river, and there being no other kind of craft than canoes to cross in, they fastened two together, and placing their horses with their hinder feet in one and their fore feet in the other thus paddled to the shore, at the eminent peril of their lives!

This section of the country, naturally productive, had suffered a material deterioration of quality, and was indeed almost "worn out," by a hard system of tillage, when the introduction of clover and plaster in the year 1800, established a new era in the husbandry of the neighborhood, and gradually produced a considerable melioration of the soil. At present the spirit of "liming" is gaining ground rapidly in Newberry and the adjoining townships, and promises very fairly to effect a material increase of productiveness.

There is also a great change of system in the husbandry

of this section which is doing much for the land. Formerly the farmer depended mainly upon keeping a large stock, and enriching his land by the *manure* which he would thus be enabled to make, *at the expense of all the hay and grass on the farm*. At present he keeps a comparatively small stock, except where there are extensive meadows, and depends more upon ploughing a clover lay and liming. It is to be remarked also that his quantity of manure is not *lessened* by this curtailment of the stock of his farm; but with care may in fact thus be *increased*, and his land greatly benefitted. For instead of putting all his hay and straw *into* them, he turns some under with the plough, leaves some to shade the ground, and saves a goodly portion to put under them.

We have now fairly settled those parts of the county which were first to be inhabited by whites. Those parts of which we have made no mention in noticing the early settlements, were not in fact taken up by emigrants to York county; but became populated from the stock which we have introduced to our readers. In the course of time the Kreutz creek settlement increased in population, and gave inhabitants to a large tract of country surrounding it, including parts of Hellam, Springgarden, York and Shrewsbury townships. The few early settlers of the region in which Hanover stands gave population to several townships in that quarter of the county. The number of families in the "Redlands" and thereabout was for some time annually augmented by fresh emigrants from Chester county—the small portion of territory at first chosen became too small for the increased population, and the whole northern division of the county, comprising Newberry, Fairview, Monahan, Warrington, Franklin and Washington townships, were partially settled as early as 1740-50.

A considerable portion of the inhabitants of the townships we have just named, are members of the society of friends. There are also methodists, lutherans, and reformed presbyterians.

CHAPTER IV.

ERECTION OF THE COUNTY.

THE lands within the present limits of the county of York were a part of Chester county from the commencement of the provincial government until the 19th of May, 1729, when they became part of a then newly erected county called Lancaster. As at that time there were but few inhabitants in what is now York county, little or no inconvenience was experienced from being at a distance from the courts of justice or from the public offices. But when the population had become more dense, and wealth had increased, it became the subject of no small complaint among the inhabitants of these parts, that they were obliged to cross the Susquehanna, and visit the borough of Lancaster, or else remain without the means of defending their rights or of redressing their grievances. At last they acquainted the governor and assembly with the great hardships to which they were subjected. They represented "how difficult it was to secure themselves against thefts and abuses, frequently committed amongst them by idle and dissolute persons who resorted to the remote parts of the province, and, by reason of the great distance from the court or prison, frequently found means of making their escape." In compliance with the earnest petitions of the inhabitants, and to remedy the above mentioned inconveniences, the governor with the general assembly on the 19th of August 1749, made a division of Lancaster county, the western part of which they erected into the county of York. York was the first county west of the Susquehanna.

York county was, when first erected, bounded on the North and West by a line running from the river Susquehanna along the ridge of the South Mountain, until it intersected the Maryland line; it was bounded on the South by the Maryland line, and on the East by the Susquehanna. In the year 1750 Cumberland county was erected; and the boundary line between that and York county was declared to be the creek called the *Yellow Breeches*, from its mouth where it empties into the Susquehanna, up the several courses of it to the mouth of a run of water called *Dogwood run*, and thence one continued straight line to the ridge of the South Mountain, and thence along the ridge of the South Mountain until it intersects the Maryland line. Such continued to be the boundaries of York for about fifty years, when at last our county was destined to undergo a division.

The controversy between the inhabitants of the western and those of the eastern parts of the county concerning a division, commenced early, and was continued with warmth. Many essays were written, meetings held and petitions presented. The disputes however were at last settled, on the 22d of January 1800, when the western part of York was erected into a new county, thenceforth called Adams. That tract of land which was taken from the county of York, to be erected into a new county, is contained within the following lines, as made at the time, viz: "Beginning in the line of *Cumberland* county where the road from *Carlisle* to *Baltimore* leads through *Trent's Gap;* thence along the said road to *Binder's;* thence a straight line to *Conewago* creek opposite to the mouth of *Abbot's* run; thence along the line of *Berwick* and *Paradise* townships, until it strikes the line of *Manheim* township; thence along the line of *Manheim* and *Berwick* westwardly, until it strikes the road leading from *Oxford* to *Hanover-town;* and from thence a due south course until it strikes the *Maryland* line; thence along the *Maryland* line to the line of *Franklin* county; thence along the line of *Franklin* and *Cumberland* counties to the place of beginning." The governor on the 2d of October 1800, appointed three commissioners to run and mark the dividing line between the two counties; the commissioners were Jacob Spangler, deputy surveyor of York county, Samuel Sloan, deputy surveyor of Adams county, and Mr. William Waugh.

TOWNSHIPS.

The following townships were laid out and erected while York was a part of Lancaster county, that is before the year

1749,—Hellam, Chanceford, Fawn, Shrewsbury, Codorus, Manchester, Newberry, Dover, Warrington, Monahan, Paradise, Manheim, Heidelberg, Huntingdon, Reading, Tyrone, Strabane, Menallen, Cumberland, Hamilton's Ban, Mountjoy, Germany, Mount-pleasant, and Berwick; a part of which townships are now within the limits of Adams county.

Those erected since 1749, have been York in 1753, Windsor in 1759, Hopewell in 1768, West Manchester in 1800, Washington in 1803, Fairview in 1803, Lower Chanceford in 1807, Franklin in 1809, Peachbottom in 1817, Conewago in 1818, Springgarden in 1822, Carroll in 1831.

CHAPTER V.

YORK TOWN.

WHAT is now the borough of York was by no means the earliest settlement of our county. Although there were many habitations in its neighborhood, yet so late as the year 1740 there was not one building within the present limits of the borough of York. The "queen of wilderness" then held "her solitary throne" where now the "city full" is cheered with everything that art and industry can render lovely or attractive.

The "tract of land on both sides of Codorus Creek," within the manor of Springettsbury, upon which the town of York was to be laid out and built, was, by the special order and direction of the proprietaries, surveyed by Thomas Cookson, then deputy surveyor of Lancaster county, in the month of October, 1741. The part east of Codorus, was immediately laid out into squares, after the manner of Philadelphia. For doing this the following instructions were originally given. "The squares to be 480 feet wide, 520 long; lots 230 by 65; alleys 20; two streets 80 feet wide, to cross each other, and 65 feet square to be cut off the corner of each lot to make a square for any public building or market of 110 feet each side: the lots to be let at 7 shillings sterling, or value in coin current according to the exchange; the squares to be laid out the length of two squares to the eastward of Codorus when any number such as 20 houses are built." On the margin of the original draught of the town as then laid out, are these words, "the above squares count in each 480 feet, on every side, which in lots of 60 feet front, and 240 feet deep, will make 16 lots; which multiplied by the number of squares, (viz. 16, for the original draught contains no more) gives 256 lots; which together with the streets, at 60 feet wide, will not take up above 102 acres of land."

After the town had been thus laid out, if any one wished for a lot therein he applied at the proper office, or in the words of his certificate he "entered his name for a lot in the town of York, in the county of Lancaster, No." &c.

The first application or entry of names for lots in York town was in November 1741. In that month 23 lots were taken up, and no more were taken up until the 10th and 11th of March 1746, when 44 lots were disposed of. In 1748, and the two years following, many applications were made, for York had then become a county town. The names of the persons who first applied for and took up lots in York, (Nov. 1741,) are as follows, viz: John Bishop, No. 57, Jacob Welsch, 58; Baltzer Spengler, No. 70; Michael Swoope, No. 75; Christopher Croll, No. 85; Michael Laub, No. 86; George Swoope, No. 87, 104, 124 and 140; Zachariah Shugart, No. 92; Nicholas Stuke, No. 101; Arnold Stuke, No. 102; Samuel Hoake, No. 105; Hermanus Bott, No. 106; George Hoake, No. 107 and 117; Jacob Crebill, No. 108; Matthias Onvensant, No. 118; Michael Eichelberger, No. 120; Andrew Coaler, No. 121; Henry Hendricks, No. 122 and Joseph Hinsman, No. 123.

The manner of proceeding to obtain a lot was this: the person wishing for one, applied for and requested the proprietors, to permit him to "take up a lot." They then received a certificate of having made such application; the lot was then surveyed for him.

The paper given to the applicant certifying that he had entered his name and mentioning the conditions was then usually called *"a ticket,"* or else the particular applicant was named, as *"George Swoope's ticket."* These tickets were transferable; the owner of them might sell them, assign them, or do what he pleased with them. The possession of a ticket was by no means the same as owning a lot. It only gave a right to build, to obtain a patent; for the lots were granted upon particular conditions strenuously enforced.

One of the usual conditions was this, viz: "that the applicant build upon the lot, at his own proper cost, one substantial dwelling-house, of the dimensions of sixteen feet square at least, with a good chimney of brick or stone, to be laid in or built with lime and sand, within the space of one year from the time of his entry for the same." A continual rent was to be paid to the proprietors, Thomas Penn and Richard Penn, for every lot taken up. This was a "yearly rent of seven shillings, sterling money of Great Britain, or the value thereof in coin current, according as the exchange should be between the province and the city of London." Beside this, the lot was held "in free and common soccage, by fealty only in lieu of all other services."

When the applicant had built or in some cases had begun to build, he received if he so wished, a patent. But this patent most explicitly stated the conditions; and if these conditions were not fulfilled, he was deprived of his lot, and it was granted to some one else.

The building of York town proceeded but slowly: for though many took up lots, yet few were enabled fully to comply with the conditions; the consequence was, the lots were forfeited, and thereby honest industry discouraged. And indeed the fear of not being able to accomplish, in so short a period, what they wished to commence, deterred many from beginning what might end in folly. It should be remembered that at that time, the conveniences for house-building were few. It appears from a statement made by George Stevenson on the 10th April, 1751, that at that time there were fifty lots built on, agreeably to the tickets. Three of these lots were then occupied by churches, viz: two by the German Lutheran, and one by the German Reformed. Hence there could not have been at that time more than forty-seven dwelling-houses in the town of York, and many of them must have been truly miserable.

At about this period, York must have been a most desert place, very unlike what she now is in the "splèndour of her domes" and the "richness of her profusion." In an old record it is alleged as a heavy offence against George Hoak that "within the very limits of York, he had cut down the proprietaries' timber in large quantities for burning brick and lime." In a letter written in 1750, it is said that "sundry persons have cut off the wood of the town land to burn brick, and are now burning brick on lots not granted, to the damage of the inhabitants, who ought to have the wood for firing, and of the purchasers of the ungranted lots, which are spoiled by clay holes."

In the first settlement of York many inconveniences and difficulties arose from persons taking possession of lots without having in the first place, secured a legal title. Some erected small houses on different lots "without licence or entry;" but for this they were reported to the governor and were obliged to leave their tabernacles. Of this many instances are found recorded in old papers. Thus Jac. Billmayer built on lot No. 55, Jacob Falkler on lot No. 60, and Avit Shall on lot No. 74, "without the proprietaries' licence." Each of them was obliged to deliver up possession: and this they did on 10th April 1751, "to Nicholas Scull, Esq., agent for the honourable proprietaries."

The early settling of York town was one continual scene of disturbance and contention; there were warring rights and clashing interests. It often happened that different men wanted the same lot; and when the lot was granted to one, the others were watchful to bring about a forfeiture. The loss of lots by not fulfilling conditions was for a long time a serious evil, concerning which clamours were loud.

We will here insert a letter dated at Lancaster, the 24th April, 1750, and addressed by Thomas Cookson, "to Geo. Stevenson Esq. at York."

"Sir,

Christian Oyster in his life time entered for a lot in York, No. 82. The time for building expired, but no new entry was made till lately, as I understood, with you. The widow is since married; and her husband has put up logs for a house on the lot. He told me that he applied to you, and acquainted you with his intentions of building, and that you had promised him that no advantage should be taken of the forfeiture of the lot, and that he might proceed to build, and since, through neglect, you have suffered another person to enter for that lot, who insists on a right to it, notwithstanding the building erected on it. I find that taking advantage of the forfeiture of lots is a greatspur to the people's building. But where there is an intent and preparation for building, I would not be too strict in insisting on the forfeiture, as the sole intent is to have the town improved; and if the first takers up of lots will build and settle, their priority of application should be favored. A few examples will be necessary to be made; and they should be made of such persons as take up lots for sale without improvement. There are some others here about their forfeited lots. But I am well satisfied that you will do every thing that is reasonable and equitable to the people, and for the advancement of the proprietor's interest. Our court being so near, I could not spare time to come to York. Please to let me know in what forwardness my house is.

I am your most humble servt.

THO. COOKSON.

Lancaster, April 24, 1750."

The following letter is of a much later date, and shows that difficulties still continued. It is dated at York, the 8th June 1764, and is addressed by George Stevenson to William Peters, Secretary of the land office.

"Yesterday at 6 o'clock P. M. Mr. Homel and myself met the two Doudels together, with sundry other inhabitants of the place, to try to settle the difference between them about the lots lately granted to Michael, on west side of Codorus creek, and south side of High street continued. After many things said on both sides, Michael proposed to bind himself by any reasonable instrument of writing, not to build a tan-yard on the said lots for the space of five years next to come; which I thought was reasonable. But nothing would satisfy Jacob but the lots; and he offered to give Michael the two opposite lots on the other side High street, and to plough them and fence them, (for Michael has ploughed and fenced his.) This offer gave great offence to all the company, "what, said they, is no body to have a lot but the two Doudels?" For my own part, I do acknowledge they are industrious men, and deserve a lot as well as their neighbors; but at the same time there are other people who have paid dear for lots here, and have improved them well, and deserve lots as well as they. Sundry persons are building on the proprietors' lots on the east side of the creek, saying they deserve and want lots as well as the Doudels. I think an immediate stop ought to be put to this; otherwise it will be productive of great trouble to you. I make free to write this account of these things to put you upon your guard, and beg leave to advise you not to grant any other lots, until I see you, which will be in about two weeks. In the mean time, I shall lay out the parson's lot for his pasture, and shall bring down an exact draught of it and of all the low bottom lands. Pray let me hear from you about these people that will build, and have built. *Fas aut nefas*, I am &c."

It is said that Thomas Cookson who surveyed the York town lands in 1741, never returned the survey into office. To supply this deficiency George Stevenson re-surveyed them in December 1742 when he found them to contain 436 acres and a half. The "tract of land situate on both sides of Codorus creek, whereon the town of York stands" was again surveyed in July 1768. John Lukens who made the survey, found the tract to contain "the quantity of 421 acres and 37 perches, with allowance of six per cent. for roads and high-ways, or 446 acres and a half, neat measure."

York town was not incorporated during the first forty-six years after it was laid out. On the 24th of September 1787, it was erected into "the Borough of York." The first burgesses were Henry Miller Esq. and David Cantler, whereof the former was chief burgess. The first assistant burgesses were Baltzer Spengler, Michael Doudel, Christian Lauman, Peter Mundorf, David Grier Esq. and James Smith Esq. The first high-constable was Christian Stoer, and the first town clerk was George Lewis Leoffler.

The population of the town of York, in 1790, was 2076, in 1800, as taken by John Edie was 2503, in 1820, as taken by Penrose Robinson, was 3545, and in 1830, 4772.

About the year 1814 a considerable addition, (but within the limits of the borough) was made to the town of York. The heirs of John Hay deceased, owning 60 acres and some perches in the northern part of the borough, laid the same out into lots after the manner of the rest of the town, extending the streets and alleys north through the tract and laying out an entirely new street (called "Water street," the second of the same name) running nearly east and west. The lots were sold by the heirs to the highest bidders, and the amount of the sum received therefor was 25,000 dollars. Those lots, now partly built upon, are known by the name of "Hay's Addition."

The number of houses in the borough of York in April, 1751, was 47—in 1780, 290—in 1820, 548—in 1825, 567—and at the present time more than 600.

In October, 1780, there were 43 slaves for life in York town.

At present there are in York

9 ministers of the gospel,
19 attorneys at law,
17 physicians,
17 teachers of schools, (exclusive of those in the theological and classical institutions),
5 wagon-makers,
23 joiners and carpenters,
5 wheelwrights,
12 saddlers,
16 tailors,
11 blacksmiths,
40 cordwainers,
4 dyers,
4 gunsmiths,
20 butchers,
1 silverplater,
4 brewers,
10 masons,
6 watch and clock makers,
8 tanners,
25 tavern keepers,
9 coppersmiths and tinners,
7 tobacconists,
5 chair makers,
1 book binder,
3 book-sellers,
5 weavers,
1 cutler,
15 storekeepers (exclusive of small shopkeepers in various parts of the town),
12 coopers,
4 locksmiths,
13 hatters,

1 distiller,
1 brass founder.
1 iron founder,
5 printers,
2 pump makers,
2 bakers,
1 engraver,
1 machinist,
4 surveyors,
18 lumber merchants,
1 coal merchant,
4 coach makers,
4 confectioners,
2 sicklesmiths,
6 apothecaries,
13 magistrates,
8 plasterers,
7 house & sign painters,
1 augur maker,
10 cabinet makers,
2 soap & candle manufacturers,
8 barbers,
1 basket maker.

The public buildings in the Borough of York are the following:

A Courthouse in the Centre Square, with Register's and Prothonotary's offices adjoining. (*Note.*—In this ancient Courthouse it was that Congress sat while in York.)

A commodious market house in the same square.

A German Reformed Church on Main, between George and Beaver streets.

A Lutheran Church in South George street.

St. John's Episcopal Church in North Beaver street.

A Methodist Episcopal Church in Newberry street.

A Presbyterian Church near the extreme eastern end of Main street.

A Moravian Church in Princess street.

A Roman Catholic Church in South Beaver street.

A Jail in South George street.

An African Church in North Duke street.

An Academy in North Beaver street, and a Theological Seminary in Main street, west of the bridge. (*Note.*—A particular account of each of these institutions will be found in another part of this volume.)

A few pages back we gave a list of the names of those who first "took up" lots in the borough. We think it may not be uninteresting to show what parts of the town were first chosen by the early settlers in it.

The first lot taken up in York town was that on which the tavern stands, now owned by John Hartman and occupied by Daniel Eichelberger.

Then the adjoining lot toward the Courthouse, was taken up.

The next lots were that on which Nes' Brewery stands, in North George street, and another east of it, the latter of which is still vacant.

Then a lot nearly opposite the German Reformed church, and the two lots adjoining it on the west.

Then were chosen at about the same time, the lot on which Isaac Baumgardner's dwelling house stands; that occupied by the house of John Lay, on the corner of Main and Water streets; that occupied by the house of *Doll*, gunsmith; those by Judge Barnitz, Charles Hay's store, the York bank, William Sayres, and the house on the S. W. corner of Main and Beaver streets, belonging to the estate of David Cassat, Esq. deceased.

CHAPTER VI.

THE EVANGELICAL LUTHERAN CONGREGATION IN YORK.

THE first settlements made by *Germans* west of the Susquehanna were undoubtedly at Kreutz Creek and in the region where Hanover now stands—the circuit of the York congregation was inhabited by white men somewhat later. At first the inhabitants of the whole region from ten to fifteen miles around York composed but one congregation; they now worship the God of their fathers in fifteen different churches.

So early as the year 1733, four and twenty heads of families, who, for the most part had emigrated from Wuertemberg, came here together, and, joining themselves in one fraternal band, formed an evangelical Lutheran congregation. They purchased a baptismal book, which is still in the possession of the congregation, and therein they recorded their names as members to this new association, for the eternal remembrance of their posterity.

Among these venerable twenty-four founders of the congregation, all of whom have long since mouldered in the grave, we find many, whose descendants at the present day may be traced by their names. Such are Christian Groll, Philip Ziegler, Heinrich Shultz, George Schwaab, John Adam Diehl, Jacob Sherer, Mathias Schmeiser, George Schmeiser, Martin Bauer, George Adam Zimmerman, George Ziegler, Joseph Beyer, Jacob Ziegler, Valentine Schultz, &c. &c. Other names, less familiar at the present day, are Michael Walch, Carl Eisen, Paul Burkhardt, Henrich Zauck, Gotfried Manch, Christian Kraut, &c. &c.

The first Baptism in the Lutheran church, and consequently in York county, was of two children on the 23d of September, 1733.

From the year 1733, onward, the congregation was visited by different teachers whose hearts were devoted to the faithful service of their heavenly master. Among these may be mentioned the Rev. Mr. Candler, Dr. H. M. Muhlenburg, Rev. Friedrich Handshuh, and Rev. Mr. Brunnholtz. In its early days, this congregation was poor, and held divine service but here and there in private houses.

In the year 1744, the first church was built in York, and the material used in its construction was wood. Soon after the completion of the building, the congregation called the Rev. Mr. Schaum to be their settled preacher. Mr. Schaum served the congregation but a few years, and was succeeded by the Rev. Messrs. Hochheimer, Bager and Raus, in the order in which their names are here mentioned.

As in the time of the Rev. Mr. Raus the congregation had increased to a numerous multitude, the old wooden church was much too small for convenience, it was determined to build a new church; and in July, 1760, the corner stone of a building, 67 by 40 feet, was laid. The material of this building was stone—It was finished in 1762, and was solemnly consecrated in October of that year. The congregation at that time consisted of 550 members.

In the stone church, the following persons preached as regularly called teachers:

1. The Rev. Mr. Hornell, in whose time sacramental vessels were purchased.

2. The Rev. Mr. Bager [Baugher] for the second time.

3. The Rev. Nicolaus Kurtz, who served the congregation twenty years with great fidelity, and died as *senior reverendi ministerii,* in the seventy-fourth year of his age. He was an upright and diligent servant of Jesus Christ.

4. The Rev. Jacob Goering, who administered to the congregation one and twenty years. He was a man of extensive knowledge and of powerful eloquence. Universally beloved by a numerous congregation, he entered into the peace of his Lord in the fifty-third year of his age.

Since the first of August, 1809, the Rev. John George Schmucker has served this congregation, in connexion with a number of others in the country. As the old stone building was fast going to decay, the corner stone of a new brick church, (the one now standing,) was laid on the 2d of July, 1812. This church was not long afterward completed and consecrated. Its dimensions are 75 feet in length by 60 in depth.

The Rev. Mr. Schmucker has now served the congregation 25 years, during which period it has greatly increased in numbers and in wealth, embracing many of the most respectable and wealthy families in the county.

Since the year 1831, the Rev. Jonathan Oswald has preached to this congregation in the English language, Dr. Schmucker officiating principally in the German language.

THE ENGLISH EPISCOPAL CHURCH OF ST. JOHN'S IN YORK.

The year 1765 is the first certain date we have with respect to this church; for though before that time divine service had been performed here according to the rites and ceremonies of the Church of England yet it was not till the above date that measures were taken for the erection of a house of worship. In that year Thomas Minshall was appointed to receive subscriptions towards building a church; some gave money, some timber, and others offered labour. On the 15th February in the same year, the General assembly of the province kindly lent their assistance. They authorized the raising, by way of lottery, of the sum of 3003 pounds and fifteen shillings to be supplied towards the payment of the arrears of debt due for finishing St. *Peter's* and St. *Paul's* Episcopal churches in the city of *Philadelphia;* and towards finishing the Episcopal church at *Carlisle,* and building an Episcopal church in each of the towns of *York* and *Reading,* and repairing the Episcopal church at *Molattin* in Berks county, and the Episcopal church in *Huntingdon* in *York* (now *Adams*) county; and for repairing the Episcopal churches at *Chester* and *Concord* and purchasing a glebe for the Church of *Chester,* in the county of *Chester.* The time limited for drawing the lottery was afterwards, in 1776, prolonged. By the lottery, 315 pounds was to be applied towards building the church in York, but as all the tickets were not sold, the sum raised for that purpose, was but 257 pounds 5 shillings.

In the year 1776 the Rev. Doctor Peters obtained, upon application to the proprietors, a lot of ground in York, 80 feet in front and 250 feet in depth, for the site of the church and a burial-ground, at the yearly rent of 1 shilling sterling, if demanded. The warrant for the lot was granted to Samuel Johnston, Thomas Minshall and Joseph Aldum, trustees for the congregation.

The sum arising from the lottery being by no means sufficient to defray the expenses of building the church, the members of the congregation solicited their friends in Philadelphia, Lancaster, and elsewhere, from whom they received somewhat more than 150 pounds. Mr. Johnston received the money arising from the lottery and from the subscription of some of his particular friends; the subscription of the people in York county were received by Mr. Aldum, and those in Philadelphia and Baltimore by Thomas Usher. The subscription made by different attornies at law, were received by Thomas Hartley. Out of the money collected by Mr. Usher, the silver communion cup was purchased.

A second and third subscription were afterwards opened among the members of the congregation. But the sums received being still insufficient, the Rev. John Andrews, then missionary in York and Cumberland counties, from the society for the propagation of the gospel, went to Philadelphia, and by subscription in that city, obtained 57 pounds and 6 pence. By means of this subscription, and of a collection made at the first opening of the church, the debts contracted for the completion of the building were nearly discharged. In a short time afterwards every demand was satisfied; and thus by unwearied and praiseworthy exertions this church was at last built.

The ladies of York made the hangings for the pulpit and desk, of crimson Damask, which they had purchased of their own generosity.

The Church being completely finished, the seats were yearly hired at a half yearly rent for the support of the minister of the church for the time being, all subscriptions for him having then been discontinued.

During the revolutionary war, (with exception of a short interval) there was no divine service held in the church: it was for some time used as an arsenal. Being very much out of repair, through violence, and through long disuse, it was after the revolutionary war fitted for a place of worship.

A petition that the church might be incorporated was presented to the legislature on the 13th December 1786; and the legislature granted the petition on the 20th of September, 1787.

In the fall of 1810, (the sum of 1300 dollars having been given for the purpose by the friends of the church) the inside of the building was repaired and very much altered. The pulpit* and reading desk were removed from the north side of the west end of the building; a door was made at the east end, and in the place of the former door in the south side was made a window. A gallery was erected. A chandelier was likewise purchased in the city of Baltimore (for the sum of three hundred dollars) principally given by gentlemen who resided in that city. In this year a small house was erected near the church for the use of a sexton.

* In removing this Pulpit, several pounds of powder were found concealed under it: it was probably placed there at the commencement of the revolution by some one who had evil designs upon the Rev. Mr. Batwell.

There have been a great many divines connected with this church: the name of the Rev. Mr. Andrews has already been mentioned, but besides him there were a number of others who preached here occasionally, and at irregular intervals. The first regular preacher whose name is mentioned in the records, was the Rev. Daniel Batwell. His residence was at the parsonage house in Huntingdon, now belonging to Adams county, but he preached statedly to the congregations in York. He was a missionary from England and commenced his services in this country, a short time before the revolution. His feelings, with respect to that event, all conflicted with those of the people in this neighborhood. Having come from Huntingdon township, he preached at York on the sabbath, and on Monday following was seized by some rude and boisterous friends of liberty, by whom he was at three several [separate ?] times ducked in Codorus Creek. Being freed he set out on his return to his dwelling house but he had hardly arrived there when a company of armed men from York roughly seized him, and, returning, confined him in the public prison.† After some time Mr. Batwell was released, when he returned to England. Though his political views did not coincide with those of Americans, yet it is due to his worth to say that he was an accomplished scholar and a good man. After his return, he obtained a church preferment in the county of Kent, where he ended his days.

---

†On the 2d of Oct., 1777, a memorial from Mr. Batwell was read in Congress. It sets forth "that on a charge of being concerned in a conspiracy to destroy the continential magazines in this state, he was in custody of the keeper of the jail of York county, by virtue of a commitment, until Congress or the supreme executive council of this state should take further order touching him or until he should be otherwise discharged according to law." It appeared to Congress "by the certificate of Dr. D. Jameson that the memorialist was so much emaciated by a complication of disorders that his life would be endangered unless he was removed from the said jail." Congress however, referred the memorial to the president and supreme executive council of the state, in the mean time permitting him to remove from jail, and receive every indulgence, yet still remaining in safe keeping.

There was no divine service performed now for about five years. In the year 1778 or '79 the Rev. Dr. John Andrews, late Provost of the University of Pennsylvania, came here and continued to preach somewhat more than a year. The church was then vacant until 1784, when on the 6th of July in that year, the Rev. John Campbell accepted of an invitation to come to York, and administer to the spiritual concerns of the congregation. He continued here until the year 1804, when he went to Carlisle, at which place he died in May 1819.

The church was now vacant until the 1st of April 1810, when the Rev. John Armstrong became the regular minister. Mr. Armstrong continued here until May 1818, when he accepted of an invitation to settle in the vicinity of Fredericktown. — Soon afterwards the Rev. Grandison Aisquith came here, who continued however but about one year.

The Rev. George B. Shaeffer was elected minister of the congregation on the 6th of March 1821. He shortly afterwards came to York, where he continued until the fall of 1822. His successor was the Rev. Charles Williams, who was invited in June 1823, and who shortly afterwards accepted of the invitation. By an account which he took of the congregation on the 1st of January 1824, it was found to consist of 153 souls.

The Rev. Mr. Williams was elected President of Baltimore college in 1825. On the 5th of March he preached his farewell sermon to his congregation and on the 29th took leave of York for Baltimore.

After a vacancy of one year, the Rev. Richard D. Hall was called and chosen Rector of St. John's church, by the vestry, his call bearing date and his services commencing on the 16th of April, 1826.

Mr. Hall's successor was the Rev. John V. E. Thorn, of Carlisle, who was elected on Easter day in 1828. Mr. Thorn continued, during his ministration, to reside in Carlisle, and to appropriate the services of every second or third Sunday to the church in York. He resigned the charge of the congregation here on the 1st of January, 1831, since which time there has been no regular ministration to the spiritual wants of the congregation, though service is held occasionally in the church, by clergymen visiting this portion of the vineyard.

The number of members at present belonging to the congregation is very small.

Before we close this article, we may mention an incident connected with the early history of St. John's church, which has just come to our knowledge:

About the year 1774, Queen Caroline of England sent three church bells as presents, one for York, one for Lancaster and one for Carlisle. The bell intended for the Episcopal church in York, weighing 500 pounds, arrived safely, and was deposited before the house of Joseph Updegraff, Esq., on the pavement; and as there was no steeple or cupola in which to place it for the use of the church, it remained there for some time. At length it was taken without any ceremony, or any opposition on the part of the vestry (if, indeed, there was such a body in existence at that time,) and placed in the steeple of the court-house, where it remains to this day. It now belongs to the county by the law of *seizibus bellorum et bungupibus in cupolarum*—(see "Old law Book," vol. 76, p. 6592)—and is further secured to the county, by the fact that it is *non comatibus in alto.* The congregation have, however, the use of the bell, as it is used to indicate the time of meeting whenever service is held in the Episcopal church.

YORK PRESBYTERIAN CONGREGATION.

Several families of the Presbyterian denomination resided in York as early as the year 1750, yet they formed no congregation and had no place of separate worship. After the building of the Episcopal Church of St. John's, the presbyterians worshipped in it, for some years, in common with the members of the Church of England.

About the year 1789 the present Brick Church was built in which from that time onward they held separate worship. The first stated preacher to the congregation was the Rev. Robert Cathcart, who was ordained and installed pastor of this and of the Hopewell congregation by the presbytery of

Carlisle, in October 1793. The congregation at the time of his ordination contained about twenty-five families. At present it consists of about thirty families, with between thirty and forty communicants.*

THE PRESBYTERIAN CHURCH AT "SLATE RIDGE," IN PEACHBOTTOM TOWNSHIP.

This congregation is of ancient origin. The *first* church was built near Muddy Creek, sometime before the year 1750. This church was afterwards burnt, and a *second* temporary building was then erected about three miles further south. The latter church was soon deserted, and a new and *third* house of worship was erected at a still different place, viz. the place where Slate Ridge church now stands. In the year 1762, a new and better and *fourth* church was built of squared logs on the same site. In or about the year 1800, the log church was burnt by an incendiary, when a *fifth* church was erected, it being the *third* one built on the same ground. This fifth church is a large stone edifice; it is still standing, and is uniformly known by the name of the "*Slate Ridge Church.*"

The first preacher in the first of these churches was the Rev. Mr. Whittlesay. As the population was very small when he commenced his labors, he administered unto the spiritual wants of those who inhabited that tract of country which is now included within the townships of Chanceford, Lower

* In connexion with the York congregation may be mentioned that of Hopewell, formerly that of "Round Hill." The Hopewell congregation was formed between the years 1768 and 1770, when a log house was erected as a place of worship. In 1790, a larger church was built in a more central situation. In the year 1793, a connection was formed between the Hopewell and the York congregation, at which time the Rev. R. Cathcart was installed their joint pastor. Previous to 1793 they regularly had preachers sent them by the presbytery, several of whom remained with them for one year. A few years ago an elegant brick church was erected, it being the third one built by this congregation.
In 1825 the congregation consisted of about fifty families, and a hundred and fifty communicants.

Chanceford, Fawn, and Peachbottom. As the population increased, other congregations and churches arose. Even during the time of Mr. Whittlesay, his infant congregation had so increased, that those, who at first worshipped in one church, worshipped in two. For during his time and under his direction a church was erected in what is now Lower Chanceford, which church by the way was a building of about 60 feet by 30, was always called the "frame meeting-house" and stood until about the year 1800, when it was removed, and the present stone church was erected on the same ground. How long Mr. Whittlesay laboured with his people cannot now be ascertained; but he did previous to the year 1750. It was during his time that the *church* was erected.

After the death of Mr. Whittlesay but before the year 1750, came the Rev. Mr. Morrison, an emigrant from Scotland. It was in his time that the *second* church was erected.

After Mr. Morrison's departure, this congregation jointly with that of what is now Lower Chanceford, was blessed with the ministry of the Rev. Mr. Black. During his time the *third* church was erected.

The successor of Mr. Black, was the Rev. John Strain, who was, in 1760, installed joint pastor of this and of the Lower Chanceford congregation. In his time the *fourth* church was erected. Mr. Strain died in March 1774. He was a man remarkable for his piety, and was distinguished for his zeal and fidelity in his holy office. His labors were much blessed; and, after he had ceased from the earth his memory was affectionately cherished.

The Rev. Mr. Smith then preached to this and the Lower Chanceford congregation for two years.

The Rev. John Slemons was then settled the joint pastor of both congregations. At *Slate Ridge,* he preached about ten years, and then resigned that part of his charge on account of the infirmities of age. He continued to labour in Lower Chanceford about four years afterwards.

The Rev. Dr. Samuel Martin then became the Pastor of the Slate Ridge congregation. When, in four years afterwards, Mr. Slemons resigned his situation in Lower Chanceford, Mr. Martin became the joint pastor of both congregations. Mr. Martin left these two congregations in about the year 1812; and in about eighteen months afterwards he became the pastor of the Lower Chanceford congregation: about the same time Mr. Parke became pastor of the Slate Ridge congregation: Each of them continues until the present time.

☞In the above account we have spoken of the *Lower Chanceford* congregation. Chanceford township was erected while York was a part of Lancaster county: it was divided in the year 1807, when Lower Chanceford was erected. Consequently the "frame Meeting-house" until 1807 was in Chanceford; and has since that time (by division of the township) been in Lower Chanceford. We preferred designating the congregation by the present name of the township, rather than by its former and (until 1806) right name, in order to avoid obscurity, and apparent inconsistency. In like manner the church-building at Slate Ridge was until 1817, in Fawn township; and since that time (by the division of Fawn) has been in a newly erected township, called Peachbottom, from a ferry in that place which had long borne the same name. The Slate Ridge Church and the Lower Chanceford Church are about eight miles apart. The *first* church was built at the junction of Scott's run* with Muddy Creek, it being east of the former, and south of the latter. The *second* was over the Maryland line on land then owned by Michael Whiteford. The present site of the Slate Ridge church is but about three-quarters of a mile from the Maryland line, the congregation consisting of people from both states.

THE GERMAN REFORMED CHURCH IN YORK.

The German Reformed Congregation is without exception one of the most ancient religious associations in the county. The exact year when the congregation was first formed, is not known; but it had existed some years before it was blessed

---

* So called from Mr. Scott, who died about the year 1828, aged nearly 100 years. This man, who lived nearly a century, furnished most of the facts contained in the above narrative.

with the instruction of a stated teacher. As the congregation, in its infancy, was not extensive, it was unable to support a settled minister; but it fast increased in strength.

On the 12th of August 1744, the elders of the church, viz. George Meyer, Philip Rothrock, &c. sent a written invitation to the Rev. Jacob Lischy to be their settled minister, Mr. Lischy declined accepting the invitation but, in the words of the Church-book, "*so hat die ganze Gemeinde ihn, im Nahmen des dreyeinigen Gottes, noch mal zu ihrem Prediger berufen.*" Mr. Lischy accepted the second invitation which was made on the 29th of May 1745; and coming to York he preached his sermon of introduction on the text in the first six verses of the second chapter of Ezekiel; and upon the same Sunday administered the Sacrament.

Soon after Mr. Lischy had come here, the trustees for the congregation, viz. Jacob Welsch and Samuel Welsch took up a lot of ground in the town of York for a meeting house. This lot No. 91, was laid out and surveyed by Thomas Cookson Esq., for the use of the congregation, on the 11th of March 1746, and is described in a draught thereof, made shortly afterwards, as "containing in front on High Street, 65 feet, and in depth, to a twenty-foot alley, 230 feet: Bounded on the *east* by a lot now in the occupation of John Hay; on the *south;* by the said alley; on the *west*, by a lot of Zachariah Shugard; and on the *north*, by High street aforesaid."† It was on this lot that the first church, which was of wood, was erected.

In the year 1750, Mr. Lischy, having received a number of invitations from another congregation, wished for a dismissal, and was about to leave York; but by a new and earn-

---

† At this early period, the congregation purchased lot No. 84 to erect a house on for their minister for the time being. The lot was originally surveyed for George Schwaab, George Meyer, Henry Wolf, Joseph Welshhans, Jacob Obb, and George Hoak, as trustees for the congregation. It is described by George Stevenson, in a certified plan thereof made on 25th January 1753, as bounded on the west by Beaver Street, on the north by lot No. 83, on the east by a twenty foot alley, and on the south by another twenty foot alley.

est request from the people of his charge, dated the 31st of December he was induced to remain with them yet a few years. In the year 1754 he again desired his dismissal, and at last preached his farewell-sermon from Acts, 20th chapter, and 21st verse. But he was again hindered in his design, for the congregation eagerly entreated him not to forsake them, and more warmly exhibited marks of fond affection: In Mr. Lischy's own words *"da die Gemeinde neuen Ernst und Eifer und Liefe bezeigte und versprach, bin ich in meinem Verhaben gehinderet, und, durch einen abermaligen neuen Beruf, bewogen worden die Gemeinde fernerhin zu bedienen."*

Mr. Lischy continued but a short time longer to administer to the congregation; and upon the cessation of his ministry, the church was for a season vacant.

The attention of the congregation was now devoted towards obtaining a successor to Mr. Lischy. Their thoughts were finally directed to the Rev. Johann Conrad Wirtz, who was born in the town and canton of Bern, in Switzerland, and was then pastor of the Churches of Rachor and Fally in Jersey. The congregation sent him a letter by the hands of Baltzer Spengler, desiring him to come to York, and preach a few sermons with the expectation that he might become their clergyman. He received the letter on the 21st of August 1761, and on the 30th, he left Jersey in company with Mr. Spengler for York. He arrived at York on Saturday the 5th of September, and preached his first sermon to this congregation, on the Sunday following. The congregation being pleased with Mr. Wirtz, gave him an invitation to become their pastor, which invitation was signed by the elders and members of the Church, and was dated the 13th of the same month in which he had arrived. Mr. Wirtz accepted the invitation on condition that he could obtain the permission of his congregations in Jersey, and of the English Presbytery, at *Braunschweig* (Brunswick) by which he had been ordained to the ministry. Returning to Jersey, he obtained the permission of the Presbytery on the 24th of October, and afterwards of his congregations; and on the 5th of May 1762 he again arrived in York, and on the following Sunday (viz.

9th May*) preached his inaugural sermon from the 10th verse of the 10th chapter of Revelations.

In Mr. Wirtz's time the congregation had considerably increased. By an account contained in the Church book dated the 1st of January 1751 it appears that there were but eighty-seven members of the several congregations, viz. those at York town, Kreutz creek, Codorus and Bermudian creek, over which Mr. Lischy then presided. From an account made by Mr. Wirtz on the 13th of May 1762, it appears that seventeen new persons had been lately added to the Church of York-town alone, and from another account dated the 24th of May 1763, it appears that there were fifty-six persons belonging to the same church.

The old church of wood, was, in this state of the congregation, too small for convenience: it was accordingly removed, and on the 24th of May 1763, the corner stone was laid for a new edifice. This church of stone was completed, in the following year, Christian Wamppler being the architect.

Mr. Wirtz did not long continue a minister to the congregation; for he died on Wednesday, the 21st of September 1763; and was buried on the following Friday.

There was now a vacancy in the church for about two years; the Rev. William Otterbein commenced his labors in September 1765, and continued to administer unto the congregation for about nine years.

In May 1774, the Rev. Daniel Wagner became the minister of the congregation, and such he continued until the year 1786, when he removed to Tulpehockin in Berks county.

The Rev. Mr. Stock and the Rev. Mr. Droldenier then administered to the congregation.

---

* On the said 9th of May 1762, the first election was held, that is recorded in the church books; though there had been regular officers for many years before that time, yet their names are not now to be found. The officers elected on the above mentioned day were Jacob Hock, Johannes Gugges [Coockas], Martin Danner and Joseph Welshhans, as Elders, John Schultz and Jacob Scheib as Deacons, and Michael Schwaab as Secretary.

In October 1793 the Rev. Mr. Wagner returned to York, and again took the pastoral charge of this congregation.

During the ministry of Mr. Wagner, the congregation suffered a great loss, for on the night of the 5th of July 1797, the church, with all its contents, was destroyed by fire. The congregation immediately took means for the erection of another building. This third church, which is built of brick, is much larger than that one which was burnt, and is erected on the same site. It was solemnly consecrated on the 11th of May 1800.

It is 65 feet in front and 55 feet deep.

The Rev. Mr. Wagner removed from York, on the 1st of October 1802, having received an invitation to settle in Fredericktown, Maryland.

After an interval of about eighteen months, the Rev. George Geistweit became a minister to this congregation in May 1804; and he continued as such until about Whitsuntide 1820; when he resigned his charge. Mr. Geistweit still continued to preach occasionally, until the close of the year.

The Rev. Lewis Mayer, was the next minister of this church. He arrived in York on the 8th of January 1821, and presided over the spiritual concerns of a numerous congregation until April 1825. Having accepted the office of professor in the theological institution at Carlisle erected by the members of the German Reformed Synod, Mr. Mayer preached his farewell-sermon at York on Sunday, the 3d day of the above-mentioned month. He left York on the 4th, and was inducted into office at Carlisle on Wednesday, the 6th of April.

Mr. Mayer was succeeded by the Rev. James R. Reily, who preached his introductory sermon on the 1st of April, 1827, the congregation having been without a regular minister for two years after Mr. Mayer left it. Mr. Reily continued to preside over the spiritual concerns of the congregation until July, 1831. His health had been feeble for a long time and at length he found himself so seriously affected, that he was induced to take leave of his congregation, in order to have time and opportunity to take measures for its restoration. He accordingly preached his valedictory sermon on the 20th of July in the above-mentioned year.

After Mr. Reily's resignation the congregation was without a regular pastor until the 1st of October, 1832, when the Rev. John Cares, in compliance with a unanimous call presented to him in the spring previous, took charge of it. During the period between the termination of Mr. Reily's and the commencement of Mr. Cares' duties as pastor, the congregation was occasionally supplied by the professors and students of the theological seminary.

Mr. Cares continues to have charge of the congregation.

ROMAN CATHOLIC CHURCH.

On the 17th of April, 1750, John Moore entered his name for a lot marked No. 295 in the general plan of the town of York, "bounded & situate on the east side of Beaver street, containing in *breadth* north and south 57 feet and 6 inches, and in *length* to a 20 foot alley, 230 feet." On the 20th of June in the same year, Moore assigned his right to Casper Stillinger who shortly afterwards erected a stone dwelling house on the lot and made other improvements. Casper died intestate, leaving as heirs, and children Michael Stillinger, Richard Stillinger, and Barbara then married to Joseph Wirt. From these three heirs by virtue of three deeds, the date of two of which is in August 1775, and of one on the 4th of May 1776, the house &c. passed into the hands of Joseph Smith, who purchased it for the use of the Roman Catholic congregation, and presented it unto them.

The former dwelling-house of Casper Stillinger now underwent alterations and repairs, by means whereof it was converted into a Roman Catholic Church. This building continued a place of divine worship until the year 1810, when, as through time and use it had lost the "glory of its first estate," it was torn down, & a second building, the present brick church, was erected on nearly the same site.

For many years there was no stated preacher to this congregation that resided in York, but preachers came to administer unto them at stated times,—at first on every sixth and afterwards on every fourth week,—from the Catholic society established in Conew.go township, Adams County, distant four miles from Hanover.

The first settled Catholic preacher who resided in York was the Rev. Lorence Huber, who came here in December 1819, and continued about six months. The second was the Rev. George D. Hogan, who came here in the summer of 1820. The third preacher was the Rev. P. J. Dween, who came here in the summer of 1822, and has continued until the present time.

The right name of this church is "Saint Patrick's Church."

THE METHODIST EPISCOPAL CHURCH, IN YORK.

The first methodist preacher who visited York was the celebrated Freeborn Garretson, who preached in the neighborhood of York on the 24th of January, 1781. The house in which the first conversion to methodism was made in this vicinity, was then known as Worley's tavern, about one mile from the borough. From that time onward the progress of methodism was continual, but not rapid, for several years. The congregation was without a place especially designed for public worship for some years after Mr. Garretson's visit. We know little of the precise condition of this society, farther back than the year 1819, at which time Andrew Hemphill was stationed here, and the congregation numbered 111 white and 11 colored members.

Mr. Hemphill was succeeded, in 1821, by the Rev. William Prettyman.

In 1822, the Rev. Robert S. Vinton and the Rev. Tobias Reily were appointed, by conference, the former to York station, the latter to York circuit.

In 1823, the Rev. Jacob Larkin was the methodist clergyman here.

In 1824, the congregation numbered 146 members, and was supplied by the Rev. Charles A. Davis.

In 1825, the Rev. Basil Barry was the clergyman of the congregation here, and was re-appointed in 1826.

In 1827, the Rev. Andrew Hemphill supplied this congregation, which at that time, numbered 208 members. Mr. Hemphill was re-appointed to this station in 1828.

In 1829, the Rev. Henry Smith and the Rev. James Brent, were sent to York station. In 1830, Mr. Smith was here alone.

In 1831 and '32, the Rev. John A. Gere supplied this station.

In 1833, conference fixed upon the Rev. Edward Smith, to take charge of the station—and at their session in 1834, re-appointed the same Rev. gentleman.

The society has been somewhat increased in number during the last year.

THE MORAVIAN CHURCH.

The Evangelical Moravian Congregation in York town, had its origin in the year 1750. The number of the members of the congregation at that time was about seventy and some odd. Their first preacher was the Rev. Philip Maurer. During the first six years of this congregation, they held divine service in a private dwelling-house.

In April 1756, the corner stone was laid of the old Moravian church. The building still stands, though it is no longer used as a church. In 1827, a neat brick church was built near the old building, the latter being now used as a parsonage.

During the first 84 years of this congregation, it had upwards of twenty different preachers, including the present pastor, the Rev. Dr. Dober.

In conclusion of this brief account we would observe, that since the commencement of the congregation to the present time, 312 members of it have been called hence to another world; their mortal parts repose in the burying-ground adjoining the church. "Our fathers—where are they?"

THE YORK COUNTY ACADEMY.

On the 31st of July, 1777, Conrad Leatherman obtained a ticket for lot No. 638, in the town of York. He continued to be the owner of the lot until the 28th of February 1785, when he sold it to the Protestant Episcopal Church of St. John's.

The Rev. John Campbell then journied throughout Pennsylvania, and the neighboring states, and obtained from the generosity of individuals, the sum of about 5000 dollars towards building a school-house or academy on the above-mentioned lot, and a parsonage house on a lot adjoining. The building of the academy was immediately commenced, and towards the close of the year 1787, although it was not fully completed, instruction first commenced. The building, as soon afterwards completed, was (and it stands the same at present) a large and convenient two-story brick edifice, having forty feet in front, and 60 feet in depth, with three spacious rooms on each floor.

The general assembly of Pennsylvania on the 20th of September 1787, incorporated the Episcopal Church to which this institution was then attached. Under the incorporation, as far as regards the academy, Thomas Hartley was the first president, Robert Hetrick the first secretary, Henry Miller the first treasurer, and Messrs. James Smith, David Grier, William Harris, and the Rev. Mr. Henderson, the first visiters. The first instructors were two, viz. James Armstrong of the English language, and Robert Hetrick, of the Latin and Greek languages. The first official meeting, particularly with respect to the academy, recorded in its archives, was held on the 28th of February 1788.

From the small number of Episcopalians belonging to the church, and from the want of proper funds, the corporation was "unable to uphold and support the academy." On this account a petition was presented to the legislature on the 13th of March 1797, the object of which was to surrender the building to the state on condition that it be used as a school-house for the county of York, and that such a sum of money be granted as would be sufficient to support it. The legislature accepted this offer of surrender, and on the first of March, 1799, incorporated and endowed the "York County Academy."

The first trustees appointed under the new charter, were James Campbell, Jacob Goering, Daniel Wagner, John Black,

Robert Cathcart, William Paxton, Thomas Hartley, James Smith, John Edie, John Clark, Jacob Hay, Jacob Rudisell, Elihu Underwood, William Ross of Chanceford, John Barnitz, Michael Schmeiser, Conrad Laub, William McLean, William Scott, Philip Gossler and George Bard. The first President of the board of trustees was the Hon. James Smith, Esq: he was elected at the first meeting, but on account of his age and infirmaties he resigned on the 8th of March 1800, when John Edie was elected his successor. The first instructor under the first incorporation was Mr. Robert Hetrick.

In the year 1811, endeavors were made to obtain a repeal of the act which incorporated the "York County Academy." On the 11th of January the rector, church-wardens and vestrymen of the Episcopal church of St. John petitioned the legislature for that purpose. On the 22d, the trustees of the academy, and some inhabitants of the borough of York remonstrated to the legislature against the above petition. On the 30th, a number of inhabitants of the borough and county petitioned. The legislature having taken the subject into consideration, resolved on the 26th of February that the petition of the rector &c. could not be granted.

In April 1817, the rector, church-wardens, and vestrymen of the church of St. John brought an action against the trustees of the Academy, in order to obtain the repossession of the lot and building. This action is still pending.

The male and female departments of this institution are now under the superintendence of excellent teachers. The Rev. Stephen Boyer, a gentleman of extensive literary attainments, has charge of the male department—and Mrs. Young is at the head of the female department.

THE THEOLOGICAL SEMINARY AT YORK.

This institution was founded by an act of the Synod of the German Reformed Church at its session at Bedford in September 1824, and commenced its operations in Carlisle on 17th of May, 1825, the inauguration of the Professor having previously taken place on the 6th of April. It was removed to York in October 1828 in pursuance of an act of

Synod at its session at Lebanon in September of the same year. The institution has a library of between 3000 and 4000 volumes, chiefly in the German language, among which are some rare works. There are two professors, viz., L. Mayer, D. D. Professor of Dogmatic Theology, and Rev. F. A. Rauch, D. P. Professor of Sacred Literature.

A Classical School under the auspices of the Synod of the German Reformed Church was founded by a resolution of Synod at Harrisburg in September 1831. It was commenced in May 1832. Mr. William A. Good, of Reading, Pa., now pastor of the Reformed congregation in Hagerstown, Md., was appointed Teacher. In September 1832, the Synod at Frederick, Md., appointed Dr. F. A. Rauch Principal of the Institution and Professor in the Theological Seminary. Rev. John H. Agnew formerly Professor of Languages in Washington College, Pa., was subsequently appointed Assistant, and upon his resignation in September 1833, the Board of Visiters elected Rev. H. Miller his successor. Rev. Charles Dober, pastor of the Moravian church in York was also engaged as assistant in May 1832, and in the Spring of 1834 on the resignation of Mr. Miller, Mr. Samuel W. Budd A. B. was appointed to the vacancy.

The Teachers at present employed in the school are Rev. Dr. F. A. Rauch, Principal, Mr. Samuel W. Budd and Rev. Charles Dober, Assistants. The number of students in the two institutions at present (July 1834) is about 80, who are generally from a distance.

CHAPTER VII.

HANOVER.

A TOPOGRAPHICAL and historical sketch of the town of Hanover cannot fail of being interesting to a large portion of the public. We are indebted for most of the facts contained in the following notice of that town, to an account of the place which was written in September 1818, and with which Mr. Daniel P. Lange very politely favored us.

Topography. Hanover is situated in York county, Pa. and is 39 degrees 46 minutes N. L. and 1 degree and 48 minutes W. of Philadelphia. It is distant six miles from the Maryland line; one, from Adams county; eighteen from York, the seat of Justice for this county; forty-two from Baltimore; forty-one, from Frederick town; sixteen from Gettysburg; thirty-six from Harrisburg; and thirty, from Carlisle. The turnpike road leading from Baltimore to Carlisle and the road from Frederick-town to Philadelphia cross each other at the centre square of the town. Along the Roads the greatest part of the houses are built; they form the different streets and derive their names from the different places to which they lead. The street leading from the square towards York, York-street; that towards Carlisle, Carlisle-street; and that towards Frederick town, Frederick-street; a 5th street in which there are a number of buildings, intersects York-street near the square, and runs in the direction of Harrisburg through Abbott's town, Berlin, Dillstown &c. and is thence often called Abbottstown-street, although the correct name is Pigeon-street, on account of its leading to the Pigeon hills. Besides these there are a number of back streets on which many neat and convenient buildings are erected. Of the several allies there is nothing particularly to be observed.

There are no water-streams of any consideration in the neighborhood of this town; the nearest are at the distance of three or four miles, and are the Conewago, Codorus &c. The very best limestone water is that daily used by the families in town.

Hanover is one of the largest villages, not a seat of justice, in the state of Pennsylvania. Of its numerous dwelling houses some are very elegant two story brick or frame buildings; others however are but one story high, and are built of various materials.

The public buildings are a very neat market house on the square, and two elegantly built churches, the one belonging to the German Lutheran, and the other to the German Reformed congregation. Almost the only religious denominations are the German Reformed and the German Lutheran:

there are however a few families of Roman Catholics whose place of worship is the chapel in Adams county, four miles from Hanover.

The language of the old and young is the German, there being but three or four English families in the town; yet the English language is much spoken by the young, and will probably at no very distant period supplant its older and more energetic sister.

We believe there is not a town in Pennsylvania where idlers and vagabonds are more rarely to be met with than in Hanover. The inhabitants are, with few exceptions industrious and economical not only in their mechanical and professional avocations, but also in their agricultural pursuits. Nearly one half of them have lots or small farms near town, from which they raise a sufficient quantity of grain for yearly home consumption, with not unfrequently, somewhat for disposal. There are few if any places in the country of the same magnitude in which there are so many wealthy and so few indigent persons; a very large majority of the inhabitants living in affluent circumstances, and many of them being independent as to their fortunes; but the "propensity for more," so natural to man, admits not of ease.

The local situation of Hanover is truly inviting, it lying as in the fields of Elysium. It is situated in the level and beautiful valley of Conewago, which extends mostly toward the north west, north, & north east, of the town & which in fertility of soil is but little inferior to the best land in the state. The descents from the square of the town are, in every direction, except one, so gentle as hardly to be perceived, and are yet sufficient to drain off the water. The common is large and beautiful, and the whole neighborhood is calculated to excite admiration and delight. About a mile from town in a south easterly direction, begins that very extensive range of country commonly called "the barrens" on account of the poorness of its soil: this neighborhood, together with the Pigeon Hills, distant about four miles in a northern direction from town, can amply supply the inhabitants of Hanover with fruit, and the wealthy farmers of Conewago with chestnut rails for all ages to come.

History. The history of Hanover is almost wholly lost in the graves of its first settlers; the following however is the result of every thing that could possibly be collected on this subject.

Hanover was laid out in lots by Richard M'Alister Esq. in the year 1763 or 1764, at which time the surrounding country had been but lately settled, and wore much the appearance of a wilderness. When the rumour of Mr. M'Alister's intentions was spread throughout the neighborhood, the people generally laughed at his project, and considered it the effect of a wild fancy. A very aged and respectable lady of a remarkably retentive memory related a few years ago the following anecdote on this subject. A certain farmer of those days returning to his family after some visits through the neighborhood, thus addressed his wife in the presence of the lady above alluded to. "Mammy," (this was then, and is yet, a very common address of the Germans to their wives) "mammy, I have great news to tell you—Richard M'Alister is going to make a town." The wife, after some enquiries and observations, said with a sarcastic smile which spoke more than words, "Ha, ha, ha! I am afraid that man will turn a fool at last.—I think he'll call his new town, *Hickory town*."—The spot on which Hanover is now in part situated, was then covered with large hickory-trees, which stood almost impenetrably thick. The above anecdote although simple is not unpleasant; for it shows how the past has been, and by contrasting that with the present, we see how the world advances. All great undertakings begin in little things, "of so much labor was it to found the walls of lofty Rome."

The account written in September, 1818, of which we have availed ourselves, says: "The farm-house or residence of Mr. M'Alister, is yet in existence. It is a two story log building in Baltimore street, occupied at present by Henry Albright, Jun. This house, in which Mr. M'Alister kept a store and a tavern, (the road from York to Fredericktown then passing his door,) is the second house to the right coming from Baltimore. The first house built on the appropriated lots, is a one story log-house in Frederick street, the second to the right coming from Fredericktown, and at present occupied by Jacob and John Rieder. It was erected in 1764, by a certain Jacob Nusser, who, from his having been the first improver of the place, was afterwards jocosely called the governor of *M'Alisterstown*, the name by which Hanover was then generally known. A short time afterwards three or four more houses were built, occupied at present by Henry Felty, Charles Barnitz, John Bardt, &c &c. Henceforward the progress of improvement was rapid, until ten or twelve years ago, when it seemed to have made a stand; there are however occasionally some buildings erected, but not more than three or four on an average every year."

Until near the commencement of the American revolution, Hanover was under very singular circumstances. It was exempt from the jurisdiction of any court, and was for many years not improperly called the "*rogue's resort.*" All refugees from Justice betook themselves to Hanover, where they were under no fear of being seized by any officer. If the Sheriff of York county could catch the delinquent one half mile out of town in a north-western direction, then he might legally make him his prisoner under the authority of the courts of this county; but neither in town nor nearer the town than that had he any ministerial power. An anecdote has been related by a respectable old gentleman of Hanover which deserves credit. A number of robbers having broken into the store of the proprietor, Mr. M'Alister, he seized them and conveyed them to York for safe confinement; but the Sheriff refused to admit them into the jail with these observations to Mr. M'Alister, "you of Hanover, wish to be independent, therefore punish your villains yourselves." The officer remembered past obstructions of justice and was not unwilling to retaliate. Although these circumstances may appear strange, yet the account we have given is strictly true.

The reason of this extraordinary exemption from all law was as follows: Charles I. granted Maryland to Cecilius Calvert, Baron of Baltimore, in Ireland, on the 30th of June 1632—Charles II. granted Pennsylvania to William Penn on the 4th of March 1681. For many years the boundary line between these two grants was not ascertained. Baltimore and Penn claimed each the neighborhood of Hanover as comprised within their several grants, and each so claiming, granted rights to lands in opposition to the other. During this uncertain state of things, consequent on the dispute, a petty nobleman, named John Digges, obtained from the proprietor of Maryland, a grant for 10,000 acres of land; it being left to the option of Mr. Digges to locate said grant on whatsoever unimproved lands he pleased within the jurisdiction of his Lordship. By the advice and under the direction of Tom, a noted Indian chief, after whom *Tom's creek* is called, Mr. Digges took up, by virtue of said grant, 6822 acres, contained at present within the townships of Conewago and Germany in Adams county, and the township of Heidelberg in York county. Hanover, which before its incorporation was a part of Heidelberg township, was situated on the south eastern extremity of "*Digges' choice.*" The course pursued by each proprietor of making individual grants at random, and in opposition to each other was the cause of Hanover and the adjacent country being exempted from all jurisdiction. The laws of neither province could be extended to a place with respect to which the mutual claims were not settled either by survey or charter. The citizens of Hanover therefore were not liable to be seized by any sheriff, or to be confined in any prison. Delinquents flew to it on the discovery of their crimes and escaped all danger of being brought to justice: the appellation of *Rogue's Resort* was therefore not inapplicable. It is unnecessary to state any of the grievous evils arising from this state of things; for any one who has any knowledge of human nature, can form a correct opinion of the confusion and disorder then prevalent.

This uncertainty of boundary continued for some years. The division line between Pennsylvania and Maryland was not finally settled till just before the revolution. Mason's and Dixon's line was run in the year 1767 and 1768, and the proceedings thereon were ratified by the king in council on the 11th of January 1769. The proclamations of the proprietaries to quiet the settlers &c. were issued in 1774, that of Pennsylvania bearing date on the 15th of September of that year. Hanover was now determined to be a part of Pennsylvania, and as such fell within the limits of the county of York.

From this time onward we find but little that is worth recording—The town has escaped, with a few exceptions, the ravages of fire: nor have there been many accidents which could operate against its improvement and prosperity. In the year 1804 however the fever and ague raged in excessive violence, and caused a considerable number of deaths.

The town of Hanover was not erected into a borough until the year 1815; the 4th of March in that year being the date of its incorporation. The statute says of the borough that it "shall be comprised within the tract of land of Richard M'Alister, deceased." The first election of burgesses and town council was held on the 4th of March 1815, at the house of Jacob Eichelberger in Frederick-street, and was superintended by Michael Hellman and Henry Welsch. A very handsome market-house was erected in this same year.

The present population of Hanover is about 1100.

CHAPTER VIII.

THE POOR HOUSE.

The legislature on the 6th of February, 1804, authorized the erecting of a house for the employment and support of the poor in York county. The persons originally appointed to determine upon and fix the place for the erection of the Poor-House, were Martin Gardner, Samuel Collins, Abraham Grafius, Christian Hetrich, Peter Small, Peter Storm, John Heneisen, Henry Grieger, and Daniel Spangler. After a number of meetings, they made their report on the 30th of June 1804. They "fixed on the spot of ground within the bounds of the borough of York, called the town commons, being the south-west part, next adjoining Codorus Creek and Water street, containing about twenty-five acres." But in consequence of different claims having been made to the site they fixed upon, it was thought improper to erect the necessary building. This was represented to the legislature: and that body on the 1st of April 1805 empowered the then directors to determine upon such a site as to them might appear eligible, and likewise to cause the necessary buildings to be erected thereon. The directors immediately proceeded on the business committed to their charge, and on the 16th of the same month, made report of their proceedings. From their written account of what they had done, it appears that they "made purchase of a certain plantation, and tract of land, of and from Andrew Robinson, Esq., called Elm-spring farm* within one mile of the borough of York, as also one piece of timber land† containing nearly one hundred acres, within two miles of the aforesaid plantation." Shortly after this, in 1805, the old buildings were erected‡ and the poor were removed thither from all parts of the county, in April 1806. The office of overseers of the poor ceased now to exist, and their duties devolved, in part, upon the directors.

The first election of directors of the poor was held on the 9th October 1804. The three persons elected met at the Court house on the 5th November following, and divided themselves into three classes. The place of the first class was to be vacated at the expiration of the first year; that of the second at the expiration of the second year; and that of the third at the expiration of the third year:—so that those who have been chosen since the first election, have been chosen to serve for three years; & one third is annually

---

* The history of this farm is as follows: On the 17th Oct. 1766, Thomas Penn and Richard Penn granted a patent to John Hahn and Michael Hahn for a tract called "Rigen." On 4th of Nov. John sold to Michael Hahn. On 20th Nov. Michael Hahn sold to Mathias Sitler. On 27th Nov. 1796, Sitler sold to George Bentz. On 15th April, 1796, Bentz sold to Henry King. On 2d March 1802 King sold to Andrew Robinson. In April, 1805, it passed to the directors of the poor, in consideration of 4400 pounds, the tract purchased containing 132 acres, 156 perches and allowance.

† This tract, which is known by the name of the "Hermitage farm," contains 159 acres and 17 perches, with allowance, and was purchased for 600 pounds.

‡ The price of "Elm-Spring" and "Hermitage" farms was $13,333.33. The cash expended for brick, lime, stone, sand, and other materials towards building the poor house amounted to $4761.34.

chosen. Their style is "The Directors of the Poor and House of employment for the county of York."

In the year 1828, another brick building was erected near the poor house, and connected with that institution. This was the elegant brick hospital which greets the eye of the stranger coming into York by the Philadelphia road, and is distinguished for its neatness, elegance and comfort. It is of brick, two stories high, its interior judiciously divided and the whole well fitted to the purpose for which it was erected.

The entire cost, in cash, to the county, of this excellent building, was $7800, a sum much less than it would have been but that a good deal of labor was performed, at its erection, by paupers supported at the poorhouse.

We cannot avoid naming the workmen who built and finished the hospital. The manner in which the work was executed reflects no little credit upon them. The mason was Mr. Jacob May—the carpenters, Messrs. Moore, Dietz and Straber.

The following is a list of the directors with the periods of their service.

FIRST CLASS.

Daniel Spangler, from October 9, 1804, to October 9, 1810.
George Barnitz, from October 9, 1810, to April 6, 1813.
George Spangler,* from April 6, 1813, to Aug. 7, 1815.
Jacob Upp,† from Aug. 7, 1815, to Oct. 8, 1816.
Michael Welsh, from Oct. 8, 1816, to Oct. 12, 1819.
John Fahs, from Oct. 12, 1819, to Oct. 1822.
Henry Stover, from Oct. 1822 to 1825.
Caspar Laucks, from 1825 to 1828.
John Emig, from 1828 to 1831.
Nicholas Diehl, from 1831 to 1834.

* Mr. Barnitz was commissioned on the 26th March, 1813, an assistant Judge of the courts of York; and it was on this account that the court of quarter sessions on the 6th April 1813, appointed Mr. Spangler as Director.

† Mr. Spangler was, after his appointment, elected Director on 12th Oct. 1813: he resigned his office on August 7, 1815, when the court appointed Mr. Upp, who was afterwards, viz. on Oct. 10, 1815, "elected" to the office.

SECOND CLASS.

Jacob Small, from Oct. 9, 1804, to April 6, 1808.
Jonathan Jessop,** from April 1808, to Oct. 10, 1809.
Martin Weiser, from Oct. 10, 1809, to Oct. 13, 1812.
Gotlieb Ziegel, from Oct. 1812, to Dec. 21, 1816.
Andrew Kramer,†† from Jan. 7, 1817, to Oct. 14, 1817.
George Spangler, from Oct. 14, 1817, to April 8, 1818.
Thomas Taylor,‡‡ from Apr. 8, 1818, to Oct. 13, 1818.
Christian Lanius, from Oct. 13, 1818, to Oct. 9, 1821.
Michael Eurich, from Oct. 9, 1821, to Oct. 12, 1824.
Clement Stillinger, from Oct. 12, 1824, to 1827.
Henry Smyser, from 1827 to 1830.
Alexander Small, from 1830 to 1833.
Christian Hildebrand, 1833 to 1836.

THIRD CLASS.

Martin Ebert, from Oct. 9, 1804, to Oct. 11, 1808.
George Lottman, from Oct. 11, 1808, to Jan. 25, 1812.
Gotlieb Ziegel,§ from April 9, 1812, to Oct. 1812.
Jacob Schaffer, from Oct. 13, 1812, to Oct. 1814.
Philip Kissinger, from Oct. 11, 1814, to Oct. 1817.
Wm. Johnston, from Oct. 14, 1817, to Oct. 10, 1820.
Jacob Laucks, from Oct. 10, 1820, to Oct. 1823.
Jacob Diehl, from Oct. 1823 to 1826.
John Strickler, from 1826 to 1829.
Henry Wolf, from 1829 to 1832.
John Rieman, from 1832 to 1835.

** Mr. Small who was elected a second time on Oct. 4, 1806, resigned on April 6, 1808, when the court appointed Mr. Jessop.

†† Mr. Ziegle, who was elected a second time on Oct. 11, 1815, died on the 21st of December 1816; and to fill the vacancy in office, the court appointed Mr. Kramer.

‡‡ Mr. Taylor was appointed in room of Mr. Spangler, resigned.

§ Mr. Lottman died on the 25th of January 1812; and the court at their next session appointed Mr. Ziegel to fill the vacancy occasioned thereby.

The *stewards* of the poor house have been John Demuth, 3 years, George Lottman, 3 years, John Becker, 1 year, William Jordan, 9 years, George Ilgenfritz, 3 years, Geo. Schank, 4 years, Martin Gardner, from 1829 to the present time.

The *Clerks* to the Directors have been, at different times, Emanuel Spangler, John Stroman, George W. Spangler, Geo. Carothers, George Haller, Daniel Heckert, Henry Welsh, George Small and Michael Bentz.

The *Physicians* of the hospital connected with the poor-house, have been the following gentlemen, in the order in which they stand, viz:

Dr. John Morris,
Dr. Thomas Jameson,
Dr. John Rouse,
Dr. Martini,
Dr. John Bentz,
Dr. Wm. McIlvaine,
Dr. Luke Rouse,
Dr. Wm. McIlvaine, (a second time),
Drs. Jacob & Michael Hay
Drs. McIlvaine and Small,
Dr. Alexander Small,
Dr. John Fisher,
Drs. Haller and Rouse.

Although the office of Overseers of the Poor is now abolished in this county, yet perhaps it may not be unpleasant to hear a word concerning them. The first appointment of Overseers of the Poor, by the courts of York county, was on the 26th of March, 1750. The record reads thus: "At a court of Private Sessions of the Peace held at York for the county of York, the 26th day of March, in the twenty-third year of the reign of our sovereign Lord, George the Second, by the grace of GOD, of Great Britain, France and Ireland, King, Defender of the Faith &c. Anno Domini 1750. Before John Day, Thomas Cox, George Swoope and Patrick Watson, Esquires, Justices assigned &c. The following persons were by the court appointed Overseers of the Poor for the several townships in this county.

York-town. William Sinkler and Michael Laub.
Hellam. Caspar Williart and Peter Gardner.
Chanceford. Robert Moreton and John Hill.
Fawn. Alexander McCandless and John Gordon.
Shrewsberry. Hugh Montgomery and Hugh Low.
Codorus. Peter Dinkle and John Worthering.
Manchester. Peter Wolf and Valentine Crans.

Newberry. Nathan Hussey and George Thauly.
Dover. Philip Couf and Andrew Spangler.
Warrington. William Griffith and George Grist.
Huntingdon. Isaac Cook and Archibald M'Grew.
Monaghan. James Carothers and George Cohoon.
Reading. William Wilson and Mathias Maloon.
Tyrone. Robert McIlvaine and Finley M'Grew.
Strabane. David Turner and James Stevenson.
Menallin. John Gilliland and John Lawrence.
Cumberland. John M'Farren and David Porter.
Hamilton's Ban. James Agnew and William Wagh.
Mountjoy. James Hunter and William Gibson.
Germany. Jacob Koontz Smith and Peter Little.
Mountpleasant. William Block and Alexander M'Carter.
Heidelberg. Peter Shultz and Andrew Schreiber.
Berwick. Caspar Weiser and George Baker.
Paradise. Clement Sludebaker and John Rode.
Manheim. Samuel Budgel and Solomon Miller."

ATTORNEYS OF YORK COUNTY.

Among the attorneys who were admitted at York, upon the first opening of the courts of the county, were William Peters, John Lawrence, George Ross, David Stout, John Renshaw, &c. Those who have been admitted since, are,

Edward Shippen, admitted	Apr. 30, 1751
John Mather, jr.	do
Samuel Morris	July 30, 1751
Joseph Galloway	do
Hugh Bay	Jan. 28, 1752
Thomas Olway	Apr. 25, 1753
William Parr	do
David Henderson	July 29, 1755
Samuel Johnson	Oct. 28, 1755
James Bisset	Jan. 23, 1759
William Atlee	July 24, 1759
William M'Clay	Apr. 28, 1760
Lindsay Coates	Jan. 29, 1765
James Reed	Apr. 30, 1765
Jasper Yeates	May 29, 1765
Andrew Allen	July 23, 1765
Alexander Wilcox	do
Henry Eleves	do
Richard Peters jr.	do
Stephen Porter	do
James Sayre	do
Robert Gilbraith	Oct. 22, 1765
William Sweney	do
Edward Biddle	do
James Wilson	Oct. 27, 1767
Jacob Moor	Jan. 24, 1769
Thomas Hood	do

Jacob Rush	Apr. 25, 1769
Stephen Watte	do
Col. Casper Witzal	do
Christian Hoake	do
Thomas Hartley	July 25, 1769
John Hubley	July 24, 1770
James Lukens	Apr. 23, 1771
David Grier	do
David Espy	do
Andrew Scott	July 23, 1771
Peter Zachariah Loyd	Apr. 28, 1772
Andrew Ross	July 28, 1772
George Ross jr.	July 27, 1773
John Reily	July 27, 1773
Robert Buchanan	do
John Stedman	Oct. 26, 1773
John M'Gill	do
Thomas Smith	Jan. 25, 1774
Charles Stedman	do
David M'Mecken	do
Jaspar Ewing	Oct. 25, 1774
William Barton	Apr. 25, 1775
James Wilson	Jan. 26, 1779
Col. Thomas Hartley	do
Maj.John Clark	Apr. 27, 1779
George Noarth	July 27, 1779
Col. Wm. Bradford	do
Stephen Chambers*	Apr. 24, 1781
James Hamilton	do
Col. Robert M'Gaw	July 24, 1781
Stephen Porter	July 23, 1782
Thomas Smith	Apr. 29, 1783
John Lawrence	July 29, 1783
Mathew M'Alister	do
John Wilkes Kittera	Oct. 28, 1783
James Riddle	Jan. 25, 1785
Jacob Hubley	do
Ross Thompson	Apr. 26, 1785
Andrew Dunlap	Oct. 25, 1785
Joseph Hubly	do
James Carson	Jan. 24, 1786
William Montgomery	Apr. 25, 1786
Peter Huffnagle	do
John Joseph Henry	do
John Woods	do
John Caldwell	July 25, 1786
James Hopkins	Apr. 26, 1787
Charles Smith	do
James Campbell	July 29, 1788
George Fisher	do
John Lukens	Jan. 27, 1789
Ralph Bowie	July 28, 1789
Thomas Nisbit	July 29, 1789
John Moore	July 30, 1789
Mathias Barton	do
John Montgomery	Apr.26, 1790
James Kelly	July 27, 1790
David Waltz	Oct.26, 1790
James Orbison	Jan. 25, 1791
Samuel Riddle	Jan. 26, 1791
John Smith	do
Charles Hall	Apr. 6, 1791
George Smith	do
Mathias Slough	Mar. 7, 1792
David Moore	June 5, 1792
Jacob Carpenter	do

* Mr. Chambers was a native of Ireland, whence he came to this country before the Revolution. During the war of our independence he signalized himself as a warm and worthy friend of the country; and afterwards was honored with several exalted stations in Pennsylvania. Among other things it may be mentioned that he was one of the council of censors in 1783, and was a member of the state convention in 1787. On Monday, the 11th May, 1789, he received a wound in a duel fought with Dr. Jacob Rieger, on Wednesday mortification was discovered, and on Saturday the 16th of the same month, he died at his house in Lancaster.

John Ross June 6, 1792
Samuel Roberts do
William Barber Mar. 2, 1793
William Ross June 3, 1793
John Shippen Dec. 2, 1793
Charles William Hartley do
Thomas Elder do
David Cassat Mar. 4, 1794
Parker Campbell June 2, 1794
Samuel Scott Gilbraith do
James Smith Sept. 7, 1795
Thomas Baily do
Thomas B. Zantzinger Sept. 4, 1797
Robert Hays Dec. 4, 1797
Joseph Miller Mar. 5, 1798
Charles Hare June 5, 1800
Richard Brooks do
Andrew Buchanan June 18,1801
James Dobbins June 19, 1801
John Strohman Feb. 19, 1805
John M'Conaughy Feb. 18, 1806
Bushnell Carter Apr. 3, 1810
Charles A. Barnitz Apr. 2, 1811
Henry Shippen Nov. 5, 1811
John Gardner Aug. 4, 1812
Jasper Slaymaker Oct. 21, 1814
John Blanchard Mar. 31, 1815
Samuel Bacon Apr. 1815
James Merrill Nov. 3, 1815
Samuel Merrill Oct. 29, 1816
Thaddeus Stevens Nov. 4, 1816
Edwin A. White Dec. 17, 1816
Daniel Raymond Jan. 6, 1817
Colin Cooke Apr. 9, 1817
Isaac Fisher July 28, 1817
Molton C. Rogers Mar. 26, 1816
Edward Coleman do
William Gemmill Apr. 6, 1818
William H. Brown May 11, 1818
Michael W. Ash May 12, 1818
John Wright Aug. 9, 1818
James Lewis Aug. 1, 1820
Daniel Durkee Oct. 30, 1820
William C. Frazer do
Thomas Kelly Oct. 31, 1820
Webster Lewis Dec. 28, 1820
Walter Franklin, jr. Jan. 2, 1821
Joseph C. Cohen Jan. 4, 1822
Jacob A. Fisher Mar. 28, 1822
Charles B. Penrose July 21, 1822
John Evans Aug. 3, 1822
Calvin Mason Aug. 5, 1822
Henry C. Campbell Aug. 8, 1822
Charles Worthington Aug. 28, 1822
George W. Klein Aug. 29, 1822
John S. Wharton Sept. 16, 1822
John Bowie Nov. 4, 1822
Eman'l C. Reigard Nov. 5, 1822
James Findlay Jan. 7, 1823
Henry H. Cassat Apr. 7, 1823
Samuel M. Barnitz do
Edward Chapin Apr. 9, 1823
F. M. Wadsworth Apr. 15, 1823
George W. Harris Aug. 6, 1823
John Smith Nov. 3, 1823
James Anderson do
Richard Porter Feb. 17, 1824
Xerxes Cushman July 27, 1824
William C. Carter Aug. 4, 1824
George A. Barnitz Nov. 16, 1824
Robert S. King Aug. 1, 1825
Wm. Willer Aug. 10, 1825
Morgan Ash May 9, 1826
James Buchanan Aug. 21, 1826

David F. Lammot	Apr. 2, 1827
George Heckert	May 14, 1827
William B. Donaldson	Nov. 7, 1827
William H. Kurtz	Jan. 7, 1828
Ellis Lewis	Jan. 10, 1828
James Kelly	Mar. 3, 1828
Miner T. Leavenworth	Aug. 9, 1828
Robert J. Fisher	Nov. 4, 1828
Benjamin Champneys	do
Thomas C. Hambly	Apr. 7, 1829
Robert M. Lee	Aug. 8, 1832
William W. Haly	Sep. 4, 1832
Ebenezer M'Ilvaine	Oct. 15, 1832
Benjamin Rush	Jan. 9, 1833
Daniel M. Smyser	Aug. 7, 1833
John L. Mayer	Feb. 20, 1834
John I. Allen	Mar. 5, 1834
E. G. Bradford	Apr. 11, 1834

CHAPTER IX.

REVOLUTION.

THERE is not a part of Pennsylvania wherein the love of liberty displayed itself earlier or more strongly than in the county of York. Military companies with a view to the resisting of Great Britain, were formed in York, while the people of the neighboring counties slept. In those days there were men here, of broad breast and firm step, who feared no power and bowed to no dominion. The first company that marched from Pennsylvania to the fields of war was a company of rifle-men from the town of York: they left this place on the first of July 1775. York county sent out more soldiers during the revolution than any one of her neighboring sisters.

We will *first* mention the companies of the town of York before and during the revolution, which, however were not formed with a view of being immediately engaged in the dangers of war, and which, as then constituted, marched to no fields of fame. Hundreds of such companies were formed throughout the county, but as an enumeration of them would be lengthy and tedious, and as they are connected with no deed of danger, we will omit all particular mention of them, and confine ourselves to the town of York.

As early as December 1774, a company was formed in the

town of York, the object of which was to make soldiers who would be well disciplined for battle in casę the disaffection then existing towards England, should proceed to open hostilities. The officers of this company were James Smith, Captain, Thomas Hartley, first Lieutenant, David Green, second Lieutenant, and Henry Miller, Ensign. Each of those officers thus early attached to the cause of liberty, was much distinguished in the subsequent history of our country. The first was a signer of the declaration of independence; the second was a colonel in the revolution, and for eleven years a member of congress; and the third and fourth were each distinguished officers, and "acquired a fame and a name" connected with the cause they supported.

The *second* company formed in the town of York was in February 1775, the officers of which were Hartman Deustch, Captain; Mr. Grubb, first Lieutenant; Philip Entler, second Lieutenant, and Luke Rause, Ensign.

In December 1775, the *third* company was formed in York town, entitled "The Independent Light Infantry company belonging to the first battalion of York County." This company drew up and signed a constitution consisting of thirty-two articles, the original manuscript of which, with the signatures of all the officers and soldiers, lies now before us. It was signed on the 16th of December by the following persons, James Smith, Colonel; Thomas Hartley, Lieut. Colonel; Joseph Donaldson, Major; Michael Swoope, Major; George Irwin, Captain; John Hay, first Lieut.; William Baily, second Lieut.; Christoph Lauman, Ensign; Paul Metzgar, Henry Walter, Jacob Gardner, and John Shultz, Sergeants; and William Scott, Clerk: then follow the names of one hundred and twenty-two private soldiers, a catalogue of which would be too lengthy. This company was commanded in 1777 by William Baily, Captain; Christoph Lauman, first Lieut., and William Scott, second Lieut.—Mr. John Hay being elected a member of the state convention held in that year.

Companies were already formed throughout all the county, and every thing spoke of freemen under arms for liberty. But confining ourselves to York-town, we will mention the other companies which were formed here at the commencement of the revolution. The *fourth* company was formed in the spring of 1776, & its officers, were Michael Hahn, Captain; Baltzer Spengler, first Lieut.; Michael Billmeyer, second Lieut.; and George Michael Spengler, Ensign. The *fifth* company was likewise formed in the spring of 1776, whereof Charles Lukens was Captain; Christian Stake, first Lieutenant; and Cornelius Sheriff, second Lieutenant. The *sixth* company was formed in May of the same year, and was commanded by Captain Rudolph Spangler. The first and second companies formed in town, had long since been dissolved, and the soldiers thereof joined and became a part of the fifth and sixth companies: so that in June 1776, there were four different military associations of the town of York. The third, fourth, fifth, and sixth companies constituted a part of those five battalions which marched to New Jersey in 1776 to form the flying camp. Though they thus marched out of the county yet it was to no warlike field, the only object being to form other companies, which shall be mentioned in their places.

We will *secondly* consider the companies, composed of the citizens both of York-town and York county, which were formed with a view for actual service, and which shared in the dangers and glory of the revolution.

1. The first company to be mentioned is the rifle-company already alluded to, which left York on the 1st of July 1775, and marched directly to Cambridge near Boston. It was at first commanded by Captain Michael Doudle, who however was soon succeeded by his first Lieutenant, Henry Miller. Those who belonged to this company may be called *enlisted volunteers;* for they actually enlisted and bound themselves to military service for the space of one year, and this they did *"of their own heads,"* without being required or even so much as requested thereto by the state or by Congress.

2. In 1776 the counties of York and Cumberland were required each to raise four companies for the forming of a regiment. Of this regiment, William Irwine, at first, was

Colonel; Thomas Hartley, Lieut. Colonel; and James Dunlap, Major. Of the four companies raised in York county, David Grier was Captain of the first, Moses M'Lean, of the second, Archibald M'Allister, of the third, the name of the Captain of the fourth we cannot give. These companies, which were enlisted for fifteen months left the county to follow the fate of war in the latter end of March. In the year 1777 this regiment formed the 11th regiment of the Pennsylvania line, and its officers were Thomas Hartley, Colonel; David Grier, Lieut. Colonel; and Lewis Bush, Major.

3. Early in May 1776, a rifle company which had been enlisted to serve fifteen months marched from the county of York to Philadelphia, where it was attached to Colonel Miles' Rifle Regiment. The Captain of this company was William M'Pherson; and the third Lieut. was Jacob Stake.

4. In July 1776, five battalions of militia marched from York county to New Jersey. Out of these five battalions there were formed in about six weeks after their arrival, two battalions of the flying camp: those who did not belong to the camp returned home. The reason of so many more than there was occasion for, being called forth from all the counties seems to have been firstly to try the spirit of the people, and secondly to show the enemy the power of the nation they warred against.

As the flying camp is closely connected with the honours and the sufferings of many men in this county, we will briefly state its history. Congress, on the 3d of June, 1776, "Resolved, that a Flying Camp be immediately established in the middle colonies, and that it consist of 10,000 men:" to complete which number, it was resolved, that the colony of Pennsylvania be required to furnish of the militia, 6,000

Maryland,	3,400
Delaware,	600
	10,000

The militia were to be engaged until the 1st of December following, that is, about six months. The conference of committees for Pennsylvania, then held at Philadelphia, resolved on the 14th of June, that 4500 of the militia should be embodied, which, with the 1500 then in the pay of the province, would make 6000, the quota required by Congress. The same conference on the 25th, recommended to the associators of York county to furnish 400 men.

Thus York county furnishing	400
The other counties, and Philadelphia city, in all	4,100
Troops under Col. Miles,	1,500
Made	6,000

The Convention of the state, on the 12th of August, resolved to add four additional battalions to the Flying Camp, York county being required to furnish 515 men toward making out the number of 2984, the amount of the four new battalions. On the same day, Col. George Ross, Vice President of the Convention, Col. Thomas Matlack of Philadelphia, and Col. Henry Schlegel, of York county, were chosen, by ballot, commissioners to go to headquarters in New Jersey, and form the flying camp.

The Flying Camp was accordingly soon formed: it consisted of three brigades. The brigadier general of the first brigade was James Ewing of York county; his brigade consisted of three battalions, the first of which was commanded by Col. Swope of York County; the second, by Col. Bull of Chester county; and the third by Col. Watts of Cumberland county, father of the late David Watts Esq. of Carlisle. Of the other brigades and battalions, we are not at present able to speak with much certainty.

As the two battalions formed from the five battalions of York county militia which marched to New Jersey, underwent the hard fate of severe war, we will be somewhat particular concerning them.

The officers of the *first* battalion were Col. Michael Swope, Lieut. Col. Robert Stevenson, and Major William Baily. It was composed of eight companies, of each of which we will give the names of the officers, as far as we have been able to learn them:

1st Company.—Michael Schmeiser, Captain.
Zachariah Shugart, First Lt.
Andrew Robinson, Sec. Lt.
William Wayne, Ensign.

2d Company.—Gerhart Graeff, Captain.
Lieutenant Kauffman.

3d Company.—Jacob Dritt, Captain.
Baymiller, First Lieut.
Clayton, Second Lieut.
Jacob Mayer, Ensign.

4th Company.—Christian Stake, Captain.
Cornelius Sheriff, First Lt.
Jacob Holtzinger, Sec. Lt.
Jacob Barnitz, Ensign.

5th Company.—John McDonald, Captain.
William Scott, First Lieut.
Robert Patten, Second Lieut.
Ensign Howe.

6th Company.—John Ewing, Captain.
John Paysley, Ensign.

7th Company.—William Nelson, Captain.
Todd, First Lieut.
Joseph Welsh, Second Lieut.
Nesbit, Ensign.

8th Company.—Captain Williams.

The officers of the *second* battalion were Col. Richard McAlister (father of Archibald McAlister, already mentioned) Lieut. Col. David Kennedy, and Major John Clark.* The Captains were Bittinger, McCarter, McCoskey, Laird, Wilson and Paxton, from York county. To this battalion were added

* We perceive, by a number of letters, now in our possession, from Gen. Washington, and Gen. Greene, &c., to Major Clark, that the latter gentleman stood very high in the confidence and esteem of the American commander in chief. He was employed, during the war, in duties for which no individual would have been selected who was not deemed true as steel.

two companies from the county of Bucks. Thus each battalion consisted of eight companies.

The above list, as to both battalions, is very imperfect; but there is not a document in existence by which it can be made better. The above information, as likewise nearly all that follows, has been communicated to us by a few men of silvered hairs, whose memories are still fresh with respect to the warlike hardships and dangers of their more youthful days.

The battalion of Col. Swope suffered as severely as any one during the revolution.

The company of Gerhart Graeff belonging to that regiment was taken at the battle of Long Island, and but eighteen of the men returned to join the regiment. Not one of this company is now alive.

But the place which proved the grave of their hopes was Fort Washington, on the Hudson, near the city of New York. The officers belonging to Swope's battalion, that were taken at that place on the 16th of November 1776, were the following fourteen, Col. Michael Swope, Major William Baily, Surgeon Humphrey Fullerton, Capt. Michael Schmeisser, Capt. Jacob Dritt, Capt. Christian Stake, Capt. John M'Donald, Lieut. Zachariah Shugard, Lieut. Jacob Holtzinger, Lieut. Andrew Robinson, Lieut. Robert Patten, Lieut. Joseph Walsch, Ensign Jacob Barnitz, Ensign and Adjutant Howe, Ensign Jacob Meyer. Of the company of Capt. Stake, we are enabled to give the names of those, beside the three officers already mentioned, who were taken prisoners: they were Serj. Pater Haak, Serj. John Dicks, Serj. Henry Counselman, Corp. John Adlum, David Parker, James Dobbins, Hugh Dobbins, Henry Miller (now living in Virginia) John Strohman, Christian Strohman, James Berry, Joseph Bay, Henry Hof, Joseph Updegraff, Daniel Miller, Henry Shultze, Bill Lukens, a mulatto, and a waiter in the company —with perhaps some more. The company of Capt. Stake consisted mostly of spirited and high-minded young men from the town of York and its vicinity.

Though each party suffered much, and the mutual slaughter was great, yet but two officers of the flying camp were wounded on that day. The first was Capt. McCarter, who was from the neighborhood of Hanover, and was about twenty-two years of age. He belonged to the battalion of Col. McAlister, and commanded the piquet guard when he was shot through the breast. His wounded fellow-officer, who lay by his side, saw him stiffened in death on the fifth day. The other was ensign Jacob Barnitz, of the town of York. Mr. Barnitz was wounded in both legs, and laid for fifteen months a comfortless prisoner without hope, his wounds still unhealed and festering. After his return he lived for years to enjoy the confidence and esteem of his fellow citizens; but, after sufferings which wrung him to the soul, he was obliged to commit himself to the skill of the surgeon, and to suffer the loss of those members which had once borne the hero and the patriot, as he proudly waved to the winds the ensign of the country's liberty,

"The stars and stripes,
"The banner of the free heart's only home."

CHAPTER X.

PENSIONERS.

CONGRESS on the 18th of March 1818, passed "an act to provide for certain persons engaged in the land and naval service of the United States in the Revolutionary war." We will here mention those of the inhabitants of York county, who became United States' Pensioners under this act and its supplement, and who were alive at the passage of the act.

John Schneider, served in Col. Hartley's regiment, Captain Grier's company from 11th Nov. 1775 until the end of one year and three months. He afterwards served in the regiment commanded by Col. Haren, in Capt. Turner's company, from the early part of the year 1777 until the end of the war. In 1818 aged 67.

Christian Pepret, served in Col. Butler's regiment, in Capt.

Bush's company from the year 1779 until the close of the war. In 1818, aged 67.

John Jacob Bauer, served in the first Pennsylvania regiment commanded by Col. Chambers, in Capt. James Wilson's company, from September 1774 until the close of the war. In 1818, aged 73.

John Deis, served in Captain David Grier's company, in the regiment commanded by Col. Hartley from March 1776 until the end of one year. In 1818, aged 62.

George Lingenfelder, served in Capt. Michael McGuire's company, in Col. Brook's regiment, of Maryland, from June 1780 until the close of the war. At the Battle of Brandywine he was severely wounded. In 1818, aged 59.

David Ramsey, served in the 1st Rifle Regiment under Col. Edward Hand, the company under Capt. Henry Miller from 1st of July 1775 until July 1776. Being then discharged, he joined Col. Mannum's regiment, and was in service until taken prisoner at the battle of Brandywine. Besides this battle he was present and took a part in those of Bunker's Hill, Long Island, and of Flat Bush, at one of which he was wounded in the head. In 1818, aged 69.

Humphrey Andrews, enlisted in Chester county, Pennsylvania, on 26th January 1776 for the term of one year, in the company then commanded by Capt. James Taylor, in the 4th Pennsylvania regiment, commanded by Col. Anthony Wayne. From Chester county, he marched by the way of New York, Albany, Ticonderoga, and Crown Point, to Montreal, at which place they met the troops under Gen. Thompson who were returning from the battle at Three Rivers. He thence returned, with his fellow soldiers, to Crown Point, where he remained until 24th January 1777, stationed between the two armies of Burgoyne and Howe. Marching to old Chester in Pennsylvania, he was discharged on 25th February 1777. Andrews was engaged in a skirmish with the British in November 1776. In 1818, aged 63.

Jacob Mayer enlisted in York county, served in Col. Wagner's regiment, in the company commanded by Capt. James Taylor from Feb. 1776 until the end of one year, when he was discharged at Chester. In 1818, aged 67.

Robert Ditcher, enlisted in the spring of 1777 in Capt. James Lee's company of Artillery then in Philadelphia, attached to the regiment commanded by Col. Laub. He was present and took a part in the battles of White Plains, Staten Island, Monmouth, Mud Island, and Germantown, and was several times wounded. In 1818, aged 57.

John Taylor, enlisted in Feb. 1778 at Mount Holly in New Jersey in the company of Capt. John Cummings, and in the 2d regiment of the New Jersey line attached to the brigade commanded by General Maxwell; and he continued in service until Oct. 1783, when he was discharged near Morristown in that state. He was at the battle of Monmouth, and at the capture of Cornwallis at York-town: he likewise served as a volunteer at the storming of Stony Point by Gen. Wayne, at which time he was slightly wounded. In 1818, aged 71.

Dedlove Shadow, served from the spring of 1776 until the close of the war, in Congress regiment commanded by Col. Moses Hazen, in the company commanded by Capt. Duncan. In 1818, aged 62.

James Hogg, served from 26th January 1779 in the 1st regiment of the Maryland line, commanded at first by Col. Smallwood, and afterwards by Col. Stone. His company was at first that of Capt. Nathaniel Ramsey, and afterwards that of Capt. Hazen. In 1818, aged 63.

Michael Shultze, served in Col. Hartley's regiment and in Capt. Grier's company from January 1776 for the term of one year. In 1818, aged 61.

Mathias Kraut, served in the 10th regiment of the Pennsylvania line, commanded by Captain Stout, from the year 1776 until the close of the war. In 1818, aged 58.

Thomas Randolph, served in the 7th regiment of the Virginia line commanded by Col. M'Lellan, in the company by [of] Capt. Peasey from the year 1775 until 1778. In 1818, aged 71. "The Soldiers Friend" thus describes this old pensioner in 1818. Thomas Randolph—better known here as old Tommy Randall, the standing bugbear of children and likely to rival the most celebrated "Boog-a-boos" of any past age. We sincerely hope his sooty note of 'sweep O'—'sweep O' will soon be exchanged for more cheerful ones. Indeed he has scarcely a *note* of any kind left, as he is now a tenant of the poor house, having been some time ago gathered to that promiscuous congregation of fatherless, motherless, sisterless, brotherless, houseless and friendless beings, each of whom is little less than *civiliter mortuus*.

Samuel Ramble, served in the 1st Regiment of the Virginia line, under Col. Campbell, in the company commanded by Capt. Moss, during the three last years of the war. In 1818, aged 60.

Frederick Boyer, served in the detachment under Col. Almon from 1777 until 1779, when he enlisted in a corps of cavalry under Capt. Selincki, and under the command of Gen. Pulaski; he served in the corps until nearly the whole of it was destroyed. In 1818, aged 67.

Henry Doll, served in the first regiment of the Pennsylvania line under Col. Stewart, and in the company under Capt. Shade, for about one year. In 1818, aged 71.

John Lockert, served in Col. Proctor's regiment of Artillery in the Pennsylvania line, in the company of Capt. Duffie from June 1777 until June 1779. In 1818, aged 66.

Thomas Burke, served in the 10th regiment of the Pennsylvania line commanded by Lieut. Col. Hazen, from June 1778 until 1781. In 1818, aged 58.

Jacob Kramer, served in the regiment commanded by Capt. Hausecker, and afterwards by Col. Weltman, in the company commanded by Capt. Paulsell and afterwards by Capt. Boyer. The term of service was from 19th July 1776, until 19th July 1779. In 1818, aged 62.

Joseph Wren, served in the 7th regiment of the Pennsylvania line, in the company of Capt. Wilson, from January 1777 until the close of the war. In 1818, aged 80. Joseph Wren made his original application for a pension through Samuel Bacon, formerly an attorney of York. Mr. Bacon thus writes concerning the old soldier in 1818.

"Joseph Wren.—This old man's body and spirit seem to be equally light. He can travel his thirty miles a day with ease. His appearance reminds you of the Egyptian Mummies so celebrated for their fresh and life-like appearance after the lapse of centuries. During the deluge (not Noah's flood, nor yet Ducalion's, as you might have supposed from his ancient date, but the deluge which buried a third part of our town in ruins, on the ever memorable 9th of August 1817) old Wren, like the lively little bird of his own name, perched himself in a snug corner of the garret of a two story house, and went to sleep. The house rose on the bosom of the deep, plunged all but the garret into the waves, and was dashed from surge to surge till it lodged against a tree. Five persons were drowned! side by side they lay in a room of the second story of the house. *Joseph slept on.* At length when the God of nature held out the olive branch of hope to the terror-struck tenants of the roofs of the tottering houses, and the flood subsided so that "the dry land appeared"—when the mighty ocean that had been as it were created in a moment and precipitated upon us, gathered itself into the mild and unassuming Codorus again, Joseph's abode of death, when youth and health, and female excellence and manly virtue, had been buried in the waves, was visited,—and *still he slept.* When he awakened he rubbed his eyes, not certain whether they were his own, or whether he was Joseph Wren any more; for he knew not where he was, unless it might be in some place on the other side of the grave. Thus, indeed has Joseph Wren had hair breadth 'scapes, in the forest wild and city full, and is spared to be made glad by something very unlike the ingratitude of republics."

Conrad Pudding, served in Armand's Legion, in Captain Sheriff's company from the spring of 1781, until the fall of 1783, when the army was disbanded. In 1818, aged 64.

Michael Warner, served in Capt. Jacob Bower's company of the Pennsylvania line from Oct. 1781 until Oct. 1783. In 1818, aged 59.

John Devinny, served in the 4th regiment commanded by Col. Anthony Wayne, in Capt. Thomas Robinson's company from the fall of 1775 until the close of one year, at which time he entered in the 5th regiment, in Capt. Bartholomew's company in which he continued to serve until the close of the war. In 1818, aged 62.

William Brown, enlisted at Philadelphia in the autumn of 1777 for the term of three years, in the company commanded by Capt. John Doyle and the 1st regiment of the Pennsylvania line commanded by Col. Hand. He was at the battle of Brandywine, at the taking of the Hessians at Trenton, and at the battle of Princeton, Monmouth, Stony Point and Paoli at the last of which he received several wounds. Having continued to serve six years, he was discharged at Lancaster. In 1818, aged 73.

John Beaty, served in the 6th Pennsylvania regiment commanded by Col. Irwin, in the company of Abraham Smith, from February 1776 until February 1777. In 1818, aged 63.

John Ohmet, served in the 10th regiment of the Pennsylvania line, commanded by Col. Richard Hampton, in the company of Capt. Hicks, from May 1777 until the close of the war. In 1818, aged 60.

Jacob M'Lean, served in Col. Hausecker's regiment called the "German Regiment," in the company of Capt. Benjamin Weiser, from July 1776 until the year 1779. In 1818, aged 60.

Frederick Huebner, served in Gen. Armand's legion, in the company of Capt. Barron for the term of about three years. In 1818, aged 64.

Adam Sc[illegible]ubman, served in the 5th Pennsylvania regiment commanded by Col. Richard Butler in Capt. Walker's company commanded by Lieut. Feldam, from the Spring of 1776 until the close of the war. In 1818, aged 66.

Joel Gray, served in Col. Hartley's regiment of the Pennsylvania line, in the company of Capt. Bush, from Oct. 1778, until the 1st of April 1781. In 1818, aged 75. Poor Joel was a client of Mr. Bacon, who thus writes of him in 1818. "Joel Gray—He may indeed be addressed in the style of the old ballad, and they may make the same response.

> O why do you shiver and shake Gaffer Gray?
> And why does your nose look so blue?
> I am grown very old,
> And the weather 'tis cold,
> And my doublet is not very new."

This old man, in 1818, says: "I have one chest worth about a dollar. I have no trade or any business whatsoever. I have no children or friends to give me any kind of assistance. My pension and the poor-house are all I have to depend upon."

Michael Weirich, served in the 6th regiment of the Maryland line under Col. Williams and Col. Stewart, and in the company of Capt. Rebelle, during the last five years of the war. In 1818, aged 64.

Zenos Macomber, served in Col. Carter's regiment from May 1775 until January 1776, when he enlisted in Col. Bond's regiment of the Massachusetts line. Having served in this regiment about two months, he was removed and placed in General Washington's foot guard. Here he continued until January 1777 when he enlisted in Gen. Washington's horse guard in which he served three years. In 1818, aged 61.

Anthony Lehman, served in the 5th regiment of the Pennsylvania line under Col. M'Gaw, in the company of Capt. Deckart, from February 1775 until January 1777. In 1818, aged 65.

Samuel Spicer, served in the 10th regiment of the Pennsylvania line, under Col. Hampton, in Capt. Weaver's company, for about 1 year before the close of the war. In 1818, aged 81.

Christopher Nerr, served in the 2d regiment of the Pennsylvania line commanded by Col. Stewart, under Capt. Patterson, from April 1777 until Jan. 1780. In 1818, aged 65.

William Smith, served in the 2d regiment of the Pennsylvania line, under Capt. Watson from February 1776 until the expiration of one year. Being then in Canada, he returned home, and enlisted in the 4th regiment of the Pennsylvania line commanded by Col. William Butler, in Capt. Bird's company. In 1818, aged 69.

Martin Muller, served in Count Pulaski's legion, in Capt. Seleski's company, for the term of eighteen months. In 1818, aged 69.

Ludwig Waltman, served in the 6th regiment of the Pennsylvania line, commanded by Col. Butler, in the company of Capt. Bush, from the fall of 1777 for the term of three years and a half. In 1818, aged 60.

William Kline, served in Col. Wayne's regiment, in Capt. Fraser's company, from Dec. 1775 until March 1777. In 1818, aged 63.

CHAPTER XI.

CONGRESS.

YORK is somewhat connected with the history of the continental congress, for that body sat here some months during the revolution. It is to this that General La-Fayette alluded when, being in York on the 2d of February 1825, he called it "the seat of the American Union in our most gloomy times."

On the 14th of September 1777, Congress, then sitting at Philadelphia, and having strong reasons to believe that that city would soon be in possession of the British, resolved that, if they should be obliged to remove from Philadelphia, Lancaster should be the place where they would meet. On the 18th of September Congress sat as usual, and after having fulfilled the regular hours of daily service, adjourned to 10 o'clock the next morning; but during the adjournment the president received a letter from Col. Hamilton, one of Gen. Washington's aids, which intimated the necessity of removing the Congress immediately from Philadelphia. Upon this the members left the city, and agreeably to a former resolution, repaired to Lancaster. Philadelphia was shortly afterwards, viz. on the 27th of September, taken by Sir William Howe, which shewed the wisdom and foresight of Congress in leaving that capital.

Congress met at Lancaster on the 27th of September, (the very day Philadelphia was taken) but as they had good reasons for fearing molestation even in that place, they determined that the Susquehanna should flow between them and the enemy, and accordingly, on the same day, adjourned to York.* The first day of their session at York was the 30th of September 1777.

Congress continued about nine months, to hold their sessions in this place and in the same court house which now

---

* The treasury books, papers, money &c. were carried from

stands. In June 1778, the British evacuated Philadelphia and marched into New Jersey, and of this Congress received information on the 20th of the same month, by a letter from Gen. Washington. They sat in York but a few days longer, for on Saturday the 27th of June 1778 they adjourned to Philadelphia, at which place they met on the 7th of July following.

Among the other business transacted by Congress during its session in York, we find the following items recorded in the Journals:

October 4, 1777.

Resolved, that a letter be written to General Gates, informing him that Congress highly approve of the prowess and behaviour of the troops under his command, in their late gallant repulse of the enemy under General Burgoyne.

Resolved, That the thanks of Congress be presented to General Stark of the New-Hampshire militia, and the officers and troops under his command, for their brave and successful attack upon, and signal victory over the enemy in their lines at Bennington; and that Brigadier Stark be appointed a Brigadier General in the army of the United States.

October 6, 1777.

Resolved, That it be recommended to the legislatures of the several states to pass laws, declaring that any person, his aider or abettor, who shall wilfully and maliciously burn or destroy, or attempt or conspire to burn or destroy, any magazine of provisions, or of military or naval stores, belonging to the United States; or if any master, officer, seaman, mariner or other person, intrusted with the navigation or care of any continental vessel, shall wilfully and maliciously burn or destroy or attempt or conspire to burn or destroy, any such vessel, or shall wilfully betray, or voluntarily yield or

---

Philadelphia to Bristol, and round by Reading to Lancaster, and thence to Yorktown.

See "Journal of Congress" for Nov. 28, 1777.

This circuitous route was on account of fear that they should fall into the hands of the enemy, who were at that time in Chester county still fresh from the battle of Brandywine.

deliver, or attempt to conspire to betray, yield or deliver, any such vessel to the enemies of the United States, such person his aider or abettor, on legal conviction thereof shall suffer death without benefit of clergy.

October 8, 1777.

Resolved, Unanimously, that the thanks of Congress be given to General Washington for his wise and well concerted attack upon the enemy's army near Germantown on the 4th instant, and to the officers and soldiers of the army for their brave exertions on that occasion: Congress being well satisfied that the best designs and boldest efforts may sometime fail by unforseen incidents, trusting that on future occasions the valour and virtue of the army will by the blessing of heaven be crowned with complete and deserved success.

October 14, 1777.

Whereas the British nation have received into their ports, and condemned in their courts of admiralty as lawful prize several vessels and their cargoes belonging to these states, which the mariners, in breach of the trust and confidence reposed in them, have betrayed and delivered to the officers of the British crown:

Resolved, therefore, That any vessel or cargo, the property of any British subject, not an inhabitant of Bermuda or of any of the Bahama Islands, brought into any of the ports or harbours of any of these United States by the masters or mariners, shall be adjudged a lawful prize & divided among the captors in the same proportion as if taken by any continental vessel of war.

October 17, 1777.

Resolved, That the committee of intelligence be authorized to take the most speedy and effectual measures for getting a printing press erected in Yorktown, for the purpose of conveying to the public the intelligence that Congress may from time to time receive.

October 31, 1777.

The secretary laid before Congress a copy of the speech with which Mr. Hancock took leave of Congress, which was ordered to be entered on the Journals and is as follows:

'Gentlemen, Friday last completed two years and five months since you did me the honor of electing me to fill this chair. As I could never flatter myself your choice proceeded from any idea of my abilities, but rather from a partial opinion of my attachment to the liberties of America, I felt myself under the strongest obligations to discharge the duties of the office, and I accepted the appointment with the firmest resolution to go through the business annexed to it in the best manner I was able. Every argument conspired to make me exert myself, and I endeavored by industry and attention to make up for every other deficiency.

'As to my conduct both in and out of Congress in the execution of your business, it is improper for me to say any thing. You are the best judges. But I think I shall be forgiven if I say I have spared no pains, expense, or labour to gratify your wishes, and to accomplish the views of Congress.

'My health being much impaired, I find some relaxation absolutely necessary after such constant application; I must therefore request your indulgence for leave of absence for two months.

'But I cannot take my departure, gentlemen, without expressing my thanks for the civility and politeness I have experienced from you. It is impossible to mention this without a heart felt pleasure.

'If in the course of so long a period as I have had the honor to fill this chair, any expressions may have dropped from me that may have given the least offence to any member, as it was not intentional, so I hope his candor will pass it over.

'May every happiness, gentlemen, attend you, both as members of this house and as individuals; and I pray Heaven that unanimity and perseverance may go hand in hand in this house; and that every thing which may tend to distract or divide your councils be for ever banished.'

It was then resolved "That the thanks of Congress be presented to John Hancock, esquire, for the unremitted attention and steady impartiality which he has manifested in discharge of various duties of his office as president since his election to the chair on the 24th day of May 1775."

November 1, 1777.

Congress proceeded to the election of a president; and the ballots being taken,

The honorable Henry Laurens was elected.

November 4, 1777.

Resolved, That the thanks of Congress in their own name, and in behalf of the inhabitants of the thirteen United States, be presented to Major General Gates, commander in chief in the northern department, and to the Majors General Lincoln and Arnold and the rest of the officers and troops under his command, for their brave and successful efforts in support of the independence of their country, whereby an army of the enemy of ten thousand men has been totally defeated, one large detachment of it, that strongly posted and entrenched, having been conquered at Bennington, another repulsed with loss and disgrace from fort Schuyler, and the main army of six thousand men, under Lieut. General Burgoyne, after being beaten in different actions and driven from a formidable post and strong entrenchments, reduced to the necessity of surrendering themselves upon terms honorable and advantageous to these states on the 17th day of October last, to Major General Gates; and that a medal of gold be struck under the direction of the board of war in commemoration of this great event, and in the name of these United States presented by the president to Major General Gates.

Resolved, That General Washington be informed, it is highly agreeable to Congress that the Marquis De La Fayette be appointed to the command of a division in the continental army.

December 11, 1777.

The board of war report, "that in their opinion the public interest will be promoted by erecting in the town of York, temporary barracks or sheds sufficient for containing six hundred men, for the purpose of accommodating such recruits and other troops as may from time to time stationed or detained at the said place, either as guards or for the purpose of equipment and discipline:" whereupon

Resolved, That the board of war be directed to cause the said barracks or sheds to be erected, with all possible dispatch, and in the most reasonable manner they can devise.

January 14, 1778.

Whereas baron Steuben, a lieutenant general in foreign service, has in a most disinterested and heroic manner offered his services to these states in the quality of a volunteer:

Resolved, That the president present the thanks of Congress in behalf of these United States to baron Steuben, for the zeal he has shown for the cause of America, & the disinterested tender he has been pleased to make of his military talents; & inform him, that Congress cheerfully accept of his service as a volunteer in the army of these states, and wish him to repair to General Washington's quarters as soon as convenient.

February 6, 1778.

That Mathew Clarkson and Major John Clark be appointed auditors for the army under the command of General Washington; and that they be authorized to appoint two clerks, and allow each of them fifty dollars a month and two rations a day.

March 28, 1778

Resolved, That count Pulaski retain his rank of brigadier in the army of the United States, and that he raise and have the command of an independent corps to consist of sixty-eight horse, and two hundred foot, the horse to be armed with lances, and the foot equipped in the manner of light infantry: the corps to be raised in such a way and composed of such men as General Washington shall think expedient and proper; and if it shall be thought by General Washington, that it will not be injurious to the service, that he have liberty to dispense in this particular instance with the resolve of Congress against enlisting deserters.

June 12, 1778.

Congress being informed that Mr. P. Livingston, one of the delegates for the state of New York, died last night, and that circumstances require him to be interred this evening;

Resolved, That Congress will in a body attend the funeral this evening at six o'clock, with a crape around the arm, and will continue in mourning for the space of one month.

June 27, 1778.

Adjourned to Thursday next, to meet at the State-House in Philadelphia.

In conclusion of this article we will mention the members of congress from York county, under the Constitution of the United States, done in convention on the 17th of September 1787.

Thomas Hartley was the first: he was elected in 1788, and continued a member of Congress until the time of his death, on the 21st of December 1800.

John Stewart, was elected by special election on the 15th of January 1801, to supply the place of Thomas Hartley deceased: and. was re-elected in October 1802.

James Kelley was elected in October 1804, and was re-elected in October 1806.

William Crawford was elected in October 1808, and was re-elected in 1810.

Hugh Glasgow was elected in October 1812, and was re-elected in October 1814.

Jacob Spengler was elected in October 1816.

Jacob Hostetter was elected in March 1818, to fill the place of Jacob Spengler resigned: he was re-elected in October of the same year.

James S. Mitchell was elected in October of the years 1822, and 1834.

Adam King was elected in October, 1826, and re-elected in 1828 and 1830.

Charles A. Barnitz was elected in 1832.

CHAPTER XII.

PRINTING.

ON THE 17th October 1777, Congress, then sitting in York, "resolved that the committee of intelligence be authorized to take the most speedy and effectual measures for getting a printing press erected in York town for the purpose of conveying to the public the intelligence that Congress might from time to time receive." The press of Hall and Sellers of Philadelphia and one of the oldest in the state, was shortly afterwards brought to York, where divers public communications were printed, as was likewise much continental money.* This was the first printing press erected in Pennsylvania, west of the Susquehanna. Congress removed from York in June 1778, and the press, with all the appurtenances, accordingly accompanied them to Philadelphia.

There was now an "aching void" for about nine years. In the year 1787, Matthias Bartgis and T. Roberts established a printing office in York; in the month of October in that year they issued the first number of their newspaper, which was entitled "The Pennsylvania Chronicle and York Weekly Advertiser." It was "printed and published by M. Bartgis and Company." This paper was continued about two years, when, Edie and Wilcocks having commenced a paper in York, the press, types &c. were shortly afterwards removed to Harrisburg, Pa.

* A circumstance connected with the printing of continental money in York, shews that some of workmen employed by Congress, or the agents of Congress, were not quite so honest as they should have been. In the year 1821 repairs were made to the house in which the continental money had been printed; and under the hearth of a room in the second story of the building, bills to the amount of some thousand dollars were found concealed, no doubt with the object of filling them up with counterfeit signatures—the execution of which object, it is presumable, was prevented by accident or the fears of those who secreted the bills.

The next paper printed in York was the "Pennsylvania Herald, and York General Advertiser," the first number of which was issued by James Edie, John Edie and Henry Wilcocks, on the 7th of January, 1789.

The types employed in the printing of the Herald were cast in Philadelphia by Mr. Bane, a gentleman who was educated in Edinburgh, in Scotland, and who had been, in this country, a partner of Dr. Wilson. The press was made in York under the direction of Henry Wilcocks, the iron work being executed by Jacob Small. The printing ink of the first number was manufactured in Germantown.

The Herald preserved its title for about eleven years, though as to minor things, such as ownership and the like, it underwent some changes; thus, for example, we find it in 1799 "printed every Wednesday by John Edie; price to subscribers fifteen shillings per annum."

In the year 1800, Mr. Edie took Mr. Robert M'Clellan as a partner; and changing the title of the Herald they commenced a new paper entitled the "York Recorder." The "Recorder" was, in truth, the "Herald" continued; its first number issued on the 29th of January 1800.

The "Recorder," although it passed through the hands of about twenty different editors, was regularly continued until the year 1830. The last editor of the "Recorder" was Samuel Wagner, Esq. The establishment passed from Mr. Wagner, into the hands of Thomas C. Hambly, by whom a paper was published at first called the "York Republican," and afterwards the "Pennsylvania Republican." Mr. Hambly transferred the establishment in 1834, to Samuel E. Clement, by whom a paper is now published bearing the title of the "Pennsylvania Republican."

Until the year 1796, there had not been two papers published in York at the same time. In the spring of that year Solomon Meyer* commenced the publication of a german paper, entitled "Die York Gazette." This was the first paper

---

* Mr. Meyer was commissioned Brigade Inspector of the first brigade, composed of the militia of York and Adams counties, on the 25th of April, 1800. He died at Winchester, Virginia, on the 28th of February, 1811.

printed in this county in the German language. It afterwards passed into the hands of Christian Schlichting, under whom it ended in the year 1804. In that year, the press, types, &c., were purchased by Mr. Daniel Heckert, by whom they were sold to Stark and Lange, of Hanover, by which latter gentlemen the "Hanover Gazette," a German paper, was established, in 1805.

The paper next established in the borough of York, was "Der Volks Berichter," the first number of which was published by Andrew Billmeyer, on the 25th of July 1799.

There were now three papers published together in York, one in the English and two in the German language.

The "Volks Berichter" was continued four years.

"Der Wahre Republicaner" was the third German paper printed in York, its first number being issued on the 20th of February, 1805. This paper, which was a continuation of the "Berichter," or rather a revival of it, was at first published by Schlichting and Billmeyer, afterward by Daniel Billmeyer alone, until his death, which was in the year 1828. Shortly after Mr. Billmeyer's decease, the establishment was purchased by Mr. Samuel Wagner, at that time Editor of the York Recorder, who from that time until the year 1830, published an English and a German paper, the latter of which bore the title of "Der Republicanishe Herold." At the time that Mr. Wagner transferred the "York Recorder" to Thomas C. Hambly, as before mentioned, he sold the "Republicanische Herold" to Messrs. Glossbrenner and May, by whom the paper was published for about two months, when Mr. Glossbrenner transferred his share of it to Benjamin Flory, and the paper was published by May and Flory, for about one year, when it was purchased by Thomas C. Hambly, and united to the establishment of the "York Republican." In 1834, Samuel E. Clement purchased both papers, and they continue to be published by him to this time.

Until the year 1808, there had not been two English papers published here at one and the same time. In the month of May in that year the first number of the "Expositor" was issued, a weekly paper printed and published every Thursday by Daniel Heckert and Daniel Updegraff. The Expositor was continued until August, 1814, when both Editors suddenly relinquished their employment, and went forth, with signal patriotism, to the field of fame and danger. After their return from North Point, whither, with other "hearts of oak," they had marched as volunteers, they did not resume the publication of the Expositor.

In the year 1815, a new German paper, entitled "Der Union's Freund," was commenced in York, the first number of which was issued on the 19th of January, 1815, by Charles T. Melsheimer and James Lewis, at that time joint editors of the "York Recorder." This paper was continued nearly two years—the last number of it was issued in October, 1816.

In the year 1815, an English paper, with the title of "The York Gazette," was commenced in York; and the first number was issued in May of that year, by William Clawson Harris. The publication of the Gazette was continued by Mr. Harris until the time of his death, (the 5th of December 1818). It immediately passed into other hands, and has been regularly continued to the present time. At this time it is edited and published by Adam King and George Augustus Barnitz.

In connexion with the above English paper, its German sister, of the same name, should be mentioned. The first number of the German York Gazette was issued on the 16th of March, 1821, by Adam King and Richard Abbott, who were at that time, partners in the publication of the English paper, then as now, printed at the same office. The present Editors of the German Gazette, are Messrs. King and Barnitz, the Editors of the English paper.

In August 1819, a monthly literary gazette was commenced at York, which was at first published by P. Hardt, at that time Editor of the "York Recorder." This periodical was called the "Village Museum," and was continued four years.

The Theological Seminary of the German Reformed Church having been removed to York in the fall of the year 1828, the "Magazine" of that church has, since that time, been published here. The first three or four numbers published in York, were printed by Samuel Wagner, since which time it has been published successively by Glossbrenner and May, May and Flory, and by Daniel May. At present, the Magazine is edited by Dr. L. Mayer, and printed by Daniel May.

In 1830, a German religious paper was commenced in York, by the Rev. John H. Dreyer. The paper was called "Die Evangelische Zeitung," and continued in existence, with occasional suspension of publication, for about two years.

In the year 1830, the publication of the "Harbinger," an English paper, which had been commenced and published for about three years at Shrewsbury, in this county, was removed to York. It is still in existence, and continues to be published, in an enlarged and improved form, by its original Editor, Mr. William C. Smyth. It now bears the title of "The Harbinger and States' Union."

In December 1831, the "York County Farmer," an English paper, was commenced. This was the first paper, of imperial size, ever published in the county. It was edited by Adam J. Glossbrenner, and published by Glossbrenner and May. The "Farmer" was discontinued at the end of its second year.

Having noticed all the periodicals ever published in the borough of York, we will proceed to look after those published in other parts of the county. There was no paper printed in what is now Adams county, before the year 1800, when it was separated from York.

The first paper printed at Hanover was a German one entitled "Die Pennsylvanische Wochenschrift," the first number of which was issued by Lepper and Stellinius, in April, 1797. Mr. Lepper became, not long afterwards, the sole proprietor of the establishment, and he continued the paper until February, 1805.

The "Wochenschrift" had but just been discontinued, when the "Hanover Gazette," another German paper, was commenced, the first number of it being issued in April, 1805. It was published under the firm of Stark and Lange, until November, 1816—from which time to the present, with the exception of a short period, during which Koehler was associated in the publication, it has been published by Daniel Philip Lange alone.

The next paper printed at Hanover was a German one of short existence, for the first number was published in August, 1809, and the last number in March, 1810, at which time one of the Editors, Mr. Melsheimer, removed to Fredericktown.

The first English paper printed at Hanover was entitled the "Hanover Guardian," the first number of which was issued by J. H. Wiestling, in September, 1818.

This paper was published but for a few years, during which time the establishment passed through a number of hands; and the publication was at last discontinued for want of sufficient patronage.

After the discontinuance of the "Guardian," another English paper, with the title of the "Hanoverian," was commenced in Hanover. This paper shared the fate of its English predecessor, perishing in a short time, for want of patronage.

In 1824, a new German paper was established in Hanover, entitled the "Intelligenzblatt," the first number of which was issued in April of that year, by P. Mueller and J. Schmuck. This paper was soon after its commencement, removed to Adams county.

The "Hanover Gazette," a German paper, is now the only paper published in Hanover.

A German paper is now published in the village of Jefferson, in this county, by George Sprung. This paper was established in April, 1834.

CHAPTER XIII.

GUBERNATORIAL ELECTIONS.

There can be no truer index of the political principles of our county, than the votes it has given at different times, for governor of the commonwealth. The office of *Governor,* in this state, was substituted for that of *President of the Council,* on the 2d of September, 1790, at which time the present Constitution of Pennsylvania was adopted. Before proceeding to state the result of the different elections in this county, for governor, we will give a list of the provincial governors, (i.e., those who exercised the supreme executive power in Pennsylvania prior to the adoption of the Constitution of 29th September 1779) and a list of the *Presidents of the Council*, an office created by the constitution of 1779.

I. Provincial Executives.

1. William Penn, from October 24, 1682, to August 12, 1684.
2. Council and President, Thomas Lloyd, from August 12, 1684, to December, 1688.
3. John Blackwell, Deputy Governor, from December, 1688, to February, 1689.
4. Council and President, Thomas Lloyd, from February, 1689, to April, 1693.
5. Benjamin Fletcher, Governor, from April, 1693, to June, 1693.
6. William Markham, Deputy Governor, from June, 1693, to December, 1699.
7. William Penn, again Governor, from December, 1699, to November, 1701.
8. Andrew Hamilton, Deputy Governor, from November, 1701, to February, 1702.
9. President and Council, from February 1702, to February 1703.
10. John Evans, Deputy Governor, from February 1703, to February 1709.
11. Charles Gookin, Deputy Governor, from March 1709, to May, 1717.
12. William Keith, Deputy Governor, from May 1717, to June 1726.
13. Patrick Gordon, Deputy Governor, from June, 1726, to 1736.
14. Council and President, James Logan, from 1736 to 1738.
15. George Thomas, Deputy Governor, from 1738 to 1747.
16. Council and President, Anthony Palmer, from 1747, to November 1748.

17. James Hamilton, Deputy Governor, from November 1748, to October 1754.

18. Robert Hunter Morris, Deputy Governor, from October 1754, to 1756.

19. William Denny, Deputy Governor, from 1756 to 1759.

20. James Hamilton, again Deputy Governor, from 1759 to 1764.

21. John Penn, son of Richard, Deputy Governor from 1764, to 1771.

22. Council and President, James Hamilton, 1771.

23. Richard Penn, Governor, from 1771, to 1773.

24. John Penn, brother of Richard, Governor, from 1773, to 1776.

II. Presidents of the Councils, under the Constitution of 1779.

There were five different persons who presided, at different periods, over the executive council of Pennsylvania. They were elected and presided in the following order:

1. Thomas Wharton.
2. Joseph Read.
3. John Dickinson.*
4. Benjamin Franklin.†
5. Thomas Mifflin.‡

---

* John Dickinson was the man after whom Dickinson College, at Carlisle, is named. He was born in Delaware—was a member of the assembly of Pennsylvania in 1764—and a member of the first Congress in 1774. He died in Wilmington, Delaware, in 1808.

† It is needless to tell an American WHO Benjamin Franklin was.

‡ Thomas Mifflin was a Quaker. Born in 1744. Member of the first Congress in 1774. Expelled from the Society of Friends in 1775 for accepting the office of Quarter Master General. Member of the convention which framed the constitution of the United States in 1787. First Governor of Pennsylvania under the constitution of 1790, in which office he continued for 9 years. Died in Lancaster in January 1800.

The first election for Governor was held on the 12th of October, 1790, at which election the votes stood in York county as follows:

Thomas Mifflin,	(votes) 1699
Arthur St. Clair,	29

Thomas Mifflin was elected.

SECOND ELECTION.—October 8, 1793.

F. A. Muhlenberg,	1265
Thomas Mifflin,	712

Thomas Mifflin was elected.

THIRD ELECTION.—October 11, 1796.

Thomas Mifflin,	1124
Peter Dinkel,	12
Henry Miller,	11
F. A. Muhlenberg,	1

Thomas Mifflin was elected.

FOURTH ELECTION.—October 8, 1799.

James Ross, of Pittsburg,	2705
Thomas McKean,	2026
Scattering,	4

Thomas McKean was elected.

FIFTH ELECTION.—October 12, 1802.

Thomas McKean,	1691
James Ross, of Pittsburgh	72

Thomas McKean was elected.

SIXTH ELECTION.—October 8, 1805.

Thomas McKean,	1883
Simon Snyder,	747
James Ross, of Pittsburg,	9

Thomas McKean was elected.

SEVENTH ELECTION.—October 11, 1808.

Simon Snyder,	2867
James Ross, of Pittsburg,	1654
John Spayd,	18

Simon Snyder was elected.

EIGHTH ELECTION.—October 14, 1811.

Simon Snyder,	1834
Scattering,	19

Simon Snyder was elected.

NINTH ELECTION.—October 11, 1814.

Simon Snyder,	1599
Isaac Wayne,	1027

Simon Snyder was elected.

TENTH ELECTION.—October 14, 1817.

William Findlay,	2918
Joseph Hiester,	1644

William Findlay was elected.

ELEVENTH ELECTION.—October 10, 1820.

William Findlay,	2621
Joseph Hiester,	2131

Joseph Hiester was elected.

TWELFTH ELECTION.—October 14, 1823.

John Andrew Shultze,	3912
Andrew Gregg,	2166

John Andrew Shultze was elected.

THIRTEENTH ELECTION.—October 10, 1826.

John Andrew Shultze,	2494
Scattering,	107

John Andrew Shultze was elected.

FOURTEENTH ELECTION.—October 13, 1829.

George Wolf,	1894
Joseph Ritner,	769

George Wolf was elected.

FIFTEENTH ELECTION.—October 9, 1832.

George Wolf,	2367
Joseph Ritner,	2357

George Wolf was elected.

The above statement exhibits the fluctuations of political opinion in this county, and affords several remarkable instances of entire revolution in public opinion in a single gubernatorial term of three years. At the first election Mifflin had 1699 votes, at the second 712, at the third 1124. At the second election F. A. Muhlenberg had a majority over Mifflin of more than 500 votes, and three years after that Mifflin beat Muhlenberg 1123 votes, the latter receiving but a single vote. These changes are observable throughout the history of gubernatorial elections in this county. The latest two elections, resulted, as will have been perceived, as follows:—In 1829, George Wolf had a majority over Joseph Ritner, of 1125 votes. In 1832, Ritner had a majority of ten over Wolf. [?]

CHAPTER XIV.

STATE SENATORS OF YORK COUNTY.

UNDER the constitution of 2d September, 1790.

1. For the district composed of the counties of York and Lancaster.

1790. Michael Schmeiser,
Sebastian Groff,
Adam Hubley, Jun.

1791. No return.
1792. Do.
1793. Do.
1794. Michael Schmeiser,
Thomas Lilly.
1795. James Ewing.
1796. No return.
1797. Do.
1798. Do.
1799. James Ewing.

2. For the district composed of the counties of York and Adams.

1800. William Reed.
1801. Do.
1802. No return.
1803. Rudolph Spangler.
1804. No return.
1805. William Miller.
1806. No return.
1807. Thomas Campbell.
1808. No return.
1809. William Gilliland.
1810. No return.
1811. John Strohman.
1812. No return.
1813. James McSherry.
1814. No return.
1815. Charles A. Barnitz.
1816. No return.
1817. William Gilliland.
1818. No return.
1819. Fred'k Eichelberger.
1820. No return.
1821. Jacob Eyster.
1822. No return.
1823. William McIlvaine.
1824. Zephaniah Herbert.
1825. Do.
1826. Henry Logan.
1827. Do.
1828. No return.
1829. Ezra Blythe.
1830. No return.
1831. Henry Smyser.
1832. No return.
1833. David Middlekauff.

The district composed of York and Adams sends two Senators in every four years. The Senator is chosen from the counties alternately—one being elected every two years. In the above table it will be perceived that Senators have been elected oftener than biennially—where this occurred, it was occasioned by the resignation, before the expiration of his time, of a Senator, when another individual was chosen to serve until the expiration of the period for which the first was elected.

GENERAL ASSEMBLY.

The following is a list of the members, for the county of York, in the General Assembly of Pennsylvania, both before and since the revolution. They were elected in October of the following years, viz:

1749.	John Wright and John Armstrong.
1750.	No sheriff's return, nor did any representative appear.
1751.	John Wright and John Witherow.
1752.	No return.
1753.	John Wright and David McConaughy.
1754.	Do. Do.
1755.	" "
1756.	" "
1757.	" "
1758.	" "
1759.	" "
1760.	David McConaughy and John Blackburn.
1761.	Do. Do.
1762.	" "
1763.	" "
1764.	" "
1765.	John Blackburn and Robert McPherson.
1766.	Do. Do.
1767.	Robert McPherson and Archibald McGrew.
1768.	Thos. Minschall and Michael Schwaabe.
1769.	Do. Do.
1770.	" "
1771.	James Ewing and Michael Schwaabe.

1772. James Ewing and John Pope.
1773. Do. Do.
1774. James Ewing and Michael Schwaabe.
1775. Do. Do.

☞On the 23d of March 1776, an act was passed to increase the number of representatives, at which time Samuel Edie and James Rankin were added as representatives from York county to serve the remainder of that session.

1776. Archibald McLean, Michael Schwaabe, David Dunwoodie, James Dickson, Michael Hahn, John Read.
1777. David Dunwoodie, James Dickson, Michael Hahn, Matthew Dill, John Agnew, John Orr.
1778. Thomas Hartley, Samuel Edie, Thomas Lilly, Michael Schmeiser, William Ross, Henry Schlegel.
1779. David Dunwoodie, James Dickson, Matthew Dill, John Orr, Henry Schlegel, James Lieper, John Hay, David Kennedy.
1780. James Dickson, Thomas Lilly, Michael Schmeiser, Moses McLean, Robert Gilbraith, James Smith, William Mitchell, James Ramsey.
1781. Michael Hahn, John Agnew, Thomas Lilly, Michael Schmeiser, Moses McLean, Robert McPherson, Jas. Ramsey, Joseph McGuffin.
1782. Michael Hahn, Thomas Lilly, Michael Schmeiser, Moses McLean, Robert McPherson, Joseph McGuffen, John Hay, Patrick Scott.
1783. Moses McLean, Robert McPherson, Joseph McGuffin, John Hay, Henry Miller, Philip Gardner, David Grier, David McConaughy.
1784. Robert McPherson, John Hay, Henry Miller, Philip Gardner, David McConaughy, James Ewing, Henry Tyson, Joseph Lilly.
1785. Henry Miller, Philip Gardner, David McConaughy, Henry Tyson, Joseph Lilly, David McLellan, Adam Eichelberger, Michael Schmeiser.
1786. David McConaughy, Henry Tyson, Joseph Lilly, David McLellan, Adam Eichelberger, Michael Schmeiser.

1787. Michael Schmeiser, Joseph Lilly, David McLellan, William Mitchell, Joseph Read, Thomas Clingan.

1788. Michael Schmeiser, Thomas Lilly, Henry Tyson, David McLellan, Joseph Read, Thomas Clingan.

1789. Thomas Lilly, Thomas Clingan, Jacob Schmeiser, John Stewart, William Godfrey, Joseph Read.

1790. Joseph Read, Philip Gardner, Henry Tyson, Wm. McPherson, John Stewart, Thomas Lilly.

1791. Thomas Lilly, John Stewart, William McPherson, Alexander Turner, Thomas Thornburg, Henry Tyson.

1792. Philip Gardner, John Stewart, Alexander Turner, Thomas Thornburg, Thomas Lilly, William McPherson.

1793. Thomas Lilly, Philip Gardner, John Stewart, Alexander Turner, Thomas Campbell, James Kelly.

1794. Philip Gardner, John Stéwart, William McPherson, Alexander Turner, Thomas Campbell, James Kelly.

1795. William McPherson, Alexander Turner, Thomas Campbell, Philip Gardner, William Miller, John Stewart.

1796. William McPherson, John Stewart, Philip Gardner, Alexander Turner, Thomas Camptell, William Miller.

1797. Thomas Campbell, William McPherson, Alexander Turner, Philip Gardner, Jacob Hostetter, James Kelly.

1798. Thomas Campbell, Alexander Turner, William McPherson, James Kelly, Jacob Hostetter, Philip Albright.

1799. William McPherson, Alexander Turner, Thomas Campbell, Jost Herbach, Alexander Cobean, Jacob Hostetter.

1800. Jacob Hostetter, Frederick Eichelberger, William Anderson, Michael Gemmill.

1801. Frederick Eichelberger, William Anderson, Michael Gemmill, Michael Hellman.

1802. Frederick Eichelberger, William Anderson, Michael Hellman, Daniel Stouffer.

1803. Michael Hellman, Daniel Stouffer, Matthew Clark, George Spengler.
1804. Michael Hellman, Matthew Clark, George Spengler, Adam Hendricks.
1805. George Spangler, Conrad Sherman, William McLellan, Benjamin Pedan.
1806. William Anderson, George Spengler, Adam Hendricks, Robert Hamersly.
1807. Conrad Sherman, Jacob Eichelberger, Robert Gemmill, John McLellan.
1808. George Spengler, Abraham Graffius, Archibald Steel, George Nes.
1809. George Spengler, Abraham Graffius, George Nes, Archibald S. Jordan.
1810. George Nes, James S. Mitchell, Moses Rankin, Rudolph Spengler.
1811. Adam Hendricks, James S. Mitchell, Moses Rankin, George Stake.
1812. James S. Mitchell, Peter Storm, Jacob Heckert, Adam Hendricks.
1813. James S. Mitchell, Jacob Heckert, Archibald S. Jordan, George Freysinger.
1814. Archibald S. Jordan, Peter Storm, Peter Small, James S. Mitchell.
1815. Frederick Eichelberger, Peter Storm, John Livingston, John Strohman.
1816. Frederick Eichelberger, Peter Storm, Michael Gardner, John Livingston.
1817. Michael Gardner, Frederick Eichelberger, Peter Storm, Moses Rankin.
1818. Jacob Doll, Peter Reider, Robert Ramsey, Henry Logan.
1819. Ditto. Ditto.
1820. Jonas Dierdorf, William Nes, John Livingston, Peter Storm.
1821. Ditto. Ditto.
1822. John Gardner, Samuel Jordan, William Diven, Christian Hetrick.
1823. Ditto. Ditto.

1824. Samuel Jordan, Christian Hetrick, William Diven, John Kauffelt.
1825. Christian Hetrick, Simon Anstine, John Eichelberger, Michael Gardner.
1826. Christian Hetrick, John Becker, Peter Wolford, Stephen T. Cooper.
1827. Stephen T. Cooper, Peter Wolford, John Becker, George Fisher.
1828. Stephen T. Cooper, Michael Doudel, Thomas Metzler, George Fisher.
1829. Michael Doudel, Geo. Fisher, Andrew McConkey.
1830. George Fisher, Andrew McConkey, John Rankin.
1831. Andrew Flickinger, John R. Donnel, John Rankin.
1832. John Rankin, John R. Donnel, Daniel Durkee.
1833. John R. Donnel, William McClellan, Henry Snyder.

CHAPTER XV.

SHERIFFS.

THE candidates for the office of sheriff, at the first election held in York county, were Hans Hamilton and Richard McAlister. At that time, and at the elections for some years following, all the voters assembled together at York, as there were no election districts as at present. The first election, which was in October, 1749, was held in York-town at the house formerly occupied by Baltzer Spangler. and afterwards by Samuel Spangler, as a public inn. The building was of logs and was not quite finished. There was but one place at which the votes were received, and that was at an opening between two of the logs of the building. During the forenoon every thing was peaceable; but in the afternoon the blood was warmed, and men were now more ready for action. Hamilton, who lived in what is now Adams county, was the "Irish candidate," and McAlister, who lived where Hanover now stands, was the "Dutch candidate." McAlister's Germans pressed hard, and were, in the stillness of voting, rather overpowering the friends of Mr. Hamilton. Displeased with this, two or three stout Irish boxers took possession of the place for handing in votes, and were determined that none but their own friends should enjoy the liberty of suffrage. A lusty German being anxious to offer his vote, went determinedly to the place of voting, and tripped up the heels of one of the Irish guards. An affray immediately commenced, and in less than five minutes the action was general. *Furor administrat arma.* A large quantity of saplings near the house were soon torn and cut from the ground to be used as weapons of offence and defence. Blows were dealt with an unsparing hand; each party giving hot battle. But victory at length perched upon the banner of the "Dutch party," for the friends of McAlister not only discomfitted the Irish, but completely routed their whole forces, and put them to flight. They drove them all beyond the Codorus; and not a member of the defeated party was to be found east of the creek during the remainder of that day. There were a few limbs broken, and considerable blood shed: but, fortunately for the honour of the country, no life was lost in the affray. The Germans, keeping possession of the ground, gave in their votes without molestation: whereby McAlister had an overwhelming majority. But this availed not: for Hamilton was a great favorite of the executive, and was, shortly after the election, commissioned as sheriff of the county of York, and as such he continued until the 10th of October, 1752.

Hamilton was, after an interval of three years, again commissioned as sheriff, the only instance to be found in the records of our county, of an individual serving more than one term as sheriff.

That the second election in York county was not conducted in a less fierce spirit than the first, appears from the following extract from the record of the court of Quarter Sessions for the 30th of October, 1750: "Whereas, Hans Hamilton, Esq., High Sheriff of this county, hath by his remonstrance in writing to this court set forth, that by reason of the tumultuous behaviour of sundry persons at the last election held here for this county, and of the ballots or tickets not having been delivered to the inspectors on three several [?] pieces of paper, as directed by an act of the General Assembly of this province, entitled "an act for raising the county rates and levies," he could not make such returns as by the aforesaid act is enjoined: It is therefore considered and ordered by the Court here, that the commissioners and assessors who served this county in their several stations the last year, shall, (in pursuance of the act aforesaid,) serve for the ensuing year, or until there shall be a new election."

As Hans Hamilton was much honored in the early part of our country's history, we deem it proper to note the following of him.

He became, several years after he had served two terms as sheriff, one of the Judges of the Court of Common Pleas, and died early in the year 1772, in Menallin township. His character as a man of integrity and general worth, stood very high. At his decease he left the following children: Thomas, (who had been Sheriff,) Sarah, (then married to Alexander McKean,) Mary, (then married to Hugh McKean,) Hans, Guiain, George, John, William and James.

Mr. Hamilton was succeeded after his first term, by John Adlum, who was elected in October, 1749. Mr. Adlum's term having expired, Mr. Hamilton's second term commenced in October, 1755—and the following is the order of his successors to the sheriffalty, and the dates of their elections respectively:

Thomas Hamilton, elected in Oct. 1756	*Dav. McConaughy Oct. 1765
Zachariah Shugard, Oct. 1758	Geo. Eichelberger, Oct. 1768
Peter Shugard, Oct. 1759	Samuel Edie, Oct. 1771
Robert McPherson, Oct. 1762	**Charles Lukens, Nov. 1774

* David McConaughy was the first collector of excise in York county, being appointed by the General Assembly on the 19th of August, 1749.

** Charles Lukens and William Rowan were elected Sheriffs in 1776, for those officers were then elected annually. But Lukens, being then engaged in other public services, was prevented from accepting the office; whereupon a com-

†William Rowan,	June 1777	John Edie,	Oct. 1786
Henry Miller,	Oct. 1780	Conrad Laub,	Oct. 1789
William Bailey,	Nov. 1783		

Though the election for sheriffs in this county is usually a matter of very warm contest, yet it never was so closely contested as in October, 1789, when Conrad Laub was elected. The two candidates were Conrad Laub and William McClellan, of whom the former had 2130 votes, the latter 2111. Immediately after the election a very pleasant article appeared in one of the York papers, which, as it will not take up much of our room, we will give a place here. It was written by Mr. William Harris, then a merchant of York.

"The first chapter of Chronicles.

1. Now it came to pass in these days when *George* (1) was President, even *George the Great*, was President over the nation, and *John*, (2) even *John* surnamed *the steady*, who had done justice and judgment among the people, had fulfilled his time, that there was a great stir among the people, whom they should choose to reign in his stead.

2. Then the *Williamites*, (3) who inhabited the western country, and the people gathered themselves together, and

---

mission was granted to William Rowan, although not the highest in votes.

Congress, in November, 1777, appointed Lukens major commissary of military stores in the department of Carlisle. It may here be remarked, that although Congress fixed upon Carlisle as a proper place for erecting laboratories and for laying up magazines of military stores, yet Gen. Washington, in a letter to that body, dated January 17th 1777, says, "General Knox, and others whom I have consulted upon this occasion, think that Yorktown would be full as safe, and more convenient than Carlisle."

† Sheriff Rowan, not long after the expiration of his term of office, removed into the state of Kentucky. His son John, who was born in this county, and who accompanied his father on his removal, has since been elected, by the Legislature of Kentucky, to represent that state in the Senate of the United States.

(1) George Washington. (2) John Edie.
(3) The friends of William McClellan.

communed one with another, and said: We will make *William* to rule over us, for he is a proper young man, & will do justice and judgment even as *John* has done, whose work is fulfilled.

3. And when these sayings went abroad among the people, there were certain men rose up and withstood the Williamites and said, God do so to us, and more also, if *William* shall rule over us at this time in the stead of *John*.

4. Then the governors, the judges, the captains of the fifties, and the rulers of the people gathered themselves together.

5. And so it was that they communed together, even the *Schlegelites* (4), the *Rudisellites* (5), the *Shermanites* (6), the *Gosslerites* (7), the *Millerites* (8), the *Campbellites* (9), the tribe of *Eli* (10), and *John the Lawyer* (11).

6. Now all entered into a covenant, and said, of a truth we will make *Conrad* (12) our ruler, for he is an upright man, and will do what is right in the eyes of the people.

7. And after these things it came to pass on the thirteenth day of the tenth month, about the eleventh hour, in the fourteenth year after the people had come out of the house of bondage, that the people strove with one another, even the Williamites on the one side, and the Conradites on the other.

8. And there was a great slaughter, for the battle continued until the going down of the sun.

9. For the Conradites came forth by hundreds and by thousands, by their tribes, as sands by the seashore for multitude.

10. And so it was, that the army of the Williamites was discomfitted.

11. Now the land will have rest for three full years."

---

(4) The friends of Henry Schiegel.
(5) The friends of Jacob Rudisell.
(6) The friends of Conrad Sherman.
(7) The friends of Philip Gossler.
(8) The friends of Henry Miller.
(9) The friends of John Campbell.
(10) Eli Lewis. (11) John Lukens. (12) Conrad Laub.

The "three full years" having come to an end, Conrad Laub was succeeded by

Godfrey Lenhart, elected in	Oct. 1792	Michael Gardner,	Nov. 1811
		John Kauffelt,	Nov. 1815
William McClellan,	Oct. 1795	Zachariah Spangler,	Oct. 1818
Nicholas Gelwicks,	Oct. 1798	Thomas Jameson,	Oct. 1821
John Strohman,	Oct. 1801	Michael Doudel,	Oct. 1824
Jacob Eichelberger,	Oct. 1804	William Spangler,	Oct. 1827
Michael Klinefelter,	Oct. 1807	Andrew Duncan,	Oct. 1830
Benjamin Hirsch,	Oct. 1810	Adam Eichelberger,	Oct. 1833

CORONERS.

Alexander Love was the first coroner, and continued in office for five years from 1749, the time of the erection of the county. He was succeeded by

Archibald McGrew, in the in the year	1754	Michael Schwaabe,	1761
Zachariah Shugard,	1755	John Adlum,	1763
William King,	1758	Joseph Adlum,	1764

Mr. Adlum continued in office fourteen years—the election for coroner in those times was held annually, and there were no limitations to his term of service. Who was coroner in 1779, 1780, & 1781, the records do not show. After that time the succession was as follows:

Jacob Rudisell,	1782	George Hay,	1799
Ephraim Pennington,	1784	George Stake,	1802
Andrew Johnson,	1786	John Spangler,	1806
John Morris,	1790	Thomas Jameson,	1808
Jacob Updegraff,	1796		

At the election in October, 1811, the votes for coroner were 1893 for Michael Gardner, and 1893 for John Rouse. Mr. Gardner, however, being appointed sheriff upon the resignation of B. Hirsch, in 1811, did not receive any commission as coroner, by reason whereof the person then in office, (Dr. Thomas Jameson,) was continued.

John Rouse,	1812	Henry Nes,	1824
Thomas Jameson,	1816	Jacob Gerry,	1830
William McIlvaine,	1818	Theodore N. Haller,	1833
Luke Rouse,	1821		

CHAPTER XVI.

COMMISSIONERS.

THE following is a list of commissioners of York county with the time on which each of them was qualified or entered on the duties of his office.

FIRST CLASS.

George Schwaabe, qualified on Oct. 31, 1749
Bartholemew Maul, Oct. 29, 1751
Peter Shugard, Oct. 1754
Martin Eichelberger, Oct. 1757
James Welsch, Oct. 1760
William Douglas, Oct. 1763
Joseph Updegraff, Oct. 1766
John Heckendorn, Oct. 31, 1769
John Hay, Oct. 20, 1772
Michael Hahn, Oct. 1775
William Ross, 1776-7
Philip Rothrock, Oct. 30, 1778
Jacob Schmeiser, Oct. 12, 1781
Michael Hahn, Oct. 29, 1784
Godfrey Lenhart Oct. 29, 1787
John Spengler, Oct. 26, 1790
Joseph Welshhans, Oct. 17, 1793
John Forsythe, Dec. 6, 1796
Daniel Spengler, Oct. 29, 1799
Christopher Lauman, Oct. 16, 1802
Abr. Graffins, Nov. 4, 1805
Jacob Heckert, Nov. 7, 1808
Peter Small, Nov. 5, 1811
Jacob Spengler, Nov. 2, 1814
John Bernitz, Nov. 5, 1817
Michael Doudel, Nov. 7, 1820
Henry Schmeiser, Nov. 1823
John Voglesong, Nov. 1826
Peter Ahl, Nov. 1829
Jacob Dietz, Nov. 1832

SECOND CLASS.

Walter Sharp, qualified on Oct. 31, 1749
William McClellan,* Oct. 30, 1750
John Mikel, Oct. 1752
Thomas M'Cartney, Oct. 28, 1755
William Delap, Oct. 1758
George Meyers, Oct. 31, 1761
Phillip Zeigler, Oct. 1764
Hugh Dunwoodie, Oct. 1767
John Menteith, Oct. 15, 1770
Henry Tyson, Oct. 20, 1773
John Hay, Oct. 1776
John Sample, Oct. 1779
Wm. Cochran, Oct. 29, 1782

* As there was no return of an election in York county in 1750, the court continued the former commissioners; but as Mr. Sharp had died, the surviving commissioners, and the assessors elected Mr. McClellan in his place. Here by the way, it may be remarked of George Schwaabe that he was requalified in Oct. 1750, for regularly his period of office had terminated.

Robt. Morrison, Nov. 1, 1785
Wm. McClellan** Nov. 1, 1786
John Morrow, Oct. 1791
Henry Welsch, Oct. 1794
David Edie, Dec. 4, 1794
Anthony Hinkel, Oct. 28, 1800
Robert Ramsey, Oct. 24, 1803
Christopher Hetrick, Nov. 3, 1806
Frederick Hoke, Nov. 7, 1809
John Kauffelt, Nov. 2, 1812
Joseph Reed, Nov. 7, 1815
Andrew Kitterman, Nov. 2, 1818
Michael Newman, Nov. 6, 1821
Matthew Clark, Nov. 1824
Philip Henise, Nov. 1827
William Patterson, Nov. 1830
John Shultz, Nov. 1833

THIRD CLASS.

Patrick Watson, qualified on Oct. 31, 1749
James Agnew, Oct. 30, 1753
Robert McPherson, Oct. 1756
John Frankelberger,† Oct. 31, 1758
John Adlum, Oct. 30, 1759
Samuel Edie, Oct. 1762
Thomas Stocton, Oct. 1765
William Gemmill, Oct. 27, 1768
William Nelson, Oct. 1792
James Black, Oct. 1795
Jas. M'Canless, Dec. 3, 1798
Samuel Nelson, Oct. 26, 1801
Jacob Heckert,‡ Nov. 19, 1802
Joseph Glancy, Oct. 29, 1804
William Collins, Nov. 6, 1807
John Klein, Nov. 5, 1810
Peter Reider, Nov. 2, 1813
Charles Emig, Nov. 5, 1816
Stephen T. Cooper, Nov. 2, 1819
Peter Wolfhart, Nov. 1822
Charles Diehl, Nov. 1825
Daniel Kimmel, Nov. 1828
John W. Hetrick, Nov. 1831
Samuel Harnish,§ 1833

** Mr. Morrison removed from the county shortly after his election to office. To complete his term Mr. McClellan was elected on Oct. 10, 1786; and when that term expired, he was re-elected on Oct. 14, 1788, for three years, and was qualified on the 29th of the same month.

† Gen. Forbes, in 1758, marched with an army from Philadelphia, and reduced fort Du Quesne, which is now Pittsburg. As Mr. McPherson joined him in this, as it was then called "Western Expedition," it was to supply his place as commissioner that Mr. Frankelberger was elected for one year.

‡ Mr. Heckert was appointed till the next election to supply the place of Samuel Nelson deceased: he was nominated by the commissioners, and the nomination was assented to by the court.

§ John W. Hetrick, was, in 1833, appointed prothonotary, and the two other commissioners, (Jacob Dietz and William Patterson,) appointed Samuel Harnish to supply the vacancy until the ensuing election. At the election in 1833, Harnish was chosen to serve out the last year of the time for which Hetrick had been elected.

The clerks to the commissioners have been ten in number, viz:

John Reed, appointed in October 1749, and succeeded by John Redick, appointed in 1757, and succeeded by Henry Harris, appointed on October 25, 1757, and succeeded by William Leas, appointed on October 30, 1764, and succeeded by John Morris, appointed in 1776, and succeeded by George Lewis Leofller, appointed in October 1780, and succeeded by Jacob Spengler, appointed in 1792, and succeeded by Peter Spengler, appointed in 1815, and succeeded by George W. Spengler, appointed in November, 1823, and succeeded by Daniel Small, the present Clerk, who was appointed in 1829.

TREASURERS.

The following is a list of the treasurers of York county from the erection thereof until the present time, with the dates of their appointments or the commencement of their services.

David McConaughy, appointed in	Dec. 1749
Thomas McCartney,	Dec. 1752
Hugh Whitford,	1754
Robert McPherson,	1755
Fred'k Gelwicks,	Nov. 1756
William Delap,	1757
John Blackburn,	Dec. 1759
David McConaughy,	Oct. 1764
John Blackburn,	Oct. 1766
*Robt. McPherson,	Aug. 1767
Michael Schwaabe,	Oct. 1769
†Michael Hahn,	Apr. 1777
John Hay,	1778
Rudolph Spangler,	Oct. 1801
John Forsyth,	Nov. 1805
John Strohman,	1808
Peter Kurtz,	Nov. 1811
George Spangler,	Nov. 1814
William Nes,	Nov. 1817
Henry Smyser,	Nov. 1820
John Voglesong,	Nov. 1823
Peter Ahl,	Nov. 1826
Jacob Bayler,	Nov. 1829
Daniel Hartman,	Nov. 1832

* Robert McPherson was appointed to supply the place of John Blackburn, deceased.

† Extract from the records of the proceedings of the Commissioners, for April 10, 1777.—"Whereas the late treasurer, Michael Schwaabe, is a prisoner of war with the enemy, and is thereby incapable of exercising and doing the duty of treasurer, and whereas it is absolutely necessary that some fit person should be appointed in the room of the late treasurer, therefore the members present unanimously voted in Michael Hahn, Esq., to be treasurer in the room of Michael Schwaabe, Esq."

JUSTICES OF THE PEACE.

THE following tables exhibit the names of all the justices of the peace and of the Court of Common Pleas for the county of York, with the dates of their respective commissions.

TABLE I.

Justices before the Revolution. ☞A number of the following gentlemen were commissioned *twice* or more frequently. We give the date of their *first* commission, only.

John Day, commissioned Sept. 1749
Thomas Cox, Do.
John Wright, Jun. Do.
George Schwaabe, Do.
Mathew Dill, Do.
Hans Hamilton, Do.
Patrick Watson, Do.
George Stevenson, Do.
John Witherow, April 1751
Walter Buchanan, Do.
John Blackburne, Do.
John Pope, Do.
William Griffith, Do.
Herman Updegraff, Do.
John Adlum, October, 1755
Thomas Armor, Do.
Richard Brown, Do.
Hugh Whiteford, Do.
Michael Tanner, Do.
Martin Eichelberger, Jan. 1760
David Kirkpatrick, Apr. 1761
Abraham Nesbit, Do.
Archibald McGrew, Do.
David Jameson, Oct. 1764
Michael Schwaabe, Do.
Samuel Johnston, Do.
Samuel Edie, Do.
Matthew Dill, (son of Matthew Dill, who was commissioned in 1749, Oct. 1764
James Welsh, Do.
Robert McPherson, Do.
John Smith, Do.
Henry Schlegel, Do.
Thomas Minshall, Do.
Cunningham Sample, Do.
William Dunlop, Do.
Joseph Hutton, Do.
William Smith, Dec. 1764
Richard McAlister, Mar. 1771
William Rankin, Do.
Joseph Updegraff, Do.
David McConaughy, April 1774
William Scott, Do.
Benjamin Donaldson, Do.
William Bailey, Do.
William Leas, Do.
William McCaskey, Sept. 1774
Josiah Scott, Do.
William McLean, Do.
Thomas Latta, Do.

TABLE II.

Justices since the Revolution, and prior to the formation of the present Constitution of Pennsylvania. These commissions were granted by the convention which framed the first constitution of Pennsylvania, and by the President and Council under that Constitution.

Robt. McPherson,	Sept. 1776	Joseph Reed,	June 1777
Martin Eichelberger,	Do.	Thomas Fischer,	Do.
Samuel Edie,	Do.	Peter Wolf,	Sept. 1777
David McConaughy,	Do.	Frederick Eichelberger,	Do.
Richard McAlister,	Do.	Jacob Eichelberger,	Mar. 1778
Henry Schlegel,	Do.	William Mitchell,	June 1779
Matthew Dill,	Do.	John Rankin,	May, 1780
William Rankin,	Do.	David Beatty,	Do.
William Leas,	Do.	Robert Chambers,	Jan. 1781
William Bailey,	Do.	Michael Schwaabe,	Nov. 1782
William Scott,	Do.	George Stake,	Do.
William Smith,	Do.	Cunningham Sample,	Aug. 1783
William McCaskey,	Do.	Michael Hahn,	Sept. 1784
Josiah Scott,	Do.	Thomas Lilly,	Do.
Thomas Latta,	Do.	William Cochran,	Oct. 1784
William McLean,	Do.	Jacob Rudisill,	Do.
John Mickel,	Do.	Michael Schmeiser,	Do.
David Jameson,	June 1777	William Gilliland,	Nov. 1784
Samuel Ewing,	Do.	Daniel May,	April 1785
David Watson,	Do.	Conrad Sherman,	June 1785
John Chamberlain,	Do.	Robert Hamersly,	July 1785
Andrew Thompson,	Do.	Jacob Barnitz,	March 1786
John Hinkel,	Do.	Henry Miller,	Aug. 1786
John Herbaugh,	Do.	David Beatty,	June 1787
Robert Stevenson,	Do.	Bernhart Zeigler,	Do.
Archibald McLean,	Do.	Robert McIlhanny,	May 1788
James Nailor,	Do.	Elihu Underwood,	June 1788
Thomas Douglas,	Do.	Jacob Dritt,	Sept. 1789
David Messerly,	Do.		
Benjamin Pedan,	Do.		

TABLE III.

Justices of the Peace under the present Constitution.

Those who resided when commissioned, within the present limits of the *first* district,* composed of York Borough and Township, and part of Springgarden, were

* The legislature on the 4th of April 1803, required the commissioners of the different counties to lay out their counties into districts for justices of the peace, & to make returns to the Secretary &c. containing the number and

Andrew Billmeyer, commissioned Aug. 29, 1791
Conrad Laub, Dec. 14, 1792
William McLean, Do.
Jacob Hay, Oct. 6, 1794
George Lewis Leoffler, Nov. 6, 1795
Andrew Johnson, Do.
John Forsythe, June 2, 1799
Jacob Heckert, June 18, 1800
Peter Mundorff, April 2, 1802
Jacob Lefever, April 2, 1804
Ignatius Leitner, Apr. 1, 1806
Ephraim Penington, Sept. 30, 1808
John Stroman, Feb. 15, 1809
Thomas Whitaker, Jan. 3, 1811
George Haller, Nov. 1, 1813
Daniel Heckert, May 15, 1815
Joseph Morris, Feb. 14, 1817
Henry Schaeffer, Mar. 31, 1817
Charles F. Fischer, Dec. 17, 1819
Martin Boyer, Nov. 1, 1820
John Youse, April 5, 1821
Louis Shive, July 17, 1821
Henry Ruthrauff, Aug. 3, 1821
Penrose Robinson, Oct. 31, 1821
George Klinefelter, Dec. 9, 1823
Francis McDermott, Dec. 11, 1823
Jacob Seitz, Dec. 12, 1823
Philip Smyser, Mar. 10, 1823
John Smith, March 26, 1824
Anthony Knisely, Do.
Michael Gardner, March 21, 1825
Francis McDermott, Nov. 9, 1825
Zachariah Spangler, Aug. 25, 1828
Geo. Lauman, Nov. 10, 1829
Benjamin Lanius, Dec. 10, 1829
Jacob Eichelberger, Dec. 14, 1829
Jacob Lehman, Feb. 19, 1830
John A. Wilson, Jan. 23, 1832
John Shaeffer, Feb. 25, 1833
Benjamin Zeigler, Do.

SECOND DISTRICT.

Composed of the townships of Heidelberg and Manheim, including the borough of Hanover.

Philip Wolfhart, [The commission is not to be found on record].
Henry Welsh, Oct. 29, 1795
John Hinkel, Jan. 8, 1803
Michael Hellman, April 1, 1805
Anthony Hinkel, Feb. 15, 1809
Peter Reider, May 6, 1814

---

description of the bounds of each district, the number of acting justices in each, and, as near as might be, the place of their residence. In pursuance of this request, the commissioners of York county met, and after having divided the county into fourteen districts, and collected the information required completed their report and set their hands and affixed the seal of office thereto on the 26th of October, 1803. From the report it appears at that time there were 5540 taxables in the county and —— acting justices.

John Hoshauer, Dec. 9, 1816
David Shultz, Dec. 18, 1816
John L. Hinkel, March 14, 1817
Peter Storm, Dec. 21, 1818
Michael Lechner, Feb. 22, 1819
David T. Storm, Dec. 11, 1820
Charles T. Melsheimer, Feb. 18, 1822
Michael Bucher, Jun. Nov. 27, 1823
Peter Overdeer, May 5, 1824
Luther H. Skinner, Oct. 20, 1825
George Freysinger, Oct. 31, 1825
John Maul, Aug. 12, 1831

THIRD DISTRICT.

Composed of the townships of Newberry and Fairview.

Martin Shetter, April 23, 1792
Henry Greiger, Mar. 8, 1796
Michael Simpson, April 19, 1797
Robert Hamersly, Feb. 18, 1799
James Todd, Mar. 28, 1799
John Spence, April 1, 1805
Adam Kister, Jan. 1, 1807
Michael Hart, Mar. 30, 1809
Robert Thornburg, March 29, 1813
Isaac Kirk, Feb. 2, 1814
Fred'k Stoner, Dec. 23, 1814
Mills Hays, Aug. 13, 1817
Isaac Spence, Mar. 2, 1818
George Ashton, Jan. 7, 1820
Henry Etter, Oct. 17, 1822
William Culbertson, Jan. 19, 1823
John C. Groom, Feb. 7, 1825
John Rankin, May 2, 1827
Jacob Kirk, Jun. Apr 15, 1830
John G. Kister, Apr 4, 1831
John Thompson, Mar. 30, 1831
James Nichols, Apr. 24, 1833
Jacob Smith, Do.
Joseph McCreary, Jan. 30, 1834

FOURTH DISTRICT.

Composed of the townships of Chanceford and Lower Chanceford.

William Morrison, October 1, 1799
William Ross, [Commission not recorded].
James Patterson, June 18, 1800
Joseph Herr, April 1, 1805
Wm. Morrison, April 1, 1806
Wm. Douglass, Oct. 20, 1808
John Geben, Mar. 22, 1811
John Finley, Oct. 9, 1814
John Lane, Jan. 11, 1816
Hugh Long, Feb. 4, 1818
Samuel Nelson, Dec. 11, 1820
Andrew Clarkson, April 1, 1822
Andrew Duncan, Do.
Hugh Ross, Mar. 31, 1823

FIFTH DISTRICT.

Composed of the townships of Warrington and Washington.

E. Underwood, Aug. 29, 1791
John Hippel, June 18, 1800
William Squibb, Oct. 24, 1807
George Huber, Mar. 29, 1808
Frederick Herman, March 28, 1811
David Bauer, Dec. 9, 1823
Jacob Stickell, Do.
William Ross, Mar. 5, 1830
John S. Smith, May 23, 1833
Abraham Griffith, Feb. 7, 1834

SIXTH DISTRICT.

Composed of the townships of Monaghan and Franklin.

Thomas Black, Nov. 22, 1797
Francis Culbertson, March 28, 1799
John Blackley Jones, Dec. 9, 1799
David Meyer, March 10, 1813
Wm. McMillan, Jan. 9, 1816
William Divin, Jan. 24, 1818
Peter Wolfhart, Mar 15, 1820
Matthew Black, April 1, 1822
Hugh O'Hail, Do.
Hugh McMullen, Dec. 5, 1823
Daniel Bailey, June 19, 1827
Robert Hamersly, April 23, 1829
Thomas Godfrey, Sept. 24, 1829
James O'Hail, July 15, 1834

SEVENTH DISTRICT.

Composed of the township of Shrewsbury including Strasburg.

Henry Rehman, June 18, 1800
Caleb Low, April 2, 1807
George Klinefelder, Nov. 1, 1813
Jacob Rothrock, May 16, 1818
Joshua Hendricks, Do.
Jacob Rothrock, June 10, 1822
Henry Snyder, Sept. 15, 1828
Jacob N. Hildebrand, May 8, 1833

EIGHTH DISTRICT.

Composed of the township of Codorus.

John Brien, Aug. 21, 1797
Henry Miller, June 18, 1800
John Drexler, Do.
Henry Strickhauser, April 2, 1802
Peter Reider, March 15, 1809
John Hendrick, Mar. 18, 1817
Graham McCamant, March 29, 1821
Daniel Lease, May 28, 1828
George Fisher, Feb. 23, 1833
Jefferson Drout, February 25, 1833
Jacob Dehoff, March 1, 1834

NINTH DISTRICT.

Composed of the townships of Dover and Conewago.

John Sharp, [Commission not recorded].	Wm. Caldwell, Jan. 20, 1814
John Bull, Dec. 3, 1799	John McCreary, June 10, 1823
Henry Stover, Feb. 15, 1809	John Auginbaugh Dec. 9, 1823
	Ross Bull, Dec. 13, 1823

TENTH DISTRICT.

Composed of the township of Paradise.

Wm. Ziegler, Aug. 25, 1796	Jacob Ernst, June 11, 1810
Henry Meyer, July 11, 1809	Henry Buse, April 4, 1833

ELEVENTH DISTRICT.

Composed of the townships of Manchester and West Manchester.

Yost Herbach, Dec. 19, 1794	Adam Wolff, March 24, 1817
George Philip Zeigler, May 21, 1799	John Weyer, April 2, 1818
Andrew Ritter, Dec. 3, 1799	Jacob Smyser, June 12, 1822
John Weyer, June 18, 1800	Charles Bishop, Mar. 26, 1824
Frederick Eichelberger, Jan. 7, 1808	Anthony Dessenberger, Feb. 6, 1833
John Quickel, Dec. 19, 1808	Samuel C. Bonham, March 25, 1833

TWELFTH DISTRICT.

Composed of the townships of Hellam and Windsor and part of Springgarden.

Henry Tyson, April 10, 1793	William White, March 2, 1821
Samuel Jago, June 20, 1797	Christian Hamaker, March 2, 1822
Jacob Liebhart, Dec. 10, 1799	Samuel Johnson, March 26, 1824
Henry Liebhart, June 18, 1800	Jacob Fries, Do.
Christian Rathfon, Jan. 2, 1804	John Ruby, Feb. 25, 1828
Anthony Hines, April 1, 1806	Adam Paules, Aug. 3, 1829
Matthias Baker, Mar 13, 1809	George Addig, June 7, 1830
John Welschans, March 29, 1813	George Shenberger, May 28, 1833
William Wilson, March 2, 1818	Samuel Landes, July 18, 1834

THIRTEENTH DISTRICT.

Composed of the township of Hopewell.

William Smith,*
Andrew Duncan, [Commission not recorded].
Thomas Jordan, Aug. 10, 1800
John Smith, Aug. 16, 1821
Adam Ebaugh, Feb. 6, 1834
Henry Fulton, Feb. 11, 1834
Sampson Smith, April 2, 1834

FOURTEENTH DISTRICT.

Composed of the townships of Fawn and Peach Bottom.

Jacob Gibson, [Commission not recorded].
John Boyd, March 7, 1799
William Anderson, March 29, 1808
James Walton, Do.
John Livingston Dec. 20, 1810
Samuel Jordan, Dec. 5, 1815
James Wilson, Jan. 24, 1818
James Johnson, Mar. 1, 1820
Robert Cunningham, March 31, 1823
Wm. Coulston, Dec. 9, 1823
Joseph James, March 26, 1824
James Ramsey, March 5, 1830
Samuel Irwin, July 8, 1830
Joseph Bennet, April 4, 1832
Thomas Henderson, Feb. 20, 1834

CHAPTER XVII.

CENSUS OF YORK COUNTY.

At all enumerations, between 1790, and 1830, inclusive.

In 1790, there were

Free white males, of 16 years and upwards, including heads of families,	9,213
Free white males under 16,	9,527

---

* Esq. Smith is mentioned in the report of the commissioners of 27th Oct. 1803; and they describe his residence as being nearly in the central part of Hopewell township.—When his commission as a Justice of the Peace for Hopewell was issued, I cannot find: but on 7th Dec. 1764 he was for the first time commissioned as a Judge of the Courts of York County; and after the revolution he was re-commissioned to the same office on 10th June 1777, and on 17th Sept. 1784. This upright magistrate, and unshaken friend of his country in the days of her darkest adversity, died in October 1810 in the 80th year of his age.

Free white females, including heads of families, ... 17,671
All other free persons, ... 837
Slaves, ... 499

Total number, ... 37,747

CENSUS OF 1800.

Free white males,
under 10 years of age, ... 4,280
of 10 and under 16, ... 2,126
of 16 and under 26, ... 2,146
of 26 and under 45, ... 2,480
of 45 and upwards, ... 1,726

Total, free white males, ... 12,758

Free white females,
under 10 years of age, ... 4,243
of 10 and under 16, ... 2,061
of 16 and under 26, ... 2,202
of 26 and under 45, ... 2,305
of 45 and upwards, ... 1,645

Total, free white females, ... 12,456
To which add, males, ... 12,758

Total free white population, ... 25,214
All other free persons, including Indians not taxed,.... 352
Slaves, ... 77

Total population in 1800, ... 25,643

CENSUS OF 1810.

Free white males, ... 15,919
Free white females, ... 15,410

Total, whites 31,329
All other free white persons, ... 607
Slaves, ... 22

Total population in 1810,...................................... 31,958

CENSUS OF 1820.

Free white males,	19,256
Free white females,	18,704
All other white persons,	12
Total white population,	37,972
Free persons of color, males,	382
Free persons of color, females,	399
Slaves, males,	2
Slaves, females,	4
Total population in 1820,	38,759

Of the population in 1820, there were

Foreigners, not naturalized,	509
Persons engaged in Agriculture,	5,710
Persons engaged in Manufactures,	2,796
Persons engaged in Commerce,	106
And the population to the square mile was	43

CENSUS OF 1830.

By townships:

Codorus,	2420
Conewago,	1093
Dover,	1874
East Manchester,	2198
Fairview,	1892
Fawn,	785
Franklin,	1003
Hellam,	1876
Hanover Borough,	998
Heidelberg,	1528
Hopewell,	1941
Lower Chanceford,	1051
Manheim,	1361
Monaghan,	1214
Newberry,	1856
Paradise,	1819
Peach Bottom,	898
Shrewsbury,	2571
Springgarden,	1603
Upper Chanceford,	1177
Washington,	1037
Warrington,	1229
Westmanchester,	1269
Windsor,	2760
York,	1181
York Borough,	4216
	42,859
Population in 1830 to the square mile,	47

CHAPTER XVIII.

PROTHONOTARIES.

The following is a list of the Prothonotaries of the Court of Common Pleas for the County of York, with the years of their several appointments to office.

George Stevenson, appointed in 1749
Samuel Johnston, 1764
Archibald M'Lean, 1777
Henry Miller, 1786
John Edie, 1794
Charles William Hartley, 1800
William Barber, 1806
Michael W. Ash, 1823
Richard Porter, 1830
John W. Hetrick, 1833

CLERKS TO THE COURT OF QUARTER SESSIONS.

George Stevenson, appointed in 1749
Samuel Johnston, 1764
Archibald M'Lean, 1777
Henry Miller, 1786
John Edie, 1794
Charles W. Hartley, 1800
William Barber, 1806
Adam King, 1818
Robert Hamersly, 1821
Adam King, 1823
Jacob Spangler, 1827
Jacob B. Wentz, 1830

CLERKS OR REGISTERS TO THE ORPHANS' COURT.

George Stevenson, appointed in 1749
Samuel Johnston, 1764
Archibald M'Lean, 1777
Henry Miller, 1786
John Edie, 1794
Charles W. Hartley, 1800
William Barber, 1806
Adam King, 1818
Robert Hamersly, 1821
Adam King, 1823
Jacob Spangler, 1827
Jacob B. Wentz, 1830

REGISTERS.

The registers for the probate of wills and for granting letters of administration, are as follows:

George Stevenson, appointed in 1749
Samuel Johnston, 1764
Archibald M'Lean, 1777
Jacob Barnitz, 1785
Jacob B. Wentz, 1824
Frederick Eichelberger, 1829
William P. Fisher, 1830
Jesse Spangler, 1830
Michael Doudel, 1833

RECORDERS OF DEEDS.

George Stevenson, appointed in	1749	Jacob Barnitz,	1785
Samuel Johnston,	1764	Jacob B. Wentz,	1824
Archibald M'Lean,	1777	Frederick Eichelberger,	1820
		Charles Nes,	1830

NOTARIES PUBLIC.

The Legislature of Pennsylvania, on the 5th of March, 1791, directed the appointment of notaries public in different parts of the state. Those of York county are as follows, viz:

John Doll, appointed in	1791	George W. Spangler,	1814
John Morris, (father),	1792	Henry Schaeffer,	1818
John Morris, (son),	1806	Charles F. Fisher,	1820
George Carothers,	1810		

CHIEF RANGER.

George Stevenson, who was so much honoured in the early days of this county,* supported an office which is now unknown to our laws. James Hamilton, deputy governor of Pennsylvania, constituted him on the 7th of January 1750, *Chief Ranger* of and for the county of York: granting "full power and authority to range, view and inspect all our woods and lands within the said county, and to seize, take up, and appropriate to our use all and every such wild colts or young horses, cattle, and swine, as shall be found within the bounds of said county, that are not marked by the owners of their dams, and are liable to be seized by law; and also all marked strays for which no lawful owner can be found, that may be taken up in the said county; and to publish every such stray in the most public places of the said county for the space of one year, and also keeping some public mark of their being strays for the said space about them hereby requiring you to sue and prosecute all persons presuming to act contrary to

* Stevenson, besides being Prothonotary, Register and Recorder, Justice, &c. &c. was likewise the first deputy surveyor of the county, he being commissioned as such on the 20th of Oct. 1749.

law in cutting down or destroying any of our timber-trees or wood, or that shall in any wise invade the powers hereby granted to you within the said county."

This commission of Chief Ranger induces us to transcribe a few passages connected therewith from the records of Quarter Sessions for the county.

"Moses Wallace of Chanceford township, his marks for horses, cattle, sheep, swine, &c. a crop on the left ear &c. Brand an I on the near shoulder and buttocks. April 25th 1751."

"James Hetrick, his marks, a crop and slit on the off ear, and a slit in the near ear. Brand a fleur-de-luce, on the near buttocks. May 2d 1751."

"Alexander Creighton, Shrewsbury township, his brand for horses &c. A. C. on the near buttocks; and marks for cattle, sheep, swine &c. a crop in the off ear, a half penny out of the forepart of the near ear. June 26th 1751."

"The marks of Jacob Shetter's hogs and cattle; the off ear cropt, and the near slit. Entered the 10th of January 1757."

CHAPTER XIX.

DELEGATES TO CERTAIN PROVINCIAL AND STATE CONVENTIONS, FROM THE COUNTY OF YORK.

1. The provincial meeting of deputies from the several counties, which was held at Philadelphia on the 15th of July 1774, and was continued by adjournments from day to day:

James Smith,	Thomas Hartley.
Joseph Donaldson,	

2. The provincial convention which was held at Philadelphia on the 23d of January 1776, and was continued by adjournments until the 28th of the same month:

James Smith, Esq.,	John Hay,
Thomas Hartley,	George Irwin,
Joseph Donaldson,	Michael Schmoiser.
George Eicholberger,	

3. The provincial conference of committees at Philadelphia, which began on the 18th of June 1776, and was continued until the 25th of the same month:

Col. James Smith,	Col. Henry Schlegel,
Col. Robert McPherson,	Mr. James Edgar,
Col. Richard McAlister,	Mr. John Hay,
Col. David Kennedy,	Capt. Joseph Read.
Col. William Rankin,	

4. The convention which was held at Philadelphia on the 15th of July 1776, and was continued by adjournments until the 27th of the following September. (This convention framed the first constitution of the State of Pennsylvania.)

John Hay,	James Smith,
James Edgar,	Robert McPherson,
William Rankin,	Joseph Donaldson.
Henry Schlegel,	

5. The council of censors, the first day of whose meeting was on the 10th of November, 1783:

Thomas Hartley,	Richard McAlister.

6. The convention which framed the second constitution of the commonwealth of Pennsylvania, viz. that of 2d September 1790.

Henry Miller,	Benjamin Tyson,
Henry Schlegel,	Benjamin Pedan,
William Read,	Matthew Dill.

FAIRS.

These joyful institutions are mentioned very early in the history of our town. Even in the original instructions for laying it out are these remarkable words. "The privilege of a fair shall be granted, for which purpose I desire to be certified the most convenient times twice in a year for the sale of cattle." The grant of this privilege however, on account of the sparsity of population, was for some time delayed. But when nature had become more divested of her rude attire, and the land had increased in the multitude of its inhabitants, our sturdy fathers began soberly to think on the enjoyment of that privilege to which many of them had been accustomed before their emigration to this wilderness. At length what they wished for, was obtained. Thomas Penn, then lieutenant governor of Pennsylvania, complied with their requests on the 29th of October, 1765; such is the date of the instrument, signed by him at Philadelphia. A part of this *charter of privileges* is as follows:

"Whereas it has been represented to us that it would be of great service and utility to the inhabitants of the town and county of York, that two fairs be held yearly in the said town, for buying and selling goods, wares, merchandise, and cattle; *Know ye*, that we, favoring the reasonable request of the inhabitants, and considering the flourishing state to which the town hath arrived through their industry, have, of our free will, granted, and do, by these presents, for us, our heirs, and successors, grant to the present and succeeding inhabitants of the town, that they shall and may, forever hereafter, have and keep in the said town, two fairs in the year, the one of them to begin on the ninth day of June yearly, to be held in High Street, and to continue that day and the day following; and the other of the said fairs to be held, in the aforesaid place, on the second day of November, every year, and the next day after it, with all the liberties and customs to such fairs belonging or incident."

This charter was received as a high & peculiar blessing. Travelling dealers in small wares then found themselves, with a punctual devotion, at these semiannual congregations. But as the number of stated merchants increased, our ancient and venerable institutions began to be shorn of their glory. Yet when, in 1787, the town was erected into a borough, the legislature particularly continued this privilege of our fathers, unto their children. But manners were changing; one part of the community was growing more refined, and another more corrupted; fairs had degenerated from the primitive purity of former years, and become but a scene of a wild merriment or of a riotous commotion. At last on account of the degeneracy of the times, the legislature on the 29th of January 1816, prohibited the holding of fairs within the borough of York, and declared such holding to be a common nuisance.* Yet so great is the inveteracy of ancient custom, the former stated days are even now but too punctually observed. A few years hence the observance of these institutions will have ceased as to our county; those who succeed us, may, proud of their own belief, look upon these days as times of a rude and unpolished wilderness.

"RATES IN TAVERNS."

The general assembly of Pennsylvania, considering that Inn-holders &c. exacted excessive rates for their wine, provender, &c. made a law on the 31st of May 1748, by which the justices of the peace, in their quarter sessions, should set such reasonable prices as they should see fit. The justices of York County on the 28th of January 1752, established the following rates and prices: we give them in an extract taken word for word from the records of the Court of Quarter Sessions.

	£.	S.	D.
"One quart sangaree made with one pint of good Maderia wine and with loaf sugar........	0	1.	6.
A bowl of punch made with one quart water with loaf-sugar and good Jamaica spirits.............	"	1.	6.
One pint good Maderia wine..............................	"	1.	3.
One pint good Vidonia wine..............................	"	0.	10.

* The immediate cause of the prohibition was this. On the 26th of October 1815, being the day of the autumn fair, a young man named Robert Dunn, lost his life in a very melancholy manner. At the court in November following, when three persons were arraigned for the murder of Dunn, the Grand Jury presented the holding of fairs as a public nuisance. In January 1816, the persons who had before been arraigned, received their trial, the end of which was a conviction of manslaughter. Petitions were now presented to the legislature, who complied with the wishes of every honest citizen.

	£.	S.	D.
One pint of good Port wine	"	1.	0.
One quart of mimbo made with West-India rum, and loaf-sugar	"	0.	10.
One quart of mimbo made with New-England rum, and loaf-sugar	"	0.	9.
One gill of good West-Indian Rum	"	0.	4.
One gill of good New-England Rum	"	0.	3.
One gill of good whiskey	"	0.	2.
One quart of good beer	"	0.	4.
One quart of good cider	"	0.	4.
One man's breakfast	"	0.	6.
One man's dinner	"	0.	8.
One man's supper	"	0.	6.
One horse at hay twenty-four hours	"	0.	10.
One horse at hay one night	"	0.	8.
Half a gallon of good oats	"	0.	3.

"The above rates were settled by the court and proclaimed by the crier in open court of general quarter sessions, in pursuance of an act of general assembly of this province in such case made and provided."

The above continued for some years to be the *tavern rates* within the county of York. But the statutes requiring them, have long since been repealed; and inn-holders are now permitted, as they ought to be, like other persons, to regulate their own prices.

CHAPTER XX.

COURTS.

THE first Court of General Quarter Sessions of the Peace for the County of York, was holden at York, on "the thirty-first day of October, in the twenty-third year of the reign of our sovereign Lord, George the Second, by the Grace of God, of Great Britain, France, and Ireland, King, Defender of the Faith, &c. Anno Domini 1749. Before John Day, Esquire, and his Associates, Justices of the said court" &c.

The second court of Quarter Sessions was held on the 30th of January 1750.

The earliest records of "An Orphans' Court held at York, for the county of York are dated on the first day of Nov. in "the twenty-third year of the reign of our sovereign Lord, George the second, by the Grace of God, of Great Britain, France and Ireland, King, Defender of the Faith, &c. Anno Domini one thousand seven hundred and forty-nine, Before John Day, Thomas Cox, and Patrick Watson, Esquires, Justices &c."

The court of Common Pleas was organized in October 1749, and the first suit was brought in January term, 1750.

The first panel of Jurors for York County was returned by Hans Hamilton on the 31st of October 1749. The jurors were seventeen in number, and these were their names, viz: Michael M'Creary, William M'Lellan, James Agnew, Richard Proctor, Hugh Brigham, John Pope, James Hall, William Proctor, William Beatty, Nathan Dicks, Jerem Louchridge, Thomas Hosack, Thomas Sellick, Samuel Moore, James Smith, Richard Brown, and Thomas Neily.

Though courts were regularly held from the first erection of the county, yet a courthouse was not built till some years afterwards. The legislature on the 19th of August, 1749, appointed Thomas Cox, Michael Tanner, George Schwaabe, Nathan Hussey and John Wright, trustees to purchase "a piece of land in some convenient place in the county, to be approved of by the governor," "and thereon erect a courthouse and prison sufficient to accommodate the public service of the county and for the ease and convenience of the inhabitants." Nothing however was effectually done towards building the courthouse until the year 1754. In that year the commissioners of the county made an agreement with William Willis of Manchester township, bricklayer, to build the walls of the house; with Henry Clark of Warrington township, to saw and deliver the scantlings, for the building, and moreover with John Meem and Jacob Klein, carpenters of York town, to do all the joiners and carpenters work. Robert Jones engaged to bring 7000 shingles from Philadelphia; and in like manner many other particular agreements were made. The work, however, progressed but slowly; for the building was not completed till early in the year 1756.* The building thus erected still stands, though it has been a number of times "internally regenerated."

Before the erection of the buildings, the courts were held in private houses. The commissioners† usually held their meetings at the house of George Schwaabe.

DISTRICT COURT.

In 1826 a district court was established for the counties of York and Lancaster, of which the Hon. Ebenezer G. Bradford was appointed president judge, and Alexander Thompson, associate. Judge Thompson being appointed president judge of the common pleas of the 16th judicial district composed of the counties of Franklin, Bedford and Somerset, the Hon. Alexander L. Hays was appointed his successor.

In 1833, York and Lancaster were formed into separate districts and a judge appointed for each district. The Hon. Alexander L. Hays was appointed judge of the Lancaster district, and the Hon. Daniel Durkee of the York district.

These courts have concurrent jurisdiction with the common pleas courts, and causes are transferable from the common pleas to the district courts.

The salary of the judge of the district court is $1600 per annum.

---

* The town clock, which graces the court-house, was obtained in the year 1815.

† Connected with the commissioners we may here mention, that they paid for wolves' heads, in the year 1749-50, twenty-six pounds and ten shillings, and in the year 1750-51, twenty-one pounds. Of [—?—] we may form an estimate from the reward as then granted by law for killing these animals, the heads of about thirty wolves must have been presented to the commissioners within one year after the erection of the county. The later minutes of the commissioners' proceedings, speak of wolves' heads being presented to them for the premium, and then being "burnt publicly before the court house door," for it had been suspected that the same head had drawn two premiums.

PRESIDENT JUDGES.

The office of a president judge was not known in Pennsylvania until after the formation of the constitution of 2d September 1790. Before that time the courts were held by justices of the peace, none of whom were by profession lawyers.

In pursuance of the direction of the new constitution, the legislature on the 13th of April, 1791, made the first division that was made, of the commonwealth into districts or circuits. At that time the second circuit was made to consist of the counties of Chester, Lancaster, York, and Dauphin. Afterwards on the 24th of February 1806, the second district was made to consist of the counties of Lancaster and York, and Dauphin, & on the 6th of February 1815 of Lancaster & York.

The first president judge of the second district, to which York county belongs, was the Hon. William Augustus Atlee, who, under the first constitution of the commonwealth, had been one of the judges of the Supreme court. The first Court held in York by Judge Atlee was on the 25th of October 1791. He continued as presiding judge until the time of his death, which happened on the 9th of September 1793, at his seat near Wright's ferry on the Susquehanna.

There was now a vacancy in the office of president judge for nearly three months. In December 1793, the Hon. John Joseph Henry was appointed the successor of Mr. Atlee.

Judge Henry, son of William Henry Esq., was born at Lancaster, Pennsylvania, on the 4th of November 1758.

At the age of fourteen, John Joseph became an apprentice to a gunsmith. At the age of 16 he joined the army. At the storming of Quebec he was taken prisoner, and after a long confinement was released. Returning to Lancaster he was confined two years from an illness occasioned by his imprisonment. He was afterwards, for four years, clerk in the office of John Hubley, prothonotary of Lancaster. He afterwards studied law under Stephen Chambers, was admitted to the bar in 1785, and was appointed Judge in 1793. He resigned his commission as judge in January 1811.

Judge Henry on the 10th of December 1810, petitioned the legislature to grant him some compensation for his services and sufferings during the revolutionary war. On the 2d of April 1811, the legislature granted him the sum of 1600 dollars, and on the 22d of the same month he died in his native town.

The successor of Judge Henry, in the office of president of the second judicial district, was the Hon. Walter Franklin, who was commissioned on the 18th of January 1811, and who has continued unto this time to preside over our courts, with dignity, ability and impartiality.

ASSOCIATE JUDGES.

Upon the organization of the courts under the constitution of 1790, the first associate Judges were the Honourable Henry Schlegel, Samuel Edie, William Scott, and Jacob Rudisell, the latter of whom was commissioned on the 17th of August 1791. Judges Schlegel, Edie and Scott who lived within the present limits of Adams county, were, after a division of the county in 1800, succeeded by John Stewart, who was commissioned on the 30th of June, and Hugh Glasgow, who was commissioned on 1st of July. Judge Stewart being elected a member of Congress, the Hon. Jacob Hostetter was commissioned on the 28th of February 1801, to be an associate Judge. Judge Glasgow in his turn, was elected member of Congress and to succeed him the Hon. George Barnitz was commissioned on the 29th of March 1813. And lastly Judge Hostetter was elected member of Congress, and, on account of the vacancy occasioned by this, the Hon. John L. Hinkel was commissioned on the 10th of December, 1818.

The Hon. Jacob Rudisell continued a judge until the time of his death. He died in Petersburg, Adams county, in the house of Jacob Winrode, on the 6th of December 1800.

The Hon. Hugh Glasgow died at his seat in Peachbottom township, on the 31st of January, 1818, in the 49th year of his age.

The associate Judges at this time are the Hon. George Barnitz of York, and the Hon. John L. Hinkel, of the Borough of Hanover.

CHAPTER XXI.

DR. DADY.

THE following account of that noted imposter, Dr. Dady, is taken nearly word for word from that written by the Hon. John Joseph Henry, and sent by him to Philadelphia with the convicted imposters. Judge Henry wrote the account from notes taken at the trial. It follows, in most things, the order of the testimony as given in by the witnesses.

Dr. Dady who was a German by birth, came to this country with the Hessians during the American revolution. Possessing a fascinating eloquence in the German language, and being very fluent in the English, he was afterwards employed as a minister of the gospel by uninformed but honest Germans.

When the sacredotal robe could no longer be subservient to his avaricious views, he laid it aside and assumed the character of a physician. As such he came to York county, and dwelt among the poor inhabitants of a mountainous part thereof, (now within the limits of Adams county,) where, in various artful ways, he preyed on the purses of the unwary.

Of all the numerous impositions with which his name is connected, and to which he lent his aid, we will mention but two. The scene of one of them is in what is now Adams county, where he dwelt; and of the other in the "barrens" of York county.

The following is an account of the Adams county imposition:

Rice Williams, or rather *Rainsford Rogers* a New Englander, and *John Hall,* a New Yorker, (both of whom had been plundering the inhabitants of the southern states by their wiles,) came to the house of Clayton Chamberlain, a neighbor of Dady, in July 1797.

On the following morning, Dady went to Chamberlain's, and had a private conversation with Williams and Hall before breakfast. After Dady had left them, Williams asked Chamberlain whether the place was not haunted. Being answered in the negative, he said that it was haunted—that he had been born with a veil over his face—could see spirits, and had been conducted thither, sixty miles, by a spirit. Hall assented to the truth of this. In the evening of the same day, they had another interview with Dady. Williams then told Chamberlain, that if he would permit him to tarry over night, he would show him a spirit. This being agreed to, they went into a field in the evening, and Williams drew a circle on the ground, around which he directed Hall and Chamberlain to walk in silence. A terrible screach was soon heard proceeding from a *black* ghost (!!!) in the woods, at a little distance from the parties, in a direction opposite to the place where Williams stood. In a few minutes a *white* ghost appeared, which Williams addressed in a language which those who heard him could not understand—the ghost replied in *the same language!* After his ghostship had gone away, Williams said that the spirit knew of a treasure which it was permitted to discover to *eleven* men—they must be honest, religious and sensible, and neither horse-jockeys nor Irishmen.

The intercourse between Williams and Dady now ceased to be apparent; but it was continued in private. Chamberlain, convinced of the existence of a ghost and a treasure, was easily induced to form a company, which was soon effected. Each candidate was initiated by the receipt of a small sealed paper, containing a little yellow sand, which was called "the power." This "power" the candidate was to bury in the earth to the depth of one inch, for three days and three nights—performing several other absurd ceremonies, too obscene to be described here.

A circle, two inches in diameter was formed in the field, in the centre of which there was a hole six inches wide and as many deep. A captain, a lieutenant and three committeemen were elected. Hall had the honour of the captaincy. The *exercise* was to pace around the circle, &c. This, it was said, propitiated and strengthened the white ghost, who was opposed by an unfriendly black ghost who rejoiced in the appellation of *Pompey.* In the course of their nocturnal exercises they often saw the white ghost—they saw Mr. Pompey too, but he appeared to have "his back up," bellowed loudly, and threw stones at them.

On the night of the 18th of August, 1797, Williams undertook to get instructions from the white ghost. It was done in the following manner: He took a sheet of clean white paper, and folded it in the form of a letter, when each member breathed into it three times: this being repeated several times, and the paper laid over the hole in the centre of the circle, the instructions of the ghost were obtained. The following is a short extract from the epistle written by the ghost:

"Go on, and do right, and prosper, and the treasure shall be yours. I am permitted to write this in the same hand I wrote in the flesh for your direction—O—————☚. Take care of your powers in the name and fear of God our protector—if not, leave the work. There is a great treasure, 4000 pounds a piece for you. Dont trust the black one. Obey orders. Break the enchantment, which you will not do until you get an ounce of mineral dulcimer eliximer; some German doctors has it. *It is near, and dear, and scarce.* Let the committee get it—but dont let the Doctor know what you are about—he is wicked."

The above is but a small part of this precious communication. In consequence of these ghostly directions, a young man named Abraham Kephart waited, by order of the committee, on Dr. Dady. The Dr. preserved his *eliximer* in a bottle sealed with a large red seal, and buried in a heap of oats, and demanded fifteen dollars for an ounce of it. Young Kephart could not afford to give so much, but gave him thirty-six dollars and three bushels of oats for three ounces of it. Yost Liner, another of these wise committee men, gave the Doctor 121 dollars for eleven ounces of the stuff.

The company was soon increased to 39 persons, many of whom were wealthy. Among those who were most miserably duped may be mentioned Clayton Chamberlain, Yost Liner, Thomas Bigham, William Bigham, Samuel Togert, John M'Kinney, James Agnew the elder, James M'Cleary, Rob. Thompson, David Kissinger, George Sheckley, Peter Wikeart, and John Philips. All these and many other men were, in the words of the indictment, "cheated and defrauded by means of certain false tokens and pretences, to wit., by means of pretended spirits, certain circles, certain brown powder, and certain compositions called mineral dulcimer elixer, and Deterick's mineral elixer."

But the wiles of these imposters were soon exerted in other parts. The following is an account of their proceedings in and about Shrewsbury township in this county. Williams intimated that he had received a call from a ghost resident in those parts, at the distance of forty miles from Dady's. Jacob Wister, one of the conspirators, was the agent of Williams on this occasion. He instituted a company of twenty-one persons, all of whom were, of course, most ignorant people. The same and even more absurd ceremonies were performed by these people, and the communications of the ghost were obtained in a still more ridiculous manner than before. The communications mentioned Dr. Dady as the person from whom they should obtain the dulcimer elixer, as likewise a kind of sand which the ghost called the "Asiatic sand," and which was necessary in order to give efficacy to the "powers." Ulrich Neaff, a committee man of this company, paid to Dr. Dady ninety dollars for seven and a half ounces of the elixer. The elixer was put into vials, and each person who had one of them, held it in his hand and shook it as he pranced round the circle; on certain occasions he annointed his head with it, and afterwards, by order of the spirit, the vial was buried in the ground.

`aul Baliter, another of the committee men, took with him to Dr. Dady's, a hundred dollars to purchase "Asiatic said," at three dollars per ounce. Dady being absent, Williams procured from the Doctor's shop as much sand as the money would purchase. In this instance, Williams cheated the Doctor, for he kept the spoil to himself, and thence arose an overthrow of the good fraternity.

Each of them now set up for himself. Williams procured directions from *his* ghost, that each of the companies should despatch a committee man to Lancaster to buy "Dederick's mineral elixer" of a physician in that place. In the mean time Williams and his wife went to Lancaster, where they prepared the elixer, which was nothing but a composition of copperas and cayenne pepper. Mrs. Williams, as the wife of John Huber, a German doctor, went to Dr. Rose, with a letter dated "13 miles from New-Castle, Delaware," which directed him how to sell the article, &c. The enormity of the price aroused the suspicion of Dr. Rose. In a few days the delegates from the committee arrived, and purchased elixer to the amount of $740.33. When the lady came for the money, she was arrested, and the secret became known. Her husband, Williams, escaped.

The Lancaster expedition having led to a discovery of the tricks of the impostors, a few days after the disclosures made by Mrs. Williams, an indictment was presented in the criminal court of York county, against Dr. John Dady, Rice Williams, Jesse Miller, Jacob Wister, the elder, and Jacob Wister, the younger, for a conspiracy to cheat and defraud. The trial took place in June following, and resulted in the conviction of Wister, the elder, and of Dr. Dady—the former of whom was fined ten dollars and imprisoned one month in the county jail, the latter fined ninety dollars and sentenced to two years confinement in the penitentiary at Philadelphia.

Dady had just been convicted of participating in the conspiracy in Shrewsbury, when he and Hall were found guilty of a like crime in Adams county—whereupon Hall was fined one hundred dollars and sent to the penitentiary for two years, and Dady was fined one hundred and sixty dollars, and sentenced to undergo an additional servitude of two years in the penitentiary, to commence in June, 1800, when his first term would expire.

Thus ended the history of a man in this county, who certainly was not devoid of talent, who possessed a most winning address, and was a thorough master in quick and correct discernment of character. He reigned, for a season, with undisputed sway, in what was then the western part of York county. His cunning, for a long time, lulled suspicion to sleep. The history of his exorcisms should teach the credulous that the ghosts which appear now-a-days are as material as our own flesh.

CHAPTER XXII.

POST OFFICES IN YORK COUNTY.

BELIEVING that a list of the post offices in York county, with the names of the respective postmasters, would not be entirely without interest and utility, we have prepared the following:

Post Offices.	Post Masters.
Bermudian,	Gideon Griest
Chanceford,	Andrew Clarkson
Codorus,	Martin Shearer
Cross Roads,	Alexander Gordon
Castle Fin,	Edward Markland
Day's Landing,	Peter Dessenberg
Dillsburg,	G. L. Shearer
Dover,	E. Melchinger
Fawn Grove,	Thomas Barton
Franklintown,	Martin Carl
Farmer's,	William Snodgrass
Guilford,	Anthony Stewart
Hanover,	Peter Mueller
Hetricks,	John Hershner
Lewisberry,	Samuel Crull
Loganville,	Samuel Keyser
Lower Chanceford,	William Cowen
Manchester,	J. T. Ubil
Margaretta Furnace,	S. C. Slaymaker
Newberrytown,	Thos. Wickersham
Peach Bottom,	James McConkey
Pigeon Hill,	Abraham Bletcher
Rossville,	Michael Wollet
Shrewsbury,	Philip Folkemmer
Siddonsburg,	James G. Fraser
Windsor,	Wm. C. Cornwell
Wrightsville,	James Kerr
Wolfram's,	Gustavus Wolfram
York Haven,	D. Winchester, Jun.
York,	Daniel Small

MARKETS.

No regular markets were held in York till some years after it had been laid out, and, in part, settled. John and Richard Penn, by their lieutenant governor, Robert Hunter Morris, granted the first privilege of holding markets here. The date of their charter for this purpose is recorded as the "eighteenth day of October, in the year of our Lord one thousand seven hundred and fifty-five, the twenty-ninth year of the reign of King George the second over Great Britain &c., and in the thirty-eighth year of our government." This grant of privilege states that "the inhabitants of the town of York, in the new county of York, are become so numerous that they find it necessary to have a public market established within the said town of York, for the better supplying and accommodating them with good and wholesome provisions, and other necessaries, under proper regulations." It then, "upon the humble request of the inhabitants of York, grants and ordains that they and their successors shall and may forever thereafter hold and keep within the town, in every week of the year, two market days, the one on Wednesday and the other on Saturday, in such commodious place or places, as is, shall, or may be, appointed for that purpose." Another clause of the charter reads thus: "And we do hereby appoint John Meem, of the town of York, to be the first clerk of the market, who, and all succeeding clerks, shall have assize of bread, wine, beer, and other things with all the powers, privileges, and immunities, by law belonging to such office."

This grateful privilege of holding markets on Wednesdays and Saturdays, has been continued down to our times. When the legislature on the 24th of September, 1787, made York a borough, they specially and particularly granted a continuance of this ancient blessing, originally conferred on us by the Penns. The first clerk of the market in the *borough* of York, i. e., under its incorporation, was Frederick Youse.

The present Master of the Market is *Henry Stroman.*

CHAPTER XXIII.

MILITIA.

THE more early laws of Pennsylvania were strangers to any thing like arms. It was not until the year 1755, that the legislature turned their attention to this subject, when they made a law "ordering and regulating such as were willing, and *desirous* of being united for military purposes." Shortly afterwards a few "associated companies of militia," were formed in York county. One was formed in Shrewsbury township, whereof Andrew Findlay was captain; William Gemmill, lieutenant; and Moses Lawson, ensign; and these received their commissions on 24th April 1759. Another was formed in Mountjoy township, whereof William Gibson was captain; William Thompson, lieutenant; and Caspar Little, ensign; and these received their commissions on the 1st of May 1756. A third company was formed in York township, whereof David Hunter was captain; John Corrie, lieutenant; and John Barnes, ensign; and they received their commissions on the 26th of May 1756. Besides these, Hugh Donwoody is mentioned as having been commissioned captain on the 19th of April 1756, but in what township his company was, or who were the other officers, does not appear. Most probably the *association*, which was entirely voluntary, was relinquished very soon after he had received his commission. The above mentioned persons were the first that ever bore military honours in York county.

The general assembly made a number of laws on military subjects, in the years 1757 and 1758. The latter of those years, was distinguished by the expedition against Fort Du Quesne, which was committed to general Forbes at the head of 8000 men. Towards that expedition, York county furnished four companies of foot-soldiers.

The Captains were

Robert M'Pherson, who took the necessary oaths of office on May 10, 1758

Thomas Hamilton, May 15, 1758
David Hunter* May 25, 1758

The lieutenants were

Andrew Findlay, who took the necessary oaths of office on April 26, 1758
James Ewing† May 10, 1758
Alexander M'Kean, May 15, 1758
Victor King, May 16, 1758

The ensigns were

William Haddin, who took the necessary oaths of office on April 25, 1758
Peter Mim, May 10, 1758
James Armstrong, May 15, 1758
William M'Dowell, May 16, 1758

From the period of the expedition against Fort Du Quesne to the commencement of the revolution, the services of the militia of York county were not required on any occasion. For an account of the militia from this county who were engaged in the war of independence, the reader is referred to the chapter under the head of "Revolution."

On the 7th of August 1794, President Washington issued a proclamation, setting forth that illegal combinations existed in the western part of Pennsylvania to "defeat the execution of the laws laying duties upon stills, and upon spirits distilled in the United States"—and that the conspirators had attacked the house of John Neville, one of the inspectors of the revenue for the state of Pennsylvania, and had seized and maltreated David Lennox, marshall of the District of Pennsylvania. The proclamation concluded with a call upon all good citizens to aid the government in "suppressing and preventing such dangerous proceedings."

Immediately upon the appearance of the President's proclamation, Gov. Mifflin, of Pennsylvania, issued a proclamation, requiring the General Assembly of the commonwealth to meet

---

* The same man who laid out Hunter's town now in Adams county.

† Afterwards Brigadier General in the revolutionary war, and vice-president of the council under the first constitution of Pennsylvania.

forthwith at the statehouse in Philadelphia, for the purpose of devising the necessary means to maintain the peace and dignity of the commonwealth. The Legislature accordingly convened in Philadelphia on the 2d of Sept. 1794, and one of their earliest acts was to provide for engaging the services of the militia of the commonwealth, in defence of the laws.

York county, ever ready to act when the public interest, honor or safety requires an appeal to arms, furnished, on this occasion, a regiment of well appointed militia, and two companies of volunteers. The regiment was commanded by Col. Daniel May. One company of volunteers was commanded by Captain Andrew Johnston. Of this company Charles Barnitz was first lieutenant, and John Greer ensign. Of the other, (which was a rifle company,) James Cross was captain.

THE LATE WAR.

In 1814, when the city of Baltimore was endangered by the approach of the British, York county was prompt in coming forward to the aid of the Baltimoreans. A number of companies in various parts of the county were immediately ready to march to the city, prepared to confront the proud invader, and, if necessary, to lay down their lives in the effort to check his progress.

Although, of the companies raised here for the purpose of defending Baltimore, but one reached that city in time to share the danger and glory of an actual engagement with the enemy—yet, the fact that they marched to the point of invasion as early as circumstances permitted, will shield all of them who did not arrive in time, from any imputation of indifference to the fate of Baltimore. When they did leave their homes, they left them in the full expectation that they were to meet any enemy flushed and insolent with success, and surpassing them in military discipline. It was no fault of theirs, that, when they arrived at Baltimore, an attack had already been made—it was no fault of theirs that they had not assisted in the gallant defence of the city and the repulse of the invader.

The "YORK VOLUNTEERS," who did arrive in time, were nearly one hundred strong, were composed principally of young men, "the flower of the county," and were commanded by Captain (afterwards Colonel) Michael H. Spangler, of the borough of York.

This gallant company marched from York on the 29th of August, 1814, without any provision other than that contributed by the citizens of the borough. Immediately upon their arrival at the city, they tendered their services to the general in command, and in consequence of their respectable appearance and discipline, were solicited to attach themselves to the fifth regiment, a fine body of Baltimore troops, under the command of Col. Sterett. They were marched with their regiment to oppose the enemy at North Point, and until overpowered by numbers, fought with the bravery of veterans. Notwithstanding the formidable host opposed to them, they resolutely maintained their ground, until a retreat, thrice ordered, became absolutely necessary to prevent their being surrounded and cut off. Two of their number were taken prisoners and several wounded—one very severely. After the battle, and until the enemy retired, their duty was of the most severe and arduous kind, and they acquitted themselves in a manner fully satisfactory to their commanders and highly honorable to themselves.

In testimony of the gallant bearing of the "Volunteers" at Baltimore, we subjoin the discharge of Gen. Smith, a private letter of Maj. Heath, and an extract from the regimental orders of the brave Col. Sterett, of September 20, 1814:

HEAD QUARTERS, Baltimore,
September 20, 1814.

"Captain Spangler and his company of volunteers from York, Pa., having honorably performed the tour of duty for which they had offered their services, are hereby permitted to return to their homes. In taking leave of this gallant corps, the major general commanding has great pleasure in bearing testimony to the undaunted courage they displayed in the affair of the 12th inst., and in tendering them his thanks for the essential aid they contributed towards the defence of the city. S. SMITH, Maj. Gen. Commanding."

"BALTIMORE, September 20, 1814.

To Captain Spangler,

Dear Sir—Hearing that you are about to depart from our city with your brave corps, I cannot do justice to my own feelings without expressing the obligations I am under to you and them for the promptness with which you uniformly executed my orders, your readiness at all times to perform your duty and the cool and manly conduct manifested by the officers and men under your command during the action with the enemy on the 12th inst. May you all return in health to the bosoms of your families, and long enjoy happiness uninterrupted.

I am, sir, with sentiments of sincere respect, your friend and humble servant,

R. K. HEATH, 1st major, 5th reg't."

REGIMENTAL ORDERS — FIFTH REGIMENT.

"BALTIMORE, SEPT. 20, 1814.

Captain Spangler's company of York Volunteers having permission to return to their respective homes, the lieutenant colonel cannot permit them to depart without thanking them for their soldier-like and orderly conduct. The few days they were attached to the 5th regiment, was a momentous period of trial—they not only had to face the dangers of battle, but to bear the inclemencies of weather and suffer all the inconveniences of fatigue, watching and hunger to which the soldier is liable in the hour of alarm—these were met and borne by them with a manly fortitude, which does them honor and entitles them to the gratitude of Baltimore, and particularly to the friendship and esteem of the officers and men of the 5th regiment, which are thus publicly and cheerfully accorded to them."

The following is a list of the officers and men composing the company of "York Volunteers," when that company marched from York on the invasion of Baltimore—August 29, 1814:

Michael H. Spangler, Captain.
Jacob Barnitz, First Lieutenant.

John M'Curdy, Second Lieutenant.
George F. Doll, Ensign.

Musicians.

John A. Leitner, Daniel Small, G. P. Kurtz.

Non-Commissioned Officers.

John Hay, Adam King, Joseph Schall, David Wilson, Charles Kurtz, Michael Hahn, John Kuntz, Daniel Updegraff.

Privates.

Peter Lanius,
Henry Sleeger,
James Gibson,
G. W. Spangler,
Hugh Ingram,
John Brickel,
Thomas Miller,
Jacob Lehman,
Jacob Wiesenthal,
Jacob Frey,
George Dunn,
John M'Clear,
George Holter,
George Reisinger,
Michael Miller,
John Devine,
John M'Anulty,
John Sinn,
Anthony T. Burns,
Jacob Gartner,
Peter O'Conner,
Charles Stroman,
Enoch Thompson,
Henry Wolf,
David Hoffart,
Richard Coody,
James Dugan,
Charles Stuck,
Hugh Stewart,
Jacob Lottman,
Jacob Sheffer,
Peter Siers,
Jacob Reisinger,
William Burns,
Jacob Glessner,
Emanuel Raab,
Jacob Rupp,
Grafton Duvall,
Samuel Hays,
George Beard,
George Brickel,
Christian Eshbach,
Joseph Kerr,
John Taylor,
John Byron,
Daniel Coyle,
Jacob Herbst,
Peter Grimes,
Hugh M'Cosker,
Abraham Keller,
Henry Mundorff,
G. M. Leitner,
Walter Bull,
William Nes,
Daniel Heckert,
James S. Connellee,
David Trimble,
J. W. Altemus,
Thomas Thompson,
Chester Smith,
E. W. Murphy,
Robert Pierson,
Daniel Baumgardner,
Frederick Witz,
Frederick Kercher,
Jacob Noell,
George Ilgenfritz,
George Laub,
Joseph Woodyear,
Joseph M'Conliken,
John Fisher,
John Giesy,
Jacob Levan,
Jacob Stoehr,

Peter Cooker,	William Warson,
Hugh M'Alear, Sen.	Dennis Kearney,
Hugh M'Alear, Jun.	Aaron Holt,
David Kauffman,	Andrew Kauffman.

Of the members of the above company, only about twenty-five are now living. The arduous duty performed at Baltimore, and the exposure to the inclemency of a number of damp and cold nights in September, to which many of them were unaccustomed, we have no doubt implanted in their systems the germs of diseases, by which they were afterwards hurried to their graves. Their gallant captain died on Sunday the 7th of September, 1834, and was attended to his grave on the following Tuesday by a vast concourse of mourning relatives and friends, by the officers of the 94th regiment, P. M., by the survivors of the "York Volunteers," and by the following volunteer companies of the borough:

THE "WASHINGTON ARTILLERISTS,"
Commanded by Capt. Jacob Upp, Jun.
THE "PENNSYLVANIA VOLUNTEERS,"
Commanded by Capt. John Evans.
THE "CITIZEN GUARDS,"
Commanded by Capt. Samuel Hay.
THE "NATIONAL GREYS,"
Commanded by Capt. Alexander H. Barnitz.
THE "YORK RANGERS,"
Commanded by Capt. Samuel E. Clement.

CHAPTER XXIV.

CONSPIRACY OF THE NEGROES IN YORK IN 1803

ON THE 23d of February, 1803, a negro woman, named Margaret Bradley, was convicted for a misdemeanor in attempting to poison Sophia Bentz, and Matilda Bentz, both of York; and in consequence thereof was sentenced to undergo an imprisonment of four years in the Penitentiary at

Philadelphia. The negroes of the place, being dissatisfied with the above conviction and sentence, determined to have revenge on the whites, and sought it in the destruction of their property. They conspired together to burn the town of York, and almost succeeded in their nefarious purpose. So secret and artful was the conspiracy, that though the fires were known to be the work of incendiaries, yet no suspicion was for a long time attached to the blacks of the place. On nearly every successive day, or night, for about three weeks, they set fire to some part of the town; but through the incessant vigilance and unwearied exertions of the citizens, their dark designs were frustrated. Numerous patrols were established; strong guards were kept on foot by the citizens; and the governor ordered out a detachment of the militia, which was constantly on duty. Indeed so great was the danger, and so high had the public fear arisen, that the governor of the state, Thomas McKean, offered by proclamation on the 17th of March, the sum of three hundred dollars to any person who should discover those who were engaged in the conspiracy for burning the borough. But happily for the town, suspicion had already been attached, and arrest made, which were followed by confessions. A negro girl, who had received instructions to set fire to Mr. Zinn's barn at *twelve o'clock*, mistaking midday for midnight, perpetrated the deed at *noon;* in consequence of the concealed crime (for she openly carried a pan of coals into the barn and scattered them on the hay,) she was arrested and confessed herself guilty; thereby lending a key to the conspiracy.—Several other negroes were immediately arrested on suspicion; and during the following week a number more were cast into prison, some of whom confessed. Fires now ceased to be kindled, and peace and safety was again restored to the town.—The persons apprehended lay in jail until May, when their trial came on in the court of oyer and terminer. One indictment was presented against twenty-one negroes and mulattoes for the crime of *arson,* that is house burning; a part of whom were convicted and sent to the Penitentiary for a goodly length of years. Thus ended this dark conspiracy, which for a long time baffled discovery.

Among the principal fires in York (for they burnt some buildings out of the borough) may be mentioned the following:

On the night of Sunday the 20th of February, the stable of Richard Koch was set on fire and burnt to the ground. This building was well selected, for it was joined to the kitchen by one and the same roof, and stood within a few feet of a stable on an adjoining lot in which there was a quantity of hay. The roof of the kitchen being torn down, the fire was, by means of the engines, confined to the stable: but had it not been discovered until a little later, it would have destroyed all the neighboring buildings.

On the night of Monday the 7th of March they set fire to the stable of Mr. Edie, then in the tenure of Dr. Spangler. The flames were communicated with uncontrolable rapidity to the stable of Dr. Jameson on the west, and to that of the widow Updegraff on the east. Those three buildings were all on fire at the same time, and sunk down in one common ruin: by uniting their flames, they formed a tremendous fire which seemed to threaten the destruction of a great part of the town.

On the 8th of March the Academy* was on fire, but the flames were quickly and fortunately extinguished. This was the fifth fire in the town within the period of nine days.

On the 14th of March, they set fire to the barn of Mr. Zinn, whence the flames were communicated to the barn of Rudolph Spangler, Jacob Spangler, G. L. Loeffler and Philip Gossler. These five barns, built of wood, filled with hay and straw, and standing near one another, formed but one fire. Through great exertions and a fortunate change of the wind, the houses and other buildings in the neighborhood were

* This fire is believed not to have been caused by the blacks, but is supposed to have originated in the carelessness of one of the teachers, who either directed or permitted hot ashes to be poured on the floor of an unoccupied room, containing some dry wood and chips which were in consequence ignited, and communicated the fire to the floor and woodwork of the room.

saved. This was the fire which led to the immediate discovery of the conspiracy.

After the fires had ceased, and most of those who had been engaged in the conspiracy were confined in prison, the justices of the peace and burgesses of the borough published a notice (on the 21st of March) "to the inhabitants of York and its vicinity to the distance of ten miles," requiring such as had negroes "to keep them at home under strict discipline and watch, and not to let them come to town on any pretence whatsoever without a written pass:" and when they came they were to leave town one hour at least before sundown "on pain of being imprisoned or at risk of their lives." Free negroes were "to get a pass from a justice of the peace, in order that they might not be restrained from their daily labor."

CHAPTER XXV.

FLOODS OF THE CODORUS.

THE Codorus originates partly in Maryland and partly in York county, and flowing in a northern direction, passes directly through the borough of York, about ten miles above its mouth. It is ordinarily a placid stream—but sometimes, forgetting its bounds, it makes an awful display of its terrible destructive power.

One of the first floods of the Codorus, was in March, 1784, the date of what is usually called the "ice flood." Though the water and ice rose to an extraordinary height on this occasion, no buildings were destroyed—the flood did not pass off however without doing considerable damage.

There was another flood in 1786. On Tuesday, the 3d of October, it began to rain, there being at the same time a high South East wind. The rain continued until Thursday night, at which time the Codorus was three feet and ten inches and a half higher than it was in 1784. This flood, like its predecessor, destroyed every bridge on the Codorus.

But the greatest flood was that of 1817, when the water

rose five feet higher than it did in 1786. On Friday, the 8th of August, 1817, at about ten o'clock in the evening, the air was uncommonly heavy—an unusual darkness soon followed, and then a moderate rain. At about 12 o'clock the rain increased considerably, and at about one, it became violent. The storm continued till nearly one o'clock on Saturday afternoon, when the sky suddenly became clear, and the sun shone brightly. The gloom of feeling caused by the unusual and incessant storm had indeed occasioned some melancholy forebodings; but all heaviness of soul was now dissipated by the view of a sky again clear and serene. Every where there was cheerfulness, without a dream of the approach of danger.

By the rain the Codorus had swollen beyond its banks. In the strength of its course, it swept away the large wooden bridge which connected George street with the York Haven turnpike road. The destruction of the bridge, however, did not excite the fears of the inhabitants. Many of them were amused at the novel sight of a bridge moving off with the current.

The water, in the mean time, was rising rapidly—it soon covered Main street from above Water street on the eastern to Newberry street on the western side of the creek. The people now removed from the lower stories of their houses; but no one forboded the approach of disaster.

At length news arrived that the large dam at Spring Forge, on the Codorus, some miles above York, had yielded to the fury of the waters. This intelligence was communicated to the people who lived west of the creek, and immediately beyond the stone bridge in Main street. They were advised to save themselves by going to some place of security, while the water might yet be waded. They apprehended however, no danger, supposing that their houses would save them—and consequently, they did not remove.

The waters of the Spring Forge dam, and of the other dams above York, broken by the discharged fury of the first, came now foaming, rolling, roaring on, acquiring new strength as they progressed, and sweeping down every thing in their course, until finally lost in the Susquehanna. Before the creek, however, had arisen to the fullness of its fearful height, Col. Michael H. Spangler, first with a horse, and afterwards with a boat, removed many people from their houses, thereby saving them, most probably, from a death amid the waters. At one time there were eight persons attached to the boat, so that it was almost impossible to make it move over the waves. A few minutes more, and it would have been too late to have saved these beings from the fury of a merciless element.

The water had now risen so high that communication between the people in their houses and those on the shores became impossible. As the danger of removing was greater than that of remaining, those who were exposed were obliged to continue where they were, each seeming affixed to the spot, fearing, each moment, that in the next, they should be precipitated into the flood.

The torrent now rolled through the streets of York, as though the foundations of the great deep had been broken up. The Codorus had swollen into a mighty river—it was from a quarter to a half mile wide, and deep enough to float the proudest war-ship that rides the ocean. On came the torrent, bearing on its broad bosom trophies of the ruin and destruction it had already spread throughout the region of its march. Bridges, the wood-work of dams, mills, houses, barns, stables, &c., from the country above, all, in rapid succession, came floating through the town.

House after house either rose on the water and was borne off or was undermined and sunk beneath the waves. As the small and less strong houses were most exposed to danger, their inhabitants betook themselves to those which were more fortified against the element. Many beat holes from room to room, thereby ascending to the tops of their dwellings; and then, by jumping from roof to roof, they escaped. In some instances, the houses deserted were swept away in less than a minute from the time they were left.

The houses in which the people mostly collected for safety, were Mrs. Margaret Doudle's, Jesse Spangler's and Jesse Love's. There were eight persons saved in Mrs. Doudle's house; six in Mr. Spangler's; and between twenty-five and thirty in Mr. Love's. The people in these houses remained for nearly four hours in continued expectation of instant death; for the houses stood in the midst of a current which was on all sides overthrowing buildings apparently as firm as they. These houses, with several others, were watched from the shore with a breathless anxiety; but though one corner after another had given, or was giving way, yet enough remained to secure the lives of those who were in them and upon them.

Helpless relatives and friends were seen extending their arms from roofs and windows for assistance, expecting that the house which sustained them, would instantly yield beneath them, or float down the torrent. The cries of the living and the dying were heard on all sides; and every one was taking, in breathless agony, a last look at some dear object of affection.

It would be a labor almost endless to recount all the hair-breadth escapes, and to detail every deed of individual prowess, for which this day will long be mentioned with a melancholy and a tearful recollection. Every thing which human power could effect, was done to aid and to save. There were a few men whose exertions on this occasion entitles them to honorable notice. Messrs. Penrose Robinson and John Wolf secured two coloured people who were floating down the torrent on the roof of a house, at the risk of their own lives. Messrs. Seacrist, Eichelberger, Leitner, Cookes, Hart, Doughen, Detterman, and John Miller exerted themselves in boats, like heroes, fearless of the waves, and despising danger.

There were ten persons who lost their lives by this flood; they were Mr. Hugh Cunningham and lady, Mr. Daniel Updegraff (formerly editor of a paper entitled "The Expositor"); Master Samuel Eichelberger (son of Martin Eichelberger,) aged about 15 years, a Miss Colvin of York county, a child of Mr. John F. Williams, aged about two years; and four persons of colour.

Mr. and Mrs. Cunningham, and Samuel Eichelberger were found in one and the same room, lying dead side by side. They were in part of Mrs. McClellan's house, which was lodged a few perches from the channel against a tree. Out of this house, Mrs. McClellan had been taken but a few minutes before it was carried away. Mr. Joseph Wren, a soldier of the revolution, was found alive in the garret of the same house.* Mrs. Williams' child was thrown from its cradle in sight of its mother, who was herself saved with difficulty.

The following is a list of most of the buildings that were ruined or carried off by the flood, between Water and Newberry streets.

Michael Doudel's large currying shop, tan-house &c. and his stock of hides and leather, all swept away.

Jacob Barnitz's stone brewery, destroyed.

Samuel Welsh's brick brewery (with all its contents,) nail-factory, and out-houses, carried off; and the brick dwelling house much injured.

Jesse Spangler's hatter shop, stable, and out-houses destroyed; and his dwelling house (occupied by him as a tavern) ruined.

Mr. Schlosser's brick dwelling-house, stable, and out-house destroyed.

Joseph Morris' kitchen, stable, and out-houses destroyed; his dwelling house greatly injured.

Mrs. Morris' stable and out-houses destroyed; dwelling-house injured.

Mr. Hantz's tavern, (occupied by Thomas Smith) stable, sheds, and out-houses carried off; the tavern and back-buildings, all of brick, nearly ruined.

Peter Ruhl's dwelling-house, kitchen, and stable carried off.

John F. Williams' brick grocery store, brick kitchen, stable, and out-houses destroyed: dwelling-house ruined.

Alexander Underwood's kitchen, stable, and out-houses destroyed: dwelling-house very much injured.

Messrs. Jessop's and Davis's jeweller's shop carried off.

Jonathan Jessop's cotton ware-house, with a large quantity of cotton; his stables, and out-houses, all carried off.

John Elgar's nail-factory, stable, and out-houses destroyed: dwelling-house greatly injured.

George Rothrock's stables and out-houses destroyed.

Mr. Lanius' stables and out-houses destroyed.

---

* See chapter under head of "Pensioners."

Martin Spangler's tan-house, two other houses, and stable destroyed: dwelling-house injured.

Jacob Smyser's tan-house &c. destroyed.

Mr. Ilgenfritz's stable carried off.

Jacob Gardner's tan-house, bark-house, barn &c. carried off: dwelling-house injured.

Israel Gardner's new two-story brick-house (occupied by George Lauman) with all its contents carried off: back-buildings injured.

Thomas Owing's back-building and stable carried off: dwelling-house ruined.

John Love's tan-house, bark-house, stable &c. carried off.

The Rev. Michael Dunn's stable and out-houses carried off: dwelling-house injured.

Weirich Bentz's two dwelling-houses, stables, and out-houses carried off.

Mrs. Margaret Doudel's tan-house and out-houses carried off: her large and strong two-story brick dwelling-house very much injured by the falling in of the whole west gable end.

Mrs. Rummel's stable, and Mr. Carnan's stable carried off.

Mr. Behler's log-house and still-house in Water street carried off.

Mr. Siechrist's shed full of bricks, carried off.

The whole of the curtain and wing walls of the stone bridge in High street broken down.

In most of these cases the buildings and improvements were either entirely carried off, or were so much injured as to be incapable of repair.

The tenants who suffered and who mostly lost their all, were Martin Eichelberger, Mrs. McClellan, G. K. Kane, Samuel Hartman, George Lauman, Abner Thomas, and several others.

One account of the flood* says that "seven tan yards, two taverns, three stores, two breweries, one candle and soap

* The same account says "The expanse of several miles of water below the town was covered with ruins:—Roofs floating down with people on them, reaching and crying for assistance; stables with dogs, fowls and other domestic animals; wrecks covered with tables, beds, bedsteads, chairs,

factory, one whip factory, two nail factories, one jeweller's shop, one coppersmith's shop and several other shops, besides other buildings, in all *fifty-four buildings,* were destroyed." Another account says, "all the barns, stables, and out-houses, with one or two exceptions, from the creek to Newberry street were carried away. The buildings swept away or injured, such as dwelling-houses, barns, stables and work-shops, could not be far from one hundred."

It is estimated that the damage to York and its immediate vicinity amounted to more than two hundred thousand dollars. Nearly fifty families were nearly ruined. In short many people worth from one to seven thousand dollars on Saturday morning were in a few hours reduced to poverty.

As this great and awful inundation was a cause not of private calamities only, but of losses of a public nature, application was made to the legislature of the state for relief. That body at their first session after the flood, granted (on 13th Feb. 1818) the sum of 5000 dollars to the commissioners of the county, to be applied in building and repairing the public bridges which had been destroyed or injured; and likewise the sum of 1000 dollars to the burgesses of York, to be applied in repairing the public streets of the borough.

FLOOD OF 1822.

In the year 1822, York suffered from another flood. A snow of between fifteen and eighteen inches deep, fell on the 18th of February. On the evening of the 20th, a south wind arose,

---

desks, bureaus, clocks and clock cases, trunks, cradles, sideboards, and many other articles both of furniture and cloathing; dry goods and groceries; barrels, hogsheads, timber and mill-wheels; trees, wheat and rye sheaves, corn, oats, fences, &c. all passing along with lifeless bodies, down the torrent.

In the country there was great distress. The saw-mill of J. P. King was carried away. A house occupied by Samuel Boyer, who lived at King's paper mill, was swept off, and with it went every thing Mr. Boyer had except the clothes on his back. The bridges on the Baltimore road were broken down: the stage was unable to travel the road on Monday. The large bridge over the Conewago on the York Haven road was destroyed. And so of a thousand other things."

accompanied with heavy rain: the snow dissolved with unexampled rapidity; and on the 21st, the Codorus was swollen to a river. The water was within four feet and four inches, of being as high as on the memorable 9th of August, 1817. From the vast quantity of floating ice, the flood was very destructive to bridges,† mill-dams, &c.

The following is an account of the principal sufferers in York Borough.

The tannery of Michael Doudel was much injured: he lost moreover, a shop and a considerable quantity of hides and leather.

The dwelling-house and brew-house of Samuel Welsh were much injured: he lost a framed store-house.

Jacob Schlosser lost his still house and distillery.

The stables of Jesse Spangler, of Joseph Morris Esq., and of Andrew Newman were carried off.

Jacob Siechrist sustained considerable loss in his brick yard.

Though this flood did much damage, and was well an object of terror, yet the remembrance of it loses much of its interest and its dread, on account of the greater power and far more destructive consequences of its predecessor.

CHAPTER XXVI.

RIOT IN 1786.

THERE was an affray in the Borough of York in December, 1786, which may not be unworthy of a brief notice, it being a matter still fresh in the recollections of many of the inhabitants of the town. This was a riot occasioned by the excise-law then existing.

A certain man in Manchester, viz., Jacob Bixler, was unwilling to pay his tax or rather excise: whereupon his cow was *distrained* or taken by the collector, for the payment.

† In particular it may be mentioned that three arches of the bridge in Main street, York, and five arches on the then new stone bridge over Conewago, at Berlin, were thrown down by the ice, &c. the briges being thereby destroyed.

It was to *rescue* (i. e. forcibly take from the hands of the officer) this cow, that the affray happened. The beast had been driven by the officer from Manchester to York town, and, by advertisement, was on a certain day to be exposed to sale. On the day of the sale a company of about 100 men set out from the neighborhood of the poor animal's former residence, armed some with clubs, others with pistols or guns; and directing their march towards York, they crossed *chicken* bridge [at the end of north George street] and in single or Indian file marched into town. Their captain, who was Godfrey King, led them on, with dread determination, to the place where her *vaccine* excellence was exposed to *vendition*. This was the square where Main and Beaver streets cross each other. The appearance of such a body of men so armed for outrage, was the subject of an instant alarm. They had hardly proceeded to commit violence when the whole town, as on the alarm of fire, was assembled together. The inhabitants met the rioters with the like weapons, clubs, pistols, guns and swords. One justice half deprived of his senses hastened to the spot and supporting himself with both hands against a corner said "I command *thee* in *my* name to keep peace." But something more forcible was found in the weapons of Henry Miller, John Hay, John Edie, William Bailey &c. all well prepared for the battle. Miller during the affray, struck with his sword at one Hoake, who leaping over a waggon-tongue, just escaped the blow; the sword falling upon the wagon tongue, sunk into it about an inch.

After some boxing and striking, the party dispersed in every direction, and the whole tumult hushed. The men became ashamed of their folly and said that "they had just come in to see what became of the money."

Frederick Hoake was afterwards severely fined for cutting the rope around the cow's neck, and letting her loose, though the fact was, Peter Schneider, jun., did the very thing for which Hoake, innocent as to this, was punished.

The several rioters were shortly afterwards brought before the justices of the peace, and bound for appearance at next court, and on the 23d of January 1787, Godfrey King, Andrew Hoake, Philip King, [son of Godfrey] Philip Wintemeyer, George Miller and Adam Hoake were each bound before the court of Quarter Sessions in a considerable sum to appear at the next Supreme court to answer such bills of indictment as should be presented against them, and not to depart the court without leave and in the mean time to keep the peace to all the liege subjects of the commonwealth." They accordingly appeared, and with others of their brethren, were fined, "judgment being tempered with mercy." Thus ended an affray of which many speak, and of which, from the much speaking we have been induced to write. It was in fact a *cow-insurrection;* it brought Manchester and York into a fond and loving union.

SNOW STORM.

In January 1772 there was an uncommon fall of snow in York county. On the 27th of that month the snow was three feet and a half deep. A heavy rain then came on, which, freezing, formed a thick crust.—Nearly every man and boy in the county now turned out to chase deer, for while the hunter could run fleetly on the crust, the poor animals struck through, and from the wounds received in their legs, were unable to proceed far. The consequence was that (with exception of a few that were on the mountains and in the more remote parts of the county) the race was nearly extirpated. Before that time deer were common throughout the county, yet since then but few have been found.

HAIL STORM IN 1797.

The following account of a hail storm in the year 1797, is extracted from the manuscripts left by the Hon. *Thomas Hartley.*

On the * * day of June 1797, there was a hail storm in the town of York, and in a part of the neighborhood, which as far as it extended, destroyed the gardens and broke down the winter grain in a most extraordinary manner: there was hardly a hope that any would be saved, but the farmers were able, in the harvest, to gather more than half of what they considered as lost. The Indian corn was apparently injured, but the sun brought it up again. The hail stones were prodigiously large. Several persons were in danger of losing their lives from them. Many fowls and birds were killed. Some of the stones were as large as a pullet's egg, or as the apples then growing. It is supposed that in York town and Buttstown, fully 10,000 panes of glass were broken."*

FIRE IN 1797.

As an account of the fire which raged in York town in the year 1797, we give two extracts, the first from the manuscripts of the Hon. *Thomas Hartley,* and the second from the private papers of another late member of the York bar.

"The hail-storm had made a serious impression upon the citizens; but on Wednesday night, the 5th of July, 1797, between the hours of 12 and 1 o'clock, the town was alarmed by the cry of fire, which it seems, had been communicated from an oven of Mr. John Hay. The house of Mr. John Hay was soon in flames. The Reformed German Church also took fire. The kitchen and small stable were soon on fire; the stable stood about forty feet from my back buildings. The sparks and inflamed parts of shingles ascended into the air, and were then dispersed and carried upon parts of the town, and far into the neighboring country. Between twenty and thirty houses and barns were on fire nearly at the same time; but by mighty exertions, none were materially injured beside those I first mentioned. My house, it is said, was on fire four or five times. A willow tree nearly fifty feet high, standing beyond my buildings, away from the fire, had several of its upper branches scorched and burnt.—The trees and shrubs in the garden were hurt. A small bush of a monthly

* On the 29th of May, 1821, an uncommon hail storm destroyed most of the grain in the neighborhood of York. On that same day the heat was uncommonly oppressive in the borough of Hanover, and in the evening there was violent thunder and lightning: but (a circumstance very strange) at the distance of three miles from Hanover there was a destructive hail storm.

white rose, at the distance of perhaps seventy feet from the church, was totally blasted and destroyed, never to rise again. So great was the heat, that pears hanging on espaliers in my garden, fifty feet from the flames, were in part roasted.—The circumstances of the garden, I carefully noticed on my return home (which was on the 8th of July;) and I shewed the trees and pears to several of my acquaintances, among others, to Mr. Milledge, a member of Congress from Georgia. There was scarcely any wind at York in the night of the fire, (Mr. Milledge says that at the great fire at Savannah, the air was calm, and the horizon clear and serene.) But after the flames had ascended some height in the sky, the sparks became disturbed and more scattered, and fell upon several houses, which caught fire at the same time, and drew off the people from the places at which they were first engaged to take care of their respective dwellings. What does great honour to the town is, that, though the furniture, goods, wares, and merchandise were carried out by different hands, yet scarcely a single article is, as I hear, missing.

THOMAS HARTLEY."

The second account is as follows:

"Last Wednesday night was a night of terror to the inhabitants of this place. Between the hours of twelve and one o'clock, a fire broke out in the back-buildings, adjoining the dwelling-house of John Hay, Esq. Mr. Hay, who slept in one of the back-rooms, on being awakened by the noise of the fire, immediately arose and gave alarm. But before the citizens had collected in numbers sufficient to make an effectual resistence to its progress, the fire had been communicated to the dwelling house and to the German Reformed Church, both of which were in a few minutes all in flames. The fire advanced with such rapidity that all the efforts to save those buildings were soon found to be in vain. The burning was, in a small degree, an object of terror.—Sparks of fire, and blazing shingles were thrown to a vast height, many of them falling upon houses and stables in different parts of the town. From fifteen to twenty buildings, among which was the court house, were on fire during the night. All however, except the two first mentioned, were saved through the vigilance and activity of the citizens. The buildings in the immediate neighborhood of Mr. Hay's house and of the church, were almost continually on fire; but, by the most surprising intrepidity and perseverance of the citizens, the ruinous element, which threatened general devastation, was, at last under the favor of a calm night, happily subdued.

"The citizens, animated with a sense of duty as well as danger, exerted their utmost strength in warring against the invading flames. Some were stationed on the roofs of the neighboring houses, where they remained for hours amidst fire and smoke, resisting the progress of the destroying element, which seemed every moment to be gathering with fresh fury around them: some kept the fire engines in continual operation, while others furnished a constant supply of water. Many of the fair sex, of every age, strengthened by strong apprehensions of danger, were employed the greater part of the night in conveying water, thereby contributing much to the common safety. A few strangers, who were accidently in the town, also rendered essential service.

"At about six o'clock in the morning the danger was over. No lives were lost, and but two persons were materially hurt. Mr. Hay lost part of his furniture, a large quantity of grain, &c. but his papers, and most valuable effects, it is said were saved. The church organ, bells, and records were entirely destroyed. * * *

"The fire appears to have originated from an oven, in the walls of which a wooden post was placed to support the shed above. The oven had been twice heated the preceding day; and as there was but the thickness of a brick between the fire and the wooden post, it is probable that by long and repeated use of the oven, the wall separating the fire from the wood, had been in some measure demolished, so that the wood became exposed, and, when the oven was heated, took fire; but that, for want of air, the fire made so slow a progress that it did not break out till late at night."

DROUGHT OF 1822.

Persons who had lived nearly a century had witnessed nothing like the great drought of 1822. There was no rain of any consequence from the 21st of February, the time of the flood, until sometime in September, a period of about six months. Fountains which had been considered as perennial, were dried up. Grinding was not done at one mill out of ten; and where grinding was done, the demand for flour was not supplied. Many farmers went twenty miles to mill, and then were obliged to return with a quantity of flour not sufficient to satisfy immediate want. An account of the drought written on the 13th of August says "the summer crops have almost totally failed; some fields will yield not a grain of corn, and the best fields not more than a few bushels to the acre." Shortly after this there were two showers, which greatly relieved the distress of the country: the one fell on the 23d and the other on the 24th of August. The showers, however, did not extend to the north-western part of the county, where the distress arising from the drought was still excessive. As a proof that the scarcity of water at this time was unparalleled, it may be mentioned that on the 13th of September, 1822, there was not a drop of water to be seen in the channel of the Big Conewago, at the place where the bridge is thrown across it on the Carlisle road. At low water, the stream there is generally from 90 to 120 feet wide.

CHAPTER XXVII.

GEOLOGY OF YORK COUNTY.

York county is mostly of transition formation.

A ridge of Roof Slate, commencing near the Susquehanna river in the South East corner of the county extends several miles along the Southern line of the county, and furnishes an abundance of slate of the best quality.

Above the Roof Slate, and occupying a considerable portion of the South Eastern townships of the county, is a range of Shining Argillite; passing in some places into Steatite, under which, in one or two places, Dolomite, or Magnusian carbonate of lime, have been discovered by sinking shafts.

North of this range of Argillite, is a more extensive one of Chlorite rock, alternating with, or containing veins of Quartz, overlaid with Red Shale, and Micacious Schiste, containing Garnets.

From this range, we descend into the great Limestone valley of York, containing Blue and White Limestone, with veins of very beautiful Cal. Spar Calciferous Sand Rock.

A ridge of Gray Wacke formation, and consisting of Gray Wacke Sandstone, Gray Wacke Slate, and Rubble, of the character of the Cocalico Millstones of Lancaster county, runs North of the York Limestone Valley from the Susquehanna river.

North of this Gray Wacke elevation, and nearly as extensive, is a second valley of Limestone, under which there is a thin layer, or stratum of coal, in no place more than four inches thick.

In the North part of this valley, the Conglomerate, or Breccia marble, of the range extending from the Potomac through the D. of Columbia, Frederick county, Maryland, York, Lancaster, and Berks county &c. in Penn'a., crops out in two or three places, in favorable situations for quarrying, and of a quality fit for use or ornament.

This second or North Limestone valley is terminated by the Old Red Sandstone formation of the Conewago hills, which occupies nearly the balance of the county to the North. The great Limestone valley of Cumberland county, a narrow strip of which extends into York county, succeeds to the North of the Red Sand stone formation.

MINERAL DEPOSITS.

There are in a number of townships of York county, deposits of Iron of a greater or less extent, some of which furnish ore of an excellent quality for manufacture.

Indications of Copper exist in a number of places in this county, but no extensive deposit has yet been discovered.

Sulphuret of Lead, or Galena, has been found in small portions near the Susquehanna.

Sulphuret of Iron is extensively disseminated.

Colophonite, Prase, Actynolite, Asbestos, Mag. Ox. of Iron, and Micacious ox. of Iron, exist in different parts of the county. No Fossil remains have yet been found.

Particles of Gold have been found, and very strong indications exist of pretty extensive deposits of this mineral in several townships South of the Limestone valley of York.

CHAPTER XXVIII.

INCORPORATED BOROUGHS IN YORK COUNTY.

1. The Borough of YORK was incorporated on the 24th of September, 1787. [For an account of the Borough see pages 19-27, of this volume.]

2. The Borough of HANOVER was incorporated on the 4th of March, 1815. [See pages 47-53, of this volume.]

3. The Borough of LEWISBERRY was incorporated on the 2d of April, 1832.

Lewisberry derives its name from Eli Lewis, by whom it was founded. It is agreeably situated at the western boundary of Newberry township, about 14 miles from the county seat, 18 from Carlisle, and 10 from the seat of the government of the state. The state road from Lancaster to Carlisle passes through the borough. The present population of Lewisberry is about 260. There is one Meeting House in the borough for Methodists, and one in the vicinity for Lutherans and Reformed Presbyterians. The Rev. Mr. Lauer, of Germany, is the present Lutheran Minister. There is a grist mill on Bennet's run, in the immediate vicinity of the borough, to which is attached a saw mill, and machinery for boring and grinding gun barrels. There is also a mill, within the borough boundaries, purposely constructed for boring and grinding gun barrels, and for these two establishments the barrels are forged in the borough. A variety of mechanical branches are industriously pursued, and no little business done in this pleasant little town.

4. DILLSBURG was incorporated on the 9th of April, 1833. This borough is finely situated in the new township of Carroll. In the act of incorporation the boundaries of Dillsburg are described as follows:

"Beginning at a post adjoining the lands of Frederick Eichelberger, a line bearing north eighty-six and a quarter degrees, west one hundred and four perches, to a post; thence south twelve degrees, through the land of Andrew Mumper and Peter Lightner, to a white oak; thench north one and a quarter degrees, east sixty-five perches, through lands of P. Leightner and McMullen's heirs, to a white oak; thence north one and a quarter degrees, east one hundred and fifty-seven perches, by land of Jacob Sawyer and John Mumper, to the place of beginning."

5. SHREWSBURY was incorporated on the 9th of April, 1834. This borough is situated in a township of the same name, on the turnpike road leading from York to Baltimore. Its boundaries are described in the act of incorporation as follows:

"Beginning at stones, thence by land of Peter Ruhl and others, south seventy-two degrees, west and hundred and eighteen perches and a half to stones: south six and a half degrees, west one hundred and forty-seven perches and a half, to stones; south eight degrees, east two hundred and six perches, to stones; north seventy-two degrees, east one hundred and eighteen perches and an half, to stones; north eight degrees, west two hundred and six perches, to stones; north six degrees and a half, east one hundred and forty-seven perches and an half, to the place of beginning."

6. WRIGHTSVILLE was incorporated on the 14th of April, 1834. This borough is situated on the Susquehanna, in Hellam township. It was formerly known as Wright's Ferry—but after the erection of the Columbia bridge over the river at this point, it lost its old name, and has borne that of Wrightsville for a number of years. It was at one time in contemplation to make the ground upon which Wrightsville stands, the scite [site] of the Capital of the United States. Gen. Washington was earnestly in favor of erecting the na-

ional buildings here, urging its beauty, its security, &c., in defence of his preference—but a small majority prevailed against him. Some of the events of the late war, (events which we do not very well like to speak or think of,) would perhaps not have occurred, had the wishes of Gen. Washington prevailed.

We subjoin the first section of the act of Assembly by which Wrightsville was constituted a borough.

"Be it enacted &c., That the villages of Wrightsville and Westphalia, in the county of York, shall be and the same are hereby erected into a borough, which shall be called the borough of Wrightsville, and shall be bounded and limited as follows, viz: Beginning at a birch tree on the river Susquehanna, at the foot of Bridge street and land of William Wright, south seventy-five degrees, west ninety-five perches, to a black oak on the land of James Wright; thence along said land to Fourth street; thence along the west side of said street, south twelve and a half degrees, west eighty-nine perches and a quarter, to the north side of Locust street; along the north side of said street, south seventy-seven degrees, west ninety-eight perches to a post on Jonathan Mifflin's land; thence twenty-six and a half perches, to the middle of Hellam street; thence along said street, north seventy-seven degrees, east one hundred and eighteen perches and a half, to the west side of Third street, south twenty-two degrees, east fifty-six perches, to the south side of a street adjoining land of Joseph Dewiller; thence along said street, north sixty-eight degrees, east twenty perches, to the west side of Barnes' alley; thence south twenty-three degrees, east twenty-eight perches, to a post on Joseph Detwiller's land; thence south two degrees, east forty-eight perches to a Hackbury tree; thence south thirty-six and a half degrees, east eighty perches, to a hickory stump; thence north seventy-eight and a half degrees, east eighty-six perches, to a poplar stump; thence north twelve and a half degrees, west twenty-four perches, to the river Susquehanna, at the mouth of Kreutz creek; thence north-west by the said river three hundred and sixteen perches to the place of beginning."

CHAPTER XXIX.

UNINCORPORATED TOWNS IN YORK COUNTY.

BUTTSTOWN is situated in West-Manchester township, and adjoins the borough of York. Its Main street is a continuation of the street of the same name of York Borough. It is on the turnpike road leading from York to Gettysburg.

DOVER is pleasantly situated in a township of the same name about 7 miles from the borough of York, on the state road leading from York to Carlisle.

FRANKLIN is situated in a township of the same name, near the Northern boundary of the county, being about two miles from the line of Cumberland and York counties.

FREYSTOWN is a village in Springgarden township, in the immediate vicinity of York Borough, and on the turnpike road leading from York to Lancaster.

JEFFERSON is situated in the large township of Codorus, about 14 miles South West of York Borough.

LIVERPOOL is about 7 miles North of York Borough, on the turnpike road leading from York to Harrisburg.

LOGANSVILLE is in Shrewsberry township, about 7 miles from the borough of York, on the turnpike road leading from York to Baltimore.

NEWBERRY is situated in a township of the same name, about 3 miles from the borough of Lewisberry, and about 4 and a half miles from York Haven.

NEW HOLLAND is in Manchester township. It lies on the Susquehanna, and is distant about 8 miles from the borough of York.

NEW MARKET is a flourishing village in Fairview township, in the extreme North Eastern corner of the county, on the turnpike road leading from York to Harrisburg. It is pleasantly situated near the Susquehanna river.

ROSSTOWN is in Warrington township, about a mile North of Great Conewago creek, on the state road leading from York to Carlisle.

SIDDONSBURG is a very small village in Monaghan township.

STEWARTSTOWN or MECHANICSBURG is in Hopewell township, near the southern boundary of the county, about five miles East of Shrewsbury and about 18 miles South of York Borough.

STRINESTOWN is situated in Conewago township, on the road leading from York to Newberry.

WEIGELSTOWN is a small village in Dover township, about five miles from York, on the state road leading from York to Carlisle.

YORK HAVEN, in Newberry township, is situated on the Susquehanna, about 10 miles from the borough of York, on the turnpike leading from York to Harrisburg.

CHAPTER XXX.

PUBLIC IMPROVEMENTS IN YORK COUNTY.

A TURNPIKE road traverses the county from the Susquehanna river at Wrightsville on the East to the Adams county line on the West.

A turnpike road crosses the county, from the Maryland line on the South, to the Cumberland county line on the North.

A turnpike road from Carlisle in Cumberland county, and another from Berlin, in Adams county, both leading to the city of Baltimore, cross the townships of Heidelberg and Manheim, in this county, passing through the borough of Hanover.

The Codorus creek has been rendered navigable for arks, rafts, &c., from its mouth to the borough of York, a distance of about ten miles. This improvement was completed in 1833, and is the property of a chartered association called the "Codorus Navigation Company." This Navigation will no doubt tend very much to the advantage and prosperity of the borough of York, affording a cheap and safe passage for lumber, coal, &c. from the Susquehanna to the borough. In the spring of the present year immense quantities of lumber and coal, and several large arks of grain were brought to the borough of York, through this new medium, and so far as an opportunity has been had to test the utility of the work, it has more than fulfilled the expectations of its most sanguine friends.

There are also numerous state and county roads; and all our streams are bridged wherever public convenience requires it.

Biographical Sketches

THOMAS HARTLEY.

Colonel Thomas Hartley was born in the neighborhood of Reading, Berks county, Pennsylvania, on the 7th of September, 1748. Having received the rudiments of a good classical education in that town, he removed when eighteen years of age, to York, Pa., when he commenced the study of law under the tuition of Mr. Samuel Johnson. Having pursued his law studies with diligence for the term of three years, he was admitted to practice in the courts of York on the 25th of July, 1769. He now arose in his profession with an almost unexampled rapidity, for he not only had a thorough knowledge of the law, but was acquainted with two languages, each of which was then necessary in such a county as York: his early days having been spent in Reading, then as now mostly peopled by Germans, he was from childhood acquainted with their language, which he spoke with the fluency of an orator. Another thing which favored young Hartley, much, was that he and the Hon. James Smith were for some time the only practicing lawyers of the county; Mr. Johnson with whom he had studied being then prothonotary.

Hartley was early distinguished as a warm friend of his country, both in the cabinet and in the field. In the year 1774 he was elected by the citizens of York county, a member of the provincial meeting of deputies which was held at Philadelphia on the 15th of July. In the year 1775, he was a member, from the same county, of the provincial convention which was held at Philadelphia on the 23d of January.

The war of the revolution was now approaching and Hartley was soon distinguished as a soldier. The committee of safety for Pennsylvania recommended a number of persons to Congress, for field officers to the sixth battalion ordered to be raised in that colony; and Congress accordingly on the 10th of January 1776, elected William Irwin, Esq. as

Colonel, Thomas Hartley, Esq. as Lieut. Colonel, and James Dunlap, Esq. as Major. Mr. Hartley was shortly afterwards promoted to the full degree of Colonel.

Colonel Hartley having continued about three years in faithful and laborious duty as an officer, wrote a letter to Congress on the 13th of February 1779, desiring leave to resign his commission. Congress thinking the reasons offered satisfactory, accepted his resignation, and on the same day resolved that they had "a high sense of Colonel Hartley's merit and services."

In October 1778, he was elected a member of the state legislature from the county of York.

In the year 1783, he was elected a member of the council of censors, the first day of whose meeting was on the 10th of November.

In the latter part of the year 1787, he was a member of the state convention which adopted the constitution of the United States.

In the year 1788, he was elected a member of congress, and accordingly attended their first session under the present constitution. As a new order of things had now commenced, the public mind was filled with hope and fear. The citizens of York county had taken a great interest in the establishment of the new constitution, and as Colonel Hartley was the first person who was to go forth from among them, as a member of Congress under that constitution, they determined in the warmth of their feelings, to shew him every honour. When he set out from York on the 23d of February 1789 on his way to the city of New-York, where the congress was to sit, he was accompanied to the Susquehanna by a great number of the inhabitants of the borough and its neighborhood, and was there received by a company from that part of the county and from Lancaster. The citizens then partook of a dinner, and the whole was one splendid celebration. When on the way of his return, he arrived at Wright's Ferry on the 6th of October, he was met at that place by a number of gentlemen from the borough and county of York, and was there conducted to his house in town amidst the acclamations of his friends and fellow citizens.

Colonel Hartley continued a member of Congress for about twelve years;* he was such until the time of his death.

On the 28th of April 1800, he was commissioned by governor M'Kean, as Major General of the fifth division of the Pennsylvania Militia, consisting of the counties of York and Adams.

His life of labor, usefulness, and honour was now drawing to a close. Disease was destroying his energies, and had already commenced the work of death. After a long and tedious sickness he died at his home in York, on the morning of the 21st of December 1800, aged 52 years, 3 months, and 14 days. When his mortal part was deposited in the burial ground of the Church of St. John's, the following tribute of respect to his memory was paid, by the Rev. Dr. John Campbell, his pastor and friend:

"If I could blow the trump of fame over you ever so loud and long,—what would you be the better for all this noise? yet,—let not your integrity, patriotism, fortitude, hospitality and patronage be forgotten—Another—(who need not be named)—hath borne away the palm of glory,—splendid with the never-dying honour of rearing the stupendous fabric of American freedom and empire.——Departed friend!—you hear me not,—the grave is deaf and silent.——In this work of blessings to future ages you bore, though a subordinate, yet an honourable part.——Soldiers of liberty! come drop a tear over your companion in arms.——Lovers of justice! come drop a tear over her able advocate,—and of science, come drop a tear over its warmest patron,—children of misfor-

---

* Colonel Hartley was the first gentleman from the State of Pennsylvania, that was admitted a counsellor in the Supreme Court of the United States. The first session of that court commenced at the city of New York, then the seat of Government of the United States, on Monday the 1st of February 1799. The first admission of counsellors was on Friday, the 5th of that month, when "Elias Boudinot, Esq., of New Jersey, Thomas Hartley, Esq. of Pennsylvania and Richard Harrison, Esq. of New York respectively appeared in court, took the oath for that purpose, and were appointed counsellors of the said court accordingly." These were all who were admitted during the first week of the session.

tune! come, drop a tear over your benefactor and protector. ——Brethren of this earthly lodge! rejoice that our brother is removed to the temple of the Supreme—Ministers of religion! come, drop a tear to the memory of a man, who (lamenting human frailty) was ever the friend of truth and virtue.——And thou my soul! come not into the assembly of those who would draw his reposed spirit from the bosom of his Father who is in heaven."

As an appendix to the biography of this soldier and statesman, we give the following address to his constituents which he published a short time before his decease and which is one of the last acts of his life.

Fellow Citizens:

Through want of health, and a wish to retire from a sedentary public life and to attend to my private concerns, which have been much deranged by my absence from York town, I have been induced most fixedly to decline serving in the House of Representatives in Congress after the third day of March next. Indeed it is well known that for some years past I have not wished to be elected; and should long since have declined the honor had it not been for the political condition of the world, and of our own States in particular, which have frequently suffered from two great nations;—I hope however we shall soon have peace.

A great portion of my life has been devoted to the service of my country as will appear from the following facts. I have to say that I was in two provincial conventions previous to the revolution, that I served in the revolutionary army more than three years, was one year in the assembly of the state of Pennsylvania, in the council of censors one year, was in the convention which adopted the constitution of the United States, and have been twice elected by the citizens of Pennsylvania at general elections, and four times at district elections, as a member of the house of representatives in congress. In some instances I have perhaps been useful; but I may say I have ever desired to advance the interests of the United States as far as my powers and constitution would admit. I shall endeavor to be of as much service as possible in the militia, which will occasionally require some attention and exercise.

I thank the citizens of Pennsylvania at large for shewing their frequent confidence in me, and particularly of that part of the state composing York and Adams counties, and wish them every happiness.

I am with due respect for them,

THOMAS HARTLEY.

York, Sept. 8th 1800.

N. B.—My indisposition has retarded this publication longer than I intended."

Note.—Colonel Hartley was married to a daughter of Bernhart Holtzinger of York County. He had two children, viz. a son, Charles William Hartley, for some time prothonotary of York county, and a daughter, Eleanor, married to Dr. James Hall, who was afterwards physician to the Lazaretto at Philadelphia.

HON. JAMES SMITH.

The American people have for a long time taken a deep interest in whatever concerns those illustrious worthies who signed their names to the declaration of independence. The biographies of most of them have been written, whereby the events of their lives are familiar to the public; but of some of them little is now known & but little can be collected; for the records of families have been destroyed, and the memories of friends have faded. There is not a record in manuscript or in print that gives a biography of Mr. Smith; nor are there many sources whence materials for his life can be drawn. A misfortune which happened the year before his death destroyed his private papers and with them all his family records. From relations but little can be gathered—for of all his descendants in any degree one only now lives. This quick fading of the past into the obscurity of ignorance or uncertainty should remind us how fleeting, how transitory, how like a shadow life is; fifty years hence and who will speak of *us,* if those who once directed the councils of their country and were the foremost in her senates, have passed away, leaving (with the exception of some one solitary monument of their greatness) no trace of life or deed.

Mr. John Smith, father of the Hon. James Smith, was born and educated in Ireland, in which country he was a respectable and enterprising farmer. But having a large family, he thought that in the new world he could provide better for those who would follow him; he determined therefore to visit America and take up his abode in the vallies of Pennsylvania. What induced him to prefer this one of the colonies, was that some of his brothers and uncles had emigrated hither before him, having come over with Penn when that proprietor first visited this province. Those of his relations settled in Chester county and became Quakers; their descendants still live in that county and the county of Lancaster.

Mr. John Smith being thus induced to follow his relations, sailed from Ireland with his family, and after a voyage of a few weeks, arrived at Philadelphia. His sons who came over with him were in the order of their ages, George, James and Arthur. Several daughters likewise accompanied their father to the new world; but of them little that is certain, is now known.

Mr. John Smith proceeded with his family to Lancaster county, and finally settled west of the Susquehanna in what is now York county. Here he continued to reside until about the year 1761, when he died in the neighborhood of Yorktown, at an advanced age, an example of all the happy virtues of domestic life.

George Smith, the eldest son of Mr. John Smith, studied law in Lancaster, Pennsylvania, under the tuition of Thomas Cookson, Esq. He was admitted to the bar in that place, and resided there in the practice of law until the time of his death. In company with a number of his friends he went to the river Susquehanna to bathe, opposite the place where Columbia now stands; but while in the water he was seized with the cramp; and before assistance could be given, assistance was useless. He is represented as a young man whose prospects were bright, and who seemed destined to enjoy many future honors.

Arthur, the third and the youngest son of John, and a

brother of James Smith, resided for some years as a farmer in Newberry township, in York county. He afterwards removed with a large family of children, into the Western country and has not since been heard of.

James Smith, the second son of John, and the subject of our present biography, was aged about ten years when he came with his father into this country. He resided in the paternal mansion for some years; but when his brother George had begun to practice law, he removed to Lancaster, and commenced in his office, the study of the same profession. He completed his law studies under the tuition of his brother, at the time of whose death he was aged but twenty-one.

Not long after he was admitted to the practice of the law, he removed to the neighborhood of the place where Shippensburg now stands, in company with Mr. George Ross, who was the friend and companion of Mr. Smith in early and later life. The chief occupation of Mr. Smith in his new abode, was that of surveying; though whenever occasion offered, he gave advice on subjects connected with his profession. After a few years he removed to the town of York, where he made his permanent home for the rest of his life. Here he commenced the practice of the law, and continued in it with few intermissions until near the time of his death.

Hitherto Mr. Smith had led a single life; but in or about the year 1760 he married Eleanor Armor, daughter of John Armor, who lived near New-Castle in Delaware, and who was brother of Thomas Armor, a justice and surveyor in York county before the Revolution. Eleanor, at the age of twenty-one, came to reside for a while with her uncle in York; but in less than a year after her arrival, she was wedded to one of the best of husbands.

Mr. Smith begun about this time to have a very extensive practice: he attended the courts of all the neighboring counties. With no other events in his life than those which are incident to most gentlemen of his profession, he continued in York until the beginning of the revolution. But here it should be remarked that Mr. Smith was for some time the only lawyer in York; for though Joseph Yeates and other lawyers of the neighboring counties did much business here, yet Mr.

Smith had (with the exception of perhaps of a few years) no brother in the law that resided here. When Thomas Hartley, afterwards Colonel in the revolution, and a member of congress, commenced practice here in the year 1769, there were but two lawyers in the county of York, viz. himself and Mr. Smith.*

At the commencement of the revolution, Mr. Smith was distinguished as one of the warmest friends of our liberties.

In 1774, he was chosen a deputy from the county of York to attend a provincial meeting at the city of Philadelphia; which meeting began on the 15th of June and was continued by adjournments from day to day. Mr. Smith was one of those who were appointed by this meeting or rather "committee for the province of Pennsylvania," to "prepare and bring in a draught of instructions" "to the representatives in assembly met."†

In 1775, he was elected a member for York county of the "Provincial Convention for the province of Pennsylvania, held at Philadelphia January 23d and continued by adjournments from day to day, to the 28th." In the same year he received a military honour, viz. the appointment of Colonel.

---

* For some years before and during the revolution, Mr. Smith was concerned in iron works on the Codorus creek, where the "Codorus forge" now stands. From his studious habits he was but ill calculated for business of this kind; he lost by those works about 5000 pounds, and of the two managers who were the cause of it, he said with his wonted pleasantry "that the one was a knave, and the other a fool."

From the records in the office of the Register and Recorder, I find that the forge and furnace on the Codorus Creek in the township of Hellam, were formerly owned by William Bennet; as the property of Bennet, they were sold by the Sheriff on 27th May 1771 to Charles Hamilton; Hamilton on the 9th of November in the same year sold them to Mr. Smith; and Mr. Smith on the 10th of April 1778 sold them to Thomas Neil.

† These Instructions together with the "Essay on the constitutional power of Great Britain over the Colonies in America," form the most learned state paper ever written in Pennsylvania: this may be called the commencement of the revolution in our state.

In 1776 he was deputed by the committee of York county "to join in a provincial conference of committees of the province of Pennsylvania:" the conference was held at Philadelphia and began on the 18th of June and ended on the 25th of the same month. In the same year (1776) he was elected a member of the convention for the state of Pennsylvania which commenced their session at Philadelphia on the 15th of June and ended it on the 28th of September: this convention framed the first constitution of the commonwealth. In the same year (1776) he was elected a delegate from Pennsylvania to serve in the continental congress, at which time he signed the declaration of independence.

Mr. Smith was likewise a member of Congress in the year 1777 and 1778. When Congress sat in York, the board of war was held in his law office.

After the cessation of his congressional labors, he continued to reside in York, devoting himself with great success to the practice of the law.

In October 1780, we find him elected a member of the general assembly of Pennsylvania.

Mr. Smith becoming burthened with a weight of years, and having a sufficiency of this world's goods, relinquished the practice of the law in 1801.

An event happened in the autumn of 1805, which is much to be regretted, viz. the destruction of his office by fire.* His books and papers of business, which were on the lower floor, were saved, but all his numerous private papers, which were in the upper part of the building, were destroyed. Among these were the records of the family, and manuscripts

---

* This fire, which happened on the 17th of August in the above mentioned year [1805], originated in the barn of John Hay, Esq. which was set on fire by an incendiary, and was consumed with its contents, consisting of about 700 bushels of grain. The fire was thence communicated to a number of adjoining buildings. Among those destroyed, may be mentioned a tavern-house, the property of Dr. John Rouse, and occupied by John Glessner, another dwelling house the property of Mr. Schmuck, the office of Mr. Smith, with several other buildings.

of his own connected with the history of the times, and numerous letters from Benjamin Franklin, Samuel Adams, and many other men distinguished in the revolutionary history of our country. Mr. Smith corresponded, both during and after the revolution, with many of those patriots with whom he had been in intimate connection while a member of congress: & as their letters were destroyed, the burning of the office may be considered a public loss.

Mr. Smith employed his latter days in conversation with his friends, and in reviewing and re-perusing those works which had been the delight of his youth. In view of his present and increasing infirmities, he made his will on the 25th of April 1806.† He died at his house in York on the 11th July in the same year, at a very advanced age.

There is no small difference of opinion with regard to the age of Mr. Smith. His tomb-stone erected by his son James, in the yard of the English Presbyterian Church at York, states that he was ninety-three years old at the time of his death. Many of his surviving friends say that he could not have been so old, and place his age at about eighty-seven; others say that he was not more than eighty-four or -five. Two points however we have as certain, viz. that he was but ten years of age when he came to America, and was but twenty-one years of age at the time of his brother George's death; supposing his age then to have been eighty-seven (a

---

† I have thought that in the will of Mr. Smith I could discover some traits of his originality of character: he goes, like a man of business, directly to the point. The following we have transcribed from the original in the office of the Register of wills. "I, James Smith, the elder, of the borough of York, in Pennsylvania, do hereby give and devise unto my son James Smith, his heirs and assigns forever, all that lot of ground situated on the north side of my dwelling and adjoining the alley, as the same is now under fence; and as to the rest, residue and remainder of my estate, real and personal, of whatsoever it may consist, I will and devise the same to my beloved wife, Eleanor Smith, to hold and to have during the term of her natural life. Witness my hand and seal this twenty-fifth day of April, 1806.

JAMES SMITH."

matter on which there is doubt) he must have been born in 1719 and came with his father to America in 1729, and have lost his brother George in 1740, at which time he, (James) had completed his study of the law. An obituary notice of Mr. Smith says "he was the oldest advocate in York and perhaps in Pennsylvania, for he had been in practice of the law for more than fifty years." He could not but have been a *member* of the bar between sixty and sixty-five years.

Mr. Smith, having lived through one generation and the half of another, witnessed many changes in the political world. He was born in the reign of George the first, came to America in the reign of George the second, and helped to throw off British allegiance in the reign of George the third: having witnessed the completion of his country's glory, he died in peace.

Mr. Smith was remarkable for an uncommonly retentive memory, the strength of which did not seem to be impaired by age. He was uniformly facetious and fond of anecdotes, which he always told with a happy manner. Possessing in a high degree that faculty of the mind which is defined by metaphysicians to be the tracing of resemblances or analogies between distant objects, he often exerted it in the halls of justice, producing a wild and roaring discord from all within the reach of his voice.

Mr. Smith at different times had many law students. Among them may be mentioned the Hon. Robert Smith, who began his studies here but did not complete them, and who is the same gentleman that afterwards became secretary of the navy and secretary of state under the United States government. Another of his students was Mr. David M'Mecken, who was one among the most eminent lawyers of the city of Baltimore. Another was David Bush, who was major in the revolutionary war, and who died on his bed of glory at the battle of Brandywine. Mr. David Grier, who practiced law and died in York, was likewise a student of Mr. Smith.

Mr. Smith left a widow and two out of five children surviving him: they are all now gathered to the house appointed for all living.

The above is all we have been able to collect concerning a man who was once among the earliest and warmest friends of the liberties of America.

REV. LUCAS RAUS.

The Rev. Lucas Raus, son of Lucas and Justina Raus, was born in May, 1723. His native city was Hermanstadt, the capital of Transylvania, which formerly was annexed to Hungary, but now belongs to Austria. The family to which he belonged, had produced many eminent divines in Hungary; and among them may be mentioned his own father, and his maternal grandfather.

Mr. Raus spent the first twenty years of his life in the city of his birth. There he pursued his studies under the direction of his father, preparing himself for the pulpit. Hermanstadt being mostly a catholic city, Lucas was induced to visit the institutions of other places, in order to complete his studies. Accordingly he left the paternal mansion in 1743, and proceeded to Presburg, the capital of Hungary. At this place he continued four years in the prosecution of his studies, when in May 1747, he removed to Leipsic,* in upper Saxony. In the year 1749 he removed from Leipsic to Jena, the place which, on the 14th of October, 1806, witnessed the triumph of the French over the Prussian army. At Jena he resided but a few months, for he had now completed his studies, and was, by travelling, adding the polish to the polite world to the erudition of the scholar. His intention was now to visit Holland, and then to return directly to the residence of his father. He proceeded to Amsterdam, where, at that time, there was a general spirit of migration to America. Much that was inviting was said of this part of the world; and emigrants from various parts were sailing weekly from that city. Mr. Raus caught some of the feeling which then prevailed; and as a good opportunity offered itself, he determined to cross the Atlantic, spend a few months

* The university of Leipsic was founded in the year 1469, and has long been one of the most celebrated in Europe.

in this country, which was represented as the land of promise, and then, returning to Europe, commence the labors of his holy calling. Accordingly in the year 1750, Mr. Raus sailed from Amsterdam and arrived at Philadelphia.

In a few years after his arrival in that city, he changed his views as to his future residence: for, although youthful affection still bound him to Hermanstadt, which he had not visited since he first left it in 1743, yet he determined to spend the remainder of his days in this country.

Soon after he determined to remain in this country he commenced his ministerial labors. Being invited to settle in Germantown, he accepted the invitation and preached in that place and its vicinity for three or four years, when he removed to York.

Mr. Raus was married at Germantown, in 1753, to Sophia, daughter of Mr. George Gemling, then deceased.

At York, Mr. Raus continued to reside, until the time of his death, as the minister of the German Lutheran congregation in this place. In connexion with the church in York, he presided over the spiritual concerns and occasionally preached to four or five congregations in the vicinity of the town.

This faithful servant in the vineyard of Christ, was at length called to rest from his labors. In the latter part of June, 1788, he was attacked with a billious fever. The disease raged with great fury for the space of about two weeks, when, on the 11th of July, 1788, the subject of it departed this life, in the 65th year of his age.

Mr. Raus was eminent as a scholar. Having devoted nearly all the first thirty years of his life to undisturbed and undivided study, he was not only a profound theologian but an accomplished scholar in the polite branches. Among the languages with which he was familiar, were the German, the English, the French, Latin, Greek and Hebrew.

Mr. Raus was the father of twelve children, four of whom survived him, viz., Margaret, Elizabeth, Catharine and John.

GENERAL HENRY MILLER.

General Henry Miller was born near the city of Lancaster, Pennsylvania, on the 13th of February, 1751. Early attention was paid to his education, but his father, who was a farmer, thought it necessary to place his son within the walls of a university. The high school of Miller, as of Washington and Franklin, was the world of active life.

Young Miller, having received a good English education, was placed in the office of Collison Reed, Esquire, of Reading, Pennsylvania, where he read law, and studied conveyancing. Before however he had completed his studies, he removed to York-town, in about the year 1769. At this place he pursued his studies under the direction of Samuel Johnson, Esq. At that time Mr. Johnson was Prothonotary of York county and in his office Mr. Miller acted as clerk.

The subject of our memoir was married on the 26th of June 1770, about which time he purchased a house in York-town, and furnished it. Here he supported his family mostly by the profits arising from conveyancing, and from his clerkship:* for as he found that he did not possess talents for public speaking, he devoted his industry and attention to those subjects.

The war of the revolution was now approaching; and

---

* Mr. Miller was appointed, by the general assembly, collector of the excise for York county, in October of the years 1772, 1773, and 1774. In November of the latter of these years he became clerk in the office of Charles Lukens, then sheriff of the county. In the above, among other employments, he was engaged until the time of his march to Cambridge.

Extract: "A petition from Michael Hahn, of the town of York, was presented to the house and read, praying to be appointed the collector of excise for the county of York, in place of Henry Miller, the late officer, now absent in the continental service at Boston.

"Resolved, that Michael Hahn be, and he is hereby appointed collector of excise in the county of York, for the ensuing year."

"Votes of the Assembly" for Oct. 17, 1775.

young Miller's noble soul was kindled to a generous indignation as he heard and read of the wrongs of his country. A man like him could not doubt a moment. On the 1st of June 1775, he commenced his march from York to Cambridge, Massachusetts. He went out as first lieutenant of a rifle company under the command of Captain Michael Doudel. This company was the first that marched out of Pennsylvania, and was, too, the first that arrived in Massachusetts from any place south of Long Island, or west of the Hudson. The company to which he belonged was attached to Colonel Thompson's rifle regiment, which received the first commissions issued by congress, and took rank of every other regiment.

On the arrival of the company at Cambridge, the gallantry and zeal of Miller prompted him to attempt some military act before the remainder of the regiment could arrive. His active mind immediately formed a plan to surprise the British guard at Bunker's Hill. This was on the second day after his arrival, fresh from a march of five hundred miles, a march which would have deprived ordinary men of their fire of feeling, but which left Miller in the glowing enthusiasm of a young soldier, impatient of delay. Miller submitted the plan to his captain, whose courage was more tempered with prudence & who wished to decline engaging in such an attack, alleging, as reasons against it, the small number of his own men and his want of acquaintance with the ground, and works. But Miller, who was never checked in his military career by the appearance of danger, informed his captain that if he should decline engaging personally in the attack, he would solicit General Washington to appoint him (Miller) to the command. Thus urged, the captain allowed his laudable prudence to be overcome by the ardor of his gallant young lieutenant, and his own desire to effect the capture of the guard. The attempt was made—but, as the captain had predicted, without accomplishing the object. They were obliged to retreat—though not till after several British soldiers bit the dust, and several others were prisoners in the hands of the gallant Yorkers. Captain Doudel's health being very much impaired, he was obliged to resign not long afterwards, when Miller was appointed to the command of the company. From that time onward, he was distinguished as a most enterprising, intelligent, and valuable officer.

In 1776, his company with the regiment to which he belonged, commanded at first by Colonel Thompson, and afterwards by Colonel Hand, marched to New York. In 1777, on the 12th of November, he was promoted by congress to the office of Major in the same regiment. In the year following, (1778) he was appointed lieutenant colonel commandant in the second regiment of Pennsylvania. In this latter office he continued until he left the army.

Miller was engaged, and took an active and gallant part, in the several battles of Long Island, York Island, White Plains, Trenton, Princeton, Head of Elk, Brandywine, Germantown, Monmouth, and in a considerable number of other but less important conflicts. At the battle of Monmouth, he displayed a most signal bravery. Two horses were, during that conflict, successively shot from beneath this youthful hero and patriot; but that in nothing depressed the vigour of his soul, for mounting a third, he was in the thick of battle.

A companion in arms writing of Miller, in the year 1801, says, "He was engaged in most of the battles of note in the middle states. He was selected as one of the best partisan officers. It would take much time to enumerate the many engagements he was in—as well general engagements, as such as are incident to light corps. It may, with confidence, be stated, that he must have risked his person in fifty or sixty conflicts with the British foe. He served with the highest reputation as an heroic, intelligent, and useful officer." In a letter of Washington to Congress, dated "Trenton Falls, December 12, 1776," are these words:—"Captain Miller, of Colonel Hand's regiment, also informs me, that a body of the enemy were marching to Burlington yesterday morning. He had been sent over with a strong scouting party, and, at day break, fell in with their advanced guards consisting of about four hundred Hessian troops, who fired upon him before they were discovered, but without any loss, and obliged him to retreat with his party, and to take boat." General

Wilkinson, in his memoirs, states that Major Miller of Hand's riflemen, was ordered by General Washington to check the rapid movements of the enemy in pursuit of the American army, while retreating across the state of New Jersey. The order was so successfully executed, and the advance of a powerful enemy so embarrassed, that the American troops which afterwards gained the independence of their country, were preserved from an overthrow which would have proved the grave of our liberties. In a note to the memoirs, the author says, among other things, "Gen. Miller, late of Baltimore, was distinguished for his cool bravery wherever he served. He certainly possessed the entire confidence of General Washington." To multiply quotations would be useless: suffice it to say that Miller is mentioned by many of the American historians; and always with much applause.

When Miller first engaged in the war of the revolution, he had little or no other fortune than his dwelling-house. But before the close of the war he was reduced to such necessities to support his family, that he was compelled to sell the house over the heads of his wife and children. He sometimes spoke of this as a very hard case, and in terms so pathetic as to excite the most tender emotions. At other times he would say I have not yet done all in my power to serve my beloved county;—my wife and my children I trust will yet see better days. In his pleasant manner he was heard to say that, as to the house, the sale had at least saved him the payment of the taxes. Colonel Miller being thus, through his patriotism, humiliatingly reduced in pecuniary circumstances, was obliged in the spring of 1779 to resign his commission in the army and to return to York. Here he continued to reside for some years, enjoying the love and affection of all his fellow citizens. In October 1780, he was elected high sheriff of the county of York, and as such he continued until the expiration of his term of office in November 1783. At the several elections in October of the years 1783, 1784, and 1785, he was elected a member of the legislature of Pennsylvania. In May 1786 he was commissioned as Prothonotary of York county, and in August of the same year he was appointed a justice of the peace, and of the court of Common

Pleas. In the year 1790 he was a member of the convention which framed the present constitution of the commonwealth of Pennsylvania. He continued in the office of Prothonotary until July 1794. In this year (1794) great dangers were apprehended from the encroachments of the English on our western territories. Wayne was, at that time, carrying our arms against the Indians into the western wilderness. Agreeably to the requisition of the president of the United States, contained in a letter to the secretary of war dated 19th of May 1794, Pennsylvania was required to furnish her quota of brigades towards forming a detachment of 10,768, militia, officers included. At this time Miller was general in the first brigade, composed of the counties of York and Lancaster, and belonging to the second division of Pennsylvania Militia commanded by Major General Hand. This division, with several others, was required to be in readiness to march at a moment's warning.

In the same year was the *western expedition*, an expedition occasioned by an insurrection in the four western counties to resist the laws of the Union. At this time General Miller was appointed, and went out as quarter master General. In the same year he was appointed, by General Washington, supervisor of the revenue for the district of Pennsylvania. In this office he acted with such ability, punctuality and integrity, that no one ever laid the least failure to his charge. But in 1801, Mr. Jefferson having been elected President, General Miller was removed from the office of supervisor, and was succeeded by Peter Muhlenburg.

Upon this event he left York on the 18th of November 1801, and removed to Baltimore, where he resided for some years as an honest and respectable merchant. At the commencement of the war of 1812, his soul was kindled to the former fires of youthful feeling. Relinquishing his mercantile pursuits he accepted the appointment of Brigadier General of the militia of the United States stationed at Baltimore, and charged with the defence of Fort M'Henry and its dependencies. Upon the enemy's leaving the Chesapeake bay, the troops were discharged, and General Miller again retired to private life.

In the spring of 1813, General Miller left Baltimore, and returned to his native state, Pennsylvania. He now resided on a farm at the mouth of the Juniatti [Juniata] river, in Cumberland county, devoting himself with Roman virtue, to agricultural pursuits. But his country soon called him from his retirement. The enemy having again made their appearance before Baltimore, he marched out with the Pennsylvania troops in the capacity of quarter master general. He again after a short time, returned to Pennsylvania, to reside on his farm at the mouth of the Juniata. At that place, like a Cincinnatus, away from the tumult of war, he continued to reside until the spring of 1821. At that time, being appointed prothonotary of Perry county, by Governor Hiester, he removed to Landisburg, the seat of Justice for that county. He continued to live at Landisburg, until he was removed from office, by Governor Shulze, in March 1824. On the 29th of the same month, the legislature of Pennsylvania began to make, though at a late period, some compensation for his important revolutionary services. They required the state treasurer to pay him 240 dollars immediately; and an annuity of the same sum during the remainder of his life. But General Miller lived not long enough to enjoy this righteous provision. He removed with his family to Carlisle; but he had hardly fixed his abode there, and caught the kind looks of his relatives and friends, when he was called by the messenger of peace to a distant and far brighter region where the music of war is unheard, and the storms of contention are at rest. He was seized with an inflammation of the bowels and died suddenly, in the bosom of his family, on Monday the 5th of April, 1824. On Tuesday afternoon, the mortal part of the hero and the patriot was consigned, with military honours to the small and narrow house.

In private life General Miller was friendly, social, and benevolent. He was generous even to a fault.

In public life, he had, what lord Clarendon says of Hampden, a head to contrive, a heart to persuade, and a hand to execute.

COL. MICHAEL SCHMEISER.

Col. Michael Schmeiser of York county was one of that virtuous band who in the gloomy period of 1776, when superior worth alone gave claim to distinction, were appointed to command. At the unfortunate capture of fort Washington, he was taken prisoner, & during the distressing captivity which succeeded that event, the zeal & animation with which he advocated his country's cause, inspired all his fellow prisoners with the hope that their labours were not in vain: while making use of the privilege attached to his rank as a captain, his unremitting exertions to alleviate their sufferings reflected honourably on his goodness and humanity.

During the Revolution as well as afterwards, Col. Schmeiser was repeatedly elected a member of the legislature of this state, where his intelligence and his warm attachment to our political institutions enabled him to act with honour to himself and his constituents. Possessing an enlightened, honest and independent mind, he was liberal in his views, manly in his conduct, and superior to selfish considerations. The scenes of domestic life under his influence were peaceable and happy;—and in the relative duties of friendship and society, he was warm, disinterested and benevolent.

Through his habits of temperance and moderation, the weight of nearly 70 years had but partially affected his robust constitution. He lived to exult in the 34th anniversary of his country's independence. He died on 7th July, 1810, deservedly lamented by a long train of relatives, friends and fellow citizens.

REV. SAMUEL BACON.

Samuel Bacon was born at Sturbridge, Massachusetts, on the 22d of July, 1782. Having prepared himself in an underschool, he became a student in the university of Cambridge, at which institution he was afterwards graduated. On leaving the college he went forth "in quest of fortune and a name." From New-England he went to Lancaster, Pa., and there he was for some time principal of the "Franklin College."

His leisure hours were now spent in the study of the law, and conducting the "Hive," then a periodical paper of some literary merit. From Lancaster to came to York; and this town he afterwards considered as his home. Here he was at first a classical teacher in the "York County Academy," and in this task of instruction he acquired the good will of all his pupils, and became the admiration of all that knew him. Becoming weary of the pursuit, which is at least irksome and tedious, he applied for a commission in the service of his country, and was appointed a lieutenant of marines. He was soon afterwards appointed a quarter master, with the rank of captain. In the year 1814, he was married at York to Anne Mary Bernitz, daughter of Jacob Bernitz, Esq. She died in the succeeding year, leaving a son who still lives.

Whilst yet an officer of marines, he resumed the study of the law with a distinguished advocate in the city of Washington, and was admitted to the bar in that metropolis. At the battle of Bladensburg he was attached to commodore Barney's corps, and was the officer who conducted the retreat. In the year 1815 or '16, he resigned his commission, and returning to York he commenced the practice of the law, and received the appointment of deputy attorney general for the county. About this time he began to be seriously attentive to things relating to his eternal welfare; and he evinced his sincerity by the best practical proofs. He labored continually for the establishing of Sunday schools; and owing to his extraordinary exertions there were at one time, in twenty-six schools of this county, about 2000 scholars. He commenced a course of theological reading, whilst yet in the practice of law. Upon relinquishing his profession he was ordained a deacon in the Episcopal church by Bishop White. He then travelled as an agent of the Missionary and Bible society through this and the neighboring states, soliciting donations, establishing Sunday Schools, and endeavoring to do good in the great office to which he had been called. At length he was appointed by the heads of government the agent of the United States to accompany the first adventurers of the Colonization Society to their intended settlement on the African coast. There, at an English settlement called Cape Shilling, he died of a fever incident to that country, on the 3d of May 1820, aged 38 years.

Bacon perished in a land of savages, far removed from all that could smooth his passage to the tomb, or uphold him in the hour of death. But his was the hope of a christian, & he leaned on the arm of his God. No storied urn, nor proud mausoleum mark the spot of his repose: but the poor savage as he passes over the place where his dust sleeps, will drop a tear to the memory of the friend of man.

The following remarks appeared in the Baltimore *American* shortly after Mr. Bacon's decease:

"The talents of Mr. Bacon had opened a bright scene before him;—His professional career, though short, afforded sufficient evidence of his abilities to promise honour and wealth in its pursuit. With a future so radiant, ordinary human nature would have sought no other path;—but the restlessness of his virtue held out a higher aim for a noble ambition. Greater objects opened to his view than any which the world could present;—a more serene sky shone, and a sweeter and calmer light beamed on his heart. Forsaking the bar for the pulpit, he was an able and sincere ambassador of his divine master. The same holy sentiments which gave his able mind and pious heart to the service of his God, brought from him a tear of sympathy for the wrongs and sufferings of the injured African. He embarked in the cause of justice and of feeling, & fell a noble martyr to his God and his country. What he might have been, if the blast of death had not so untimely passed over him, the blessings of posterity would have told. The same man who now reposes in death on a desert shore, might have become the Moses of his own flock—the regeneration of many an African soul. America owes a tribute to his loss, and friendship will cherish an enthusiastic feeling for his pious and patriotic martyrdom."

MICHAEL EURICH.

Michael Eurich, (father of Michael Eurich, director of the Poor House, in 1821-2,) enlisted in 1777 as a soldier in Col. Hartley's Regiment for the term of 3 years, or until the end of the revolutionary war. While he was on command at Wyoming in the winter of 1780, his feet through the inclemency of the weather were nearly frozen off, in consequence of which he was unable to continue in the service of his country. As Mr. Eurich became by this misfortune unable to provide for himself and his family, and as he had never received any donation land, the Legislature of Pennsylvania on the 29th of March 1804, granted to his heirs the donation land to which he would have been entitled, had he served to the end of the revolutionary war.

In remembrance and as a reward for his services, the Legislature of Pennsylvania on the 29th of March 1824, granted to his surviving wife, the widow Catharine Eurich, the sum of 40 dollars immediately, and an annuity of 40 dollars for life.

GEN. JAMES EWING.

James Ewing was born in about the year 1736, in Manor township, Lancaster county, Pennsylvania, of Irish parents. We have been unable to collect much information respecting the early life of Gen. Ewing—little more indeed, than that he received a liberal education and removed, when quite a youth, to Hellam township, York county, where he resided at the time of his death. He was engaged, when only about nineteen years, in the Indian, or as it is commonly called, the French war—and was, we believe, a lieutenant in Braddock's army, and present at the fatal engagement known as "Braddock's Defeat."

In 1771, Ewing was elected to represent York county in the General assembly of Pennsylvania, and was re-elected in 1772 and the three succeeding years.

At the commencement of the revolution, being then about forty years of age, he was appointed Brigadier General in the service of the United States, and was attached to what was called the "Flying Camp." During the war of the revolution, General Ewing was present at the battle of Trenton, and several other important engagements—and of his conduct as a patriot and soldier, we can speak in no higher terms than to say that it was such as to receive the warm approbation of the commander in chief.

He next appeared in the service of the public as Vice President of Pennsylvania, under the constitution of 1779, during the time that John Dickinson was President of the Supreme Executive Council of the commonwealth.

In 1795, he was elected to the Senate of this state, in which office he was continued, by annual re-election, until the year 1799.

In the year 1800, Gen. Ewing retired from public life to his country seat in Hellam township, in this county.—Here, in the enjoyment of a quiet he had not known during many years he passed the evening of his days—here, surrounded by friends who esteemed & loved him for his private virtues, he could look back with pleasure and pride upon the many proofs he had received of the confidence of his fellow citizens—a confidence which he felt was authorized by the faithfulness with which he had discharged every duty, as a man, a citizen, a soldier and a legislator, which, in a long course of active public labor, had devolved upon him.

Gen. Ewing died in March, 1806, aged about 70 years. Of him it was said, at the time of his death, what can be said of very few who die after an active life of three score and ten years: "He died without an enemy."

REV. JACOB GOERING.

The Rev. Jacob Goering, the second son of Jacob and Margaret Goering, (emigrants from Germany,) was born in Chanceford township, in this county, on the 17th of January, 1755. His father, who was a farmer, was not particularly attentive to the education of his son—yet he gave him all the advantage that could be derived from the common schools in the neighborhood. Young Goering was soon distinguished for his assiduity in the pursuit of knowledge—his days and a great part of his nights were spent in reading. His steps, in every thing he undertook, were those of a giant, and quickly led him far in advance of all his companions who had equal opportunities of advancement. Such was his economy of time, and passion for study, that scarcely a moment of his youth was spent in idleness: for in the intermissions of labor, when abroad in the field, he drew his book from his pocket, and improved the short, but by him dearly prized interval. His father had but little hope of making a farmer of his son: for the studiousness of his habits but ill accorded with that constancy of attentive labor which good husbandry always demands. Young Georing, who was a christian, was soon designed for the ministry, and with that view pursued his studies. At an early age he was a teacher of an English school in the neighborhood of his father's house; by which means he had a better opportunity of prosecuting the studies he so much delighted in.

When about eighteen years old, young Georing removed to Lancaster to pursue his studies under the direction of the Rev. Mr. Helmuth. While with Mr. Helmuth, he acquired a knowledge of the Latin, Greek and Hebrew languages. He remained in Lancaster two years, at the end of which time his theological studies were completed.

From Lancaster he went to Carlisle, and preached to the Lutheran congregations in that town and vicinity. After a few years residence in Cumberland county, he removed to Dover township, in this county, and preached to the Lutheran congregations in that neighborhood, still continuing his stated services at Carlisle. While residing in Dover township he was married* to Elizabeth, daughter of the Rev. Nicholas Kurtz, who was at that time pastor of the German Lutheran congregation in York.

About the year 1786, Mr. Goering was invited to take charge of the Lutheran congregation in York, and accepted the invitation. After preaching five or six years here, he received and accepted an invitation to preach to the congregation in Hagerstown, Maryland. During his absence from York of twelve or fifteen months, there was no preacher to the Lutheran congregation here; and such was the love entertained by the members for their former pastor, that they

* Goering had previously been married; but his first wife died young and childless.

earnestly entreated him to return, and persisted so warmly in their entreaties that he was at length induced again to take charge of the congregation.

Mr. Goering continued to minister to the congregation in York until his decease. He died at his residence in this place on the 27th of November, 1807, leaving to survive him a wife and eight children, with a numerous congregation who mourned for him in tears.

Mr. Goering wrote much, though he published but little. His manuscripts contained much that marked his original and energetic mind. These valuable papers, with all the letters he had received, he committed to the flames during his last illness. The author of the Æneiad commanded the last six books of his poem to be committed to the flames; but happily the order was not executed—and well, too, would it have been if the manuscripts of Mr. Goering had not shared that fate to which many men of genius in their last hours wish to see most of their works consigned. Viewing the world as passing away, and themselves about to take an eternal farewell of all the things of earth, they wish every thing they have done to pass with them into oblivion. The manuscripts of Mr. Goering did not contain disquisitions on theological subjects only—they embraced many inquiries into the oriental languages, with translations from the most beautiful works of Arabic poets.

As a man of profound thought and deep investigation, as an elegant scholar and eloquent public speaker, as a strict observer of every social and domestic duty, as a warm-hearted and charitable christian, *Jacob Goering* stood pre-eminent; and many generations may pass away before the world will look upon his equal.

GEN. JOHN CLARK.

Gen. Clark was born about the year 1751, in Lancaster county, Pa. When about twenty-four years old he entered the service of his country, and was distinguished during the war of the revolution by his zeal in the cause of liberty.

Early in life, General Clark held a number of civil and

military offices, the duties of all of which he faithfully discharged. Among other trusts committed to him during the revolution was his appointment by Congress, on the 6th of February, 1778, as one of the auditors for the army under General Washington.

We have now in our possession a number of original copies of letters to General Clark, from General Washington, General Greene, and other distinguished officers of the revolution; and from them we learn that Clark was a familiar correspondent of the father of our country and of many of his illustrious contemporaries.

Gen. Clark had just commenced the practice of law* when the troublesome times of the revolution came on—and receiving, shortly afterward the appointment of aid-de-camp to Gen. Greene, he abandoned his practice and devoted his whole services to his country.

Some years after the termination of the revolutionary struggle, Gen. Clark resumed the practice of law, and continued in it until the time of his death, which was in the year 1819. On the 27th of December, in that year, he attended court, and pursued his business as usual—in the evening of that day he went to bed about half past eight o'clock, in his usual health—and at nine o'clock on the same evening his race on earth was run.

At the time of his death, Gen. Clark was about 68 years of age.

George Clark, now living in York, is a son of the General. There are also several of his daughters yet residing here.

The following is a copy of a letter from Gen. Washington to Congress. We insert it as a better evidence of Gen. Clark's worth than any thing we could say in eulogy of his character.

"Head Quarters, Valley Forge, Jan. 2, 1778.

"I take the liberty of introducing Gen. John Clark, the bearer of this, to your notice. He entered the service at the commencement of the war, and has for some time past acted as aid-de-camp to Major General Greene. He is active, sen-

* He had studied under Samuel Johnson, Esq., of York.

sible and enterprising, and has rendered me very great service since the army has been in Pennsylvania, by procuring me constant and certain intelligence of the motions and intentions of the enemy. It is somewhat uncertain whether the state of his health will admit of his remaining in the military line: if it should, I shall perhaps have occasion to recommend him in a more particular manner to the favor of Congress at a future time. At present, I can assure you, that if you should, while he remains in York, have any occasion for his services, you will find him not only willing, but very capable of executing any of your commands.

Respectfully,

GEO. WASHINGTON."

GENERAL JACOB DRITT.

Gen. Jacob Dritt, of York county, was a military officer, in our revolutionary struggle, being a captain in Colonel Swope's battalion of the Pennsylvania Flying Camp. He was made prisoner at the taking of Fort Washington, and underwent, as a consequence of that event, a long and distressing captivity. When the lines of our army were attacked by the enemy, previously to the capture of the Fort, Captain Dritt with a party of men chiefly of his own company was ordered in advance to oppose the landing of the British who came in boats across Haerlem creek, below King's bridge. He defended his position with great bravery, until having lost a number of his men, and being nearly surrounded with the Hessian Riflemen on one side, and the British troops on the other, he retreated into the fort with difficulty and was there captured.

On the 19th of December 1817, Gen. Dritt, and a young man named Griffith, who had lived with the General, started at about 10 o'clock from the York shore, (in the neighborhood of Dritt's plantation) with the intention of reaching Charleston on the opposite shore where his son Col. John Dritt resided. But the Susquehanna had increased in the multitude of its waters, ice floated in it, and the cold was severe and the winds high. They were both carried away by the torrent, and drowned. The body of Gen. Dritt was found some time afterward about 30 miles down the river.

The honourable spirit and manly feelings which warmed the arm of the revolutionary patriot, Gen. Dritt, accompanied him through life. Of fifteen officers who belonged to Col. Swope's battalion of York county, and who were taken prisoners at the battle of Fort Washington, Gen. Dritt was the last survivor but one—and that one is now sleeping the sleep which knows no waking.

APPENDIX

Edited by

A. MONROE AURAND, JR.

EARLY TRAVELLERS' IMPRESSIONS OF YORK.

THE foregoing historical and biographical accounts of York county have been most ably presented. This, too, despite the fact that it appears to be the first book of its kind in the history of books in this State. The arrangement of its contents, while in "loose order," has, nevertheless, been the example which many others have followed during the past hundred years.

It pretends to be, and undoubtedly is, wholly a product of York county editing and publishing. The various biographical sketches of deceased York countians, and the various historical features, are magnanimous. It is safe to presume that Mr. Glossbrenner was entirely willing to assume responsibility for the character and worth of Mr. Carter's "notes," and where Mr. G. himself harbored a question of doubt, he must have made local inquiry for facts and incidents. This, of course, provided for points of view by men wholly resident in York county—not a disqualifying feature, but one to be improved on, perhaps, by those from outside the county, who travelled through York several decades before the *History of York County* was first contemplated and published.

It appears reasonable to say that a consensus of opinions by responsible persons would be as interesting and worth-while as the opinion of one or two persons. Therefore, let us examine some points of view of a few fairly early travellers who recorded some interesting and even important reminiscences, which they have left to us through their several writings.

Most of those whose accounts we subjoin, are men of unusual intellect, quick to observe, and a capacity for statistics, state and condition of affairs, etc.

ALEXANDER GRAYDON.

The first whom we shall call your attention to, is none other than Alexander Graydon, Esq., well known lawyer in his day, who spent the summer in York, in 1773. Graydon, in his *Memoirs of His Own Time,* edited by John Stockton Littell, Philadelphia (1846), the original title of which was *Memoirs of a Life, Chiefly Passed in Pennsylvania, Within the Last Sixty Years,* Harrisburg (1811). The account as he presents it, gives a fairly lengthy description of his sojourn at York, the relevant parts of which we herewith recount.

Mr. Graydon, a very accurate observer, was of a refractory sort, and in Chapter IV he makes bold to say

My irregular course of life had much impaired my health, for the re-establishment of which, and to enable me to pursue my studies without interruption from my free-living companions, my uncle advised my spending the approaching summer in Yorktown. Mr. Samuel Johnson, the Prothonotary of that county, was his particular friend, a respectable man who had been in the practice of the law, and had a very good library. Having been apprised of the project, he kindly offered me the use of his books, as well as his countenance and assistance in my reading. Accordingly, I submitted to become an exile from Philadelphia, with nearly the same objects and feelings of Propertius, when he left Rome for Athens. * * * Not that York was an Athens; but I was sent thither for improvement, and there were various attractions in the city from which it was, no doubt, prudent to withdraw me. It was in the spring of 1773, that I was transferred to this pleasant and flourishing village, situated about twelve miles beyond the Susquehanna. It was this circumstance which rendered it an eligible retreat for Congress in the year 1778, when General Howe was in possession of the Capitol and eastern parts of Pennsylvania. I was well received by Mr. Johnson, but with that formal, theoretical kind of politeness, which distinguishes the manners of those who constitute the "better sort," in small secluded towns: and if, in these days, the Prothonotary of a county of German population, was not confessedly the most considerable personage in it, he must have been egregiously wanting to himself. This could with no propriety be imputed to my patron. Although apparently a mild and modest man, he evidently knew his consequence, and never lost sight of it, though to say the truth, I received full as much of his attention as either I desired or had a right to expect: He repeated the tender of his books and services, complimented me with a dinner, suggested that business and pleasure could not be well prosecuted together, and consigned me to my meditations.

I established myself at a boarding-house, at whose table I found a practising attorney, a student of law, another of physic, and a young Episcopal clergyman, who had lately arrived from Dublin. The first was a striking instance of what mere determination and perseverance will do, even in a learned profession. He was an Irishman, a man of middle age—the extent of whose attainments was certainly nothing more, than in a coarse, vulgar hand, to draw a declaration; and in equally vulgar arithmetic, to sum up the interest due upon a bond. His figure was as awkward as can well be imagined, and his elocution exactly corresponded with it. From the humble post of under-sheriff, he had lately emerged to his present station at the bar, and was already in good practice. By industry and economy, his acquisitions soon exceeded his expenses; and he died not long since, in pretty affluent circumstances. Justice, however, requires it should be added, that his want of brilliant qualities, was compensated by an adequate portion of common sense, by unblemished integrity, and liberality in his dealings with the poor. Nor should it be forgotten, that after having taken part with his adopted country in the struggle for her rights, he did not, like too many of his countrymen, by a blind obedience to vindictive passions, much more than efface the merit of his services.—The law-student was from Wilmington; an easy, good-natured young man, whose talents appeared to be misplaced in their present direction. They were, probably, better adapted to the army, into which he entered on the breaking out of the war, and was killed at the battle of Brandywine, holding the rank of Major in the Pennsylvania line.—The student of physic, though with some rusticity to rub off, was yet a pretty good scholar; nor was he deficient in natural endowments. To these, he added a manly and honourable way of thinking, which made him respectable in the army, (which he had also afterwards joined,) as well as in the path of civil life, in which he possesses an honourable station in the western country.

The clergyman was only an occasional lodger, his pastoral duties often calling him to Maryland and elsewhere, which produced absences of several weeks at a time. He had probably the propensities of that species of gownman, which I have heard Whitfield call a "downy doctor;" as, whatever might have been his deportment on solemn occasions, in his intercourse with me, he did not seem to be one who considered the *enjoyment of the present* sublunary scene, by any means unworthy of regard. One day, as I was strumming a tune from the Beggar's opera, upon a fiddle I had purchased, with a view of becoming a performer upon it, he entered my apartment. "What," says he, "you play upon the violin, and are at the airs of the Beggar's opera!" He immediately began to hum the tune I had before me, from which, turning over the leaves of the note-book, he passed on to others, which he sung as he went along, and evinced an acquaintance with the piece, much too intimate to have been acquired, by any thing short of an assiduous attendance on the theatre. After amusing himself and me for some time with his theatrical recollections, "I am," said he, "to give you a sermon next Sunday, and here it is," pulling from his pocket a manuscript. Perusing the title page, he read, it was preached at such a time in such a place, and at another time in such a place, giving me to understand from the dates, that it was not of his own composition, and that he made no difficulty of appropriating the productions of others. In a word, Mr. L——— seemed in all respects to be what was then called in Pennsylvania a Maryland Parson; that is, one who could accommodate himself to his company, and pass, from grave to gay, from lively to severe," as occasion might require. Among his other accomplishments, he was a competent jockey; at least I have a right to infer so, from the results of an exchange of horses between us, a short time before my return to the city: I do not, however, insinuate that he took me in, but merely that he had the best of the bargain.

Besides my fellow boarders there were several young men in the town, whose company served to relieve the dreariness of my solitude; for such it was, compared with the scene from which I had removed. These, for the most part are yet living, generally known and respected. There was also in the place an oddity, who, though not to be classed with its young men, I sometimes fell in with. This was Mr. James Smith, [signer of the Declaration of Independence], the lawyer, then in considerable practice. He was probably between forty and fifty years of age, fond of his bottle and young company, and possessed of an original species of drollery. This, as may perhaps be said of all persons in this way, consisted more in the manner than the matter; for which reason, it is scarcely possible to convey a just notion of it to the reader. In him it much depended on an uncouthness of gesture, a certain ludicrous cast of countenance, and a drawling mode of utterance, which taken in conjunction with his eccentric ideas, produced an effect irresistibly comical;

though on an analysis it would be difficult to decide, whether the man or the saying most constituted the jest. The most trivial incident from his mouth was stamped with his originality, and in relating one evening how he had been disturbed in his office by a cow, he gave inconceivable zest to his narration, by his manner of telling how she thrust her nose into the door, and "there roared like a Numidian lion." Like the picture of Garrick between tragedy and comedy, his phiz exhibited a struggle between tragedy and farce, in which the latter seemed on the eve of predominating. With a sufficiency of various reading to furnish him with materials for ridiculous allusions and incongruous combinations, he was never so successful as when he could find a learned man to play upon: and of all men, Judge Stedman, when mellow, was best calculated for his butt. The judge was a Scotchman, a man of reading and erudition, though extremely magisterial and dogmatical in his cups. This it was which gave point to the humour of Smith, who, as if desirous of coming in for his share of the glory, while Stedman was in full display of his historical knowledge, never failed to set him raving by some monstrous anachronism, such for instance, as "don't you remember, Mr. Stedman, that terrible bloody battle which Alexander the Great fought with the Russians near the Straits of Babelmandel?" "What, sir!" said Stedman, repeating with the most ineffable contempt, "which Alexander the Great fought with the Russians! Where, mon, did you get your chronology?" "I think you will find it recorded, Mr. Stedman, in Thucidydes or Herodotus." On another occasion, being asked for his authority for some enormous assertion, in which both space and time were fairly annihilated, with unshaken gravity he replied, "I am pretty sure I have seen an account of it, Mr. Stedman, in a High Dutch almanac printed at 'Aleepo,'" his drawling way of pronouncing Aleppo. While every one at table was holding his sides at the expense of the judge, he, on his part, had no doubt that Smith was the object of laughter, as he was of his own unutterable disdain. Thus every thing was as it should be, all parties were pleased; the laughers were highly tickled, the self-complacency of the real dupe was flattered, and the sarcastic vein of the pretended one gratified; and this, without the smallest suspicion on the part of Stedman, who, residing in Philadelphia, was ignorant of Smith's character, and destitute of penetration to develope it.

York, I must say, was somewhat obnoxious to the general charge of unsociableness, under which Pennsylvania has always laboured: or if I wrong her, I was not the kind of guest that was calculated to profit of her hospitality. Perhaps I approached her under unfavorable auspices, those of a young man debauched by evil communications; or perhaps there was a want of congeniality between her manners and mine. Be it as it may, there was but a single house in which I found that sort of reception which invited me to repeat my visit; and this was the house of a Jew. In this, I could conceive myself at home, being always received with ease, with cheerfulness and cordiality. Those who have known York, at the period I am speaking of, cannot fail to recollect the sprightly and engaging Mrs. E., the life of all the gaiety that could be mustered in the village: always in spirits, full of frolic and glee, and possessing the talent of singing agreeably, she was an indispensable ingredient in the little parties of pleasure which sometimes took place, and usually consisted in excursions to the Susquehanna, where the company dined, and, when successful in angling, upon fish of their own catching. It was upon one of these occasions, the summer before I saw her, that she had attracted the notice of Mr. John Dickinson, the celebrated author of the "Farmer's Letters. He had been lavish in her praise in the company of a lady of my acquaintance, who told me of it, and thence inferred, how much I should be pleased with her when I got to York. I paid little attention to the information, having no conception that I should take any interest in the company of a married woman, considerably older than myself and the mother of several children. The sequel proved how much I was mistaken, and how essential to my satisfaction was female society; the access to a house in which I could domesticate myself, and receive attentions, not the less grateful from apparently being blended with somewhat maternal. The master of the house, though much less brilliant than the mistress, was always good-humored and kind, and as they kept a small store, I repaid as well as I could the hospitality of a frequent dish of tea, by purchasing there what articles I wanted.

After whiling away about six months, the allotted time of my exile, reading a little law in the morning, and either fowling, riding or strolling along the banks of the Codorus, a beautiful stream which passes through the town, in the afternoon, I at length set out on my return to Philadelphia. For the sake of company and yet more for the satisfaction of seeing the country, I took a circuitous route, crossing the Susquehanna at M'Call's ferry, at the "Narrows." This place is rude and romantic to a great degree. The water is extremely deep, above —— fathoms [from the account of Theodore Burr, who threw an immense arch of 360 feet, 4 inches, over the river at this place, in the winter of 1814-15, the depth of the water is 150 feet. This noble bridge was, in part, carried away by the flood of March, 1846—the greatest known within fifty years.—J. S. Littell], as it is stated in Scull's map, and the current much obstructed by rocks, which rise above the surface in huge and shapeless craggs. Leaving the river, we crossed the Octararo, which discharges itself into it; and thence, shaping our course through a pleasant country to Newark and Wilmington, we reached Philadelphia after a journey of three or four days, in the latter part of October.

In cannot take my final leave of York before mentioning, that I visited it again when Congress held their sessions there, in the year 1778. Mr. Johnson, who had been a widower, was then married to a lady from Maryland. The laws having been silenced by arms, he was no longer Prothonotary; and what was still more unfortunate for him, he had no chance of ever becoming so again, being much disaffected to the American cause. I found him extremely soured by the state of affairs: He was at no pains to conceal his disgust at it, and shook his head in fearful anticipation of future calamities. Five years had produced a considerable change in respect to the inhabitants of the town. The young men I had been acquainted with had been generally in the army, and were consequently dispersed. The E—'s were not there; or at least, I did not see them; and if my memory does not mislead me, the family had removed to Baltimore.

Although I had not made myself a lawyer, I returned to the city somewhat improved in health, as well as in my habits of living. My disposition, however, was unaltered. * *

JONATHAN WILD.

Now that the Revolution had subsided, and men were travelling again in various and sundry sections of the country east and south of the Kittatinny or Blue Mountains, we shall note what Jonathan Wild, the Irish traveller, had to say of York in 1791. Mr. Wild, whose book on travels seems to be quite scarce, gives us a "foreigner's" views of the county and its seat of government. He says that

In coming to this place [York] from Lancaster I crossed the Susquehanna River, which runs nearly midway between the two towns, at the small village of Columbia, as better boats are kept here than at either of the ferries higher up or lower down the river. The Susquehanna is here somewhat more than a quarter of a mile wide and for a considerable distance, both above and below the ferry, it abounds with islands and large rocks, over which last the water runs with prodigious velocity: the roaring noise that it makes is heard a great way off. The banks rise very boldly on each side, and are thickly wooded; the islands also are covered with small trees, which, interspersed with the rocks, produce a very fine effect. The scenery in every point of view is wild and romantic. In crossing the river it is necessary to row up against the stream under the shore, and then to strike over to the opposite side, under the shelter of some of the largest islands. As these rapids continue for many miles, they totally impede navigation, excepting when there are floods in the river, at which time large rafts may be conducted down the stream, carrying several hundred barrels of flour. It is said that the river could be rendered navigable in this neighbourhood, but the expense of such an undertaking would be enormous, and there is little likelihood indeed that it will ever be attempted, as the Pennsylvanians are already engaged in cutting a canal below Harrisburg, which will connect the navigable part of the river with the Schuylkill to the Delaware, by means of which a vent will be opened for the produce of the country bordering upon the Susquehanna, at Philadelphia. These canals would have been finished by this time if the subscribers had all paid their respective shares, but at present they are almost at a stand for want of money.

The quantity of wild fowl that is seen on every part of the Susquehanna is immense. Throughout America the wild fowl is excellent and plentiful; but there is one duck in particular found in this river, and also on Patowmac and James rivers, which surpasses all others: it is called the white or canvass-back duck, from the feathers between the wings being somewhat of the color of canvas. This duck is held in such estimation in America, that it is sent frequently as a present for hundreds of miles—indeed it would be a dainty morsel for the greatest epicure of any country.

York contains about five hundred houses and six churches, and is much another town as Lancaster. It is inhabited by Germans, by whom the same manufactures are carried on as at Lancaster.

The courts of common pleas, and those of general quarter sessions, were holding when I reached this place; I found it difficult therefore, at first, to procure accommodation, but at last I got admission in a house principally taken up by lawyers. To behold the strange assemblage of persons that was brought together this morning in the one poor apartment which was allotted to all the lodgers was really a subject of diversion. Here one lawyer had his clients in one corner of the room; there another had his: a third was shaving: a fourth powdering his own hair; a fifth noting his brief; and the table standing in the middle of the room, between a clamorous set of old men on one side, and three or four women in tears on the other, I and the rest of the company, who were not lawyers, were left to eat our breakfast.

On entering into the courts a stranger is apt to smile at the grotesque appearance of the judges who preside in them, and at their manners on the bench, but this smile must be suppressed when it is recollected, that there is no country, perhaps, in the world, where justice is more impartially administered, or more easily obtained by those who have been injured. The judges in the country parts of Pennsylvania are no more than plain farmers, who from their infancy have been accustomed to little else than following the plough. The laws expressly declare that there must be, at least, three judges resident in every county; now as the salary allowed is but a mere trifle, no lawyer would accept the office, which of course must be filled from amongst the inhabitants (this is also the case in Philadelphia, where we find practising physicians and surgeons sitting on the bench as judges in a court of justice), who are all in a happy state of mediocrity, and on a perfect equality with each other. The district judge, however, who presides in the district or circuit, had a larger salary, and is a man of a different cast. The district or circuit consists of at least three, but not more than six counties. The county judges, which I have mentioned, are "judges of the court of common pleas, and by virtue of their offices also justices of oyer and terminer, and general gaol delivery, for the trial of capital and other offenders therein." Any two judges compose the court of quarter sessions. Under certain regulations, established by law, the accused party has the power of removing the proceedings into the supreme court, which has jurisdiction over every part of the state. This short account of the courts relates only to Pennsylvania: every state in the union has a separate code of laws for itself, and a distinct judicature.

THEOPHILE CAZENOVE.

The "Journal" of Theophile Cazenove, French traveller, who made searching inquiries in a journey through New Jersey and Pennsylvania in 1794, and its subsequent translation by Prof. Raynor Wickersham Kelsey, Ph. D., of Haverford College, with the assistance of more than a score of scholars in Europe and America, has brought this more or less obscure manuscript to a full and true account of the early settlements in Pennsylvania, including some interesting phases of York county.

The original manuscript, in French, was purchased by the Library of Congress, in 1900, from a Paris dealer in books. In setting about to translate the *Journal*, and to "run down" many references, Prof. Kelsey has searched public and private libraries, and letters in Europe and America, and the results of his labors are outstanding evidence of great ability and more than ordinary patience.

M. Cazenove was of French Huguenot extraction; born in Amsterdam, October 13, 1740. He affiliated with Dutch bankers and financiers, and they, recognizing the great opportunities in the New World, and the marked ability of Cazenove, sent him to America to take an active part in its early development. While in this country he became the General Agent of the Holland Land Company, with extensive holdings and dealings in New York and Pennsylvania. It was during the period of his interest and speculation in lands that Cazenove made his journey through New Jersey and Pennsylvania.

The title of the above account is known as the *Cazenove Journal; 1794*. It was first published by the Pennsylvania History Press, in 1922, but the copyright, plates, and unsold copies were purchased by The Aurand Press, Harrrisburg, in 1928.

Cazenove's account of his travels is a notable contribution to the early history of interior Pennsylvania. On November 8, 1794, we find him in Chambersburg, the extreme western fringe of his trip through the State with a man-servant. Travelling on a saddle-horse, he had plenty of opportunity for observations, and at various stop-overs, could be well-pleased, or much annoyed, as the case might be, by the service and accommodations accorded travellers.

Leaving Chambersburg, travelling toward Philadelphia, on the above date, he next arrives

At Thompson's Tavern, 12½ miles [from Chambersburg] —bad lodging, on the top of the mountain; the road from Chambersburg here is very bad. It goes over the mountain range called here "South Ridge." It is hard work for the horses.

Here I met the York County surveyor, who was surveying the land of these high mountains for some speculators who lately located these lands at the land office for 6 pence per acre, being in the old purchase. It is to deceive buyers with the big words, "mill seats, timber," etc. There is hardly here and there a tillable piece of ground, but how to reach them! All the less bad of this very bad mountainous land had been taken a long time ago.

Left Thompson, and by 5 more miles of bad road, through the mountain, and the rest fair, [arrived] at

Russel's Tavern, [probably the tavern of Joshua Russell, and situate probably in the vicinity of the Carrie farm house, 3½ miles north of Gettysburg; or near the present Mummasburg.—Ed.] 9 miles, fair lodging for a tavern isolated on the highway, where there is no better one for 30 or 40 miles. This Russel's Tavern is in York [now Adams] County, in the plain, 3 or 4 miles from the South Mountains.

In this district the soil is of different kinds; the price in general of the "middling good land," it is "Sklit land," that is to say, clay and stones, which is not worth as much as the "lime stone land:" farms are generally from 200 to 300 acres: 140 plough land, 20 meadow, 140 woods, house and barn,—bring from £6 to £10 [per acre]. Many farm hands to hire for 2-6 in the summer, and 2 s. in the winter, ½ [dollar] at "harvest time." For £20, a hired man a—year.

The land yields 12 to 15 bushels wheat, 20 bushels corn, 15 to 40 bushels buckwheat, 1 to 1-½ tons of hay.

All meadows are sown with timothy; little clover in this district.

Price of wheat, now November 1794, 7 s.-6, corn 4-6 to 6, hay 6 dollars a ton, but not easy to sell, every one having enough; moreover many cattle are raised.

There are the mills of three flour merchants within a radius of a mile. They send the flour to Baltimore—64 miles. The carting from here to there costs 1 dollar a barrel. The load is 12 barrels of 180 [lbs.), drawn by 5 horses, or 4 strong ones.

Great complaint of the farmers about the misconduct, thefts, etc., of the now free negroes.

November 9th, left Russel's Tavern, and after 10 miles of level and bad land, although cleared, partly plowed, and pasture, poor farms,—then the country rises, slightly, broken by wide and low hills, better cultivated. The soil is red gravel.

At Abbots Town, 15 miles, had dinner with Jones, at the Sign of the Indian Queen,—fair lodging.

Mr. Abbot [John ?] a farmer, ½ mile from here, started this place as a town or village. There are about 35 houses, the principal ones are inns. The inhabitants are all Germans, descendants of Lancaster farmers. There are 2 small German churches, one Presbyterian, the other Lutheran.

Mr. Abbot is dead and his will is such that his sons cannot sell lots until their children are of age. The location of the village is on the top of a low and very large hill. He divided the land into house-lots, 4 rods front by eleven rods deep; the first lots were sold for £5 besides a perpetual quit rent of 1 dollar. They now pay for the lots from £20 to £25, and 1 dollar quit-rent. The farms, generally of 200 acres, from £4 to £6 [per acre] and for choice and best land, as much as £10. The soil is mainly red gravel, rather good for wheat.

A cord of wood, hickory and oak, sells here for 5 shillings; a pound of butter for 10 pence.

An acre yields 12 to 16 bushels wheat, 20 bushels corn, 10 to 40 bushels buckwheat, 1 to 1-½ tons of hay. Price of wheat 9 s. a bushel. There are 2 mills in this district, which sent flour to Baltimore. Price of corn 4 s.-6, price of hay 6 dollars a ton. A strong and good wagon, well built, etc., costs £30.

From Abbot's Town, the country for 6 or 8 miles is a large plain, whose land is inferior and of red gravel; few farms, but a good many fields and pasture. Then the land rises gradually, larger and broader hills; the quality of the soil becomes better, generally "limestone land;" the hollows of the valleys are well watered pastures, the slopes of the high hills and the whole of the lower ones, are grain-fields, and the places where the soil is sterile are the woods, which are part of the farms. This variety of field and forest always makes a very pleasant landscape where the country is well populated, as in the case in counties where Germans have settled; on each 200 acre farm, half or a large third remains in forest.

At York Town, county-seat of York County, 15 miles, stopped at Springel's, [probably Baltzer Spangler's], at the sign of ———, very good inn. N.B. Coming from Russel's to York Town, ... to go through Mc Collister's Town, [now Hanover], a pleasant German Catholic settlement, good road—beautiful country. The Catholic church very fine and new, on the hill-top; everything, on all sides, is cultivated or in pasture.

November 10th, stayed at York Town. The first poor German settlers arrived in this county in 1729, and in 1741

Yorktown was begun by the Proprietors, the Penns, who laid out the land for a town, and built the court-house. The lots are 56 feet front, by 250 deep, subjected to a quit-rent of from 2 to 8 dollars a lot, according to location, but the inhabitants contest this right with the Penns.

The town is in the valley, on Codorus Creek, a little river always rich in water, permitting several mills of all kinds in the neighborhood; the common is unusually spacious; otherwise the place is not pleasant, although the streets are wide and well laid out, not paved nor lighted, but a sidewalk in front of the new houses. The court-house, placed in the middle of the square, ridiculously shuts off the view of the whole of the 2 main streets.

As in every inland town of Pennsylvania, there is a quantity of taverns and inns, where the people come to talk and drink, morning and evening, as in the cafes of European cities. Also many stores where, in each one, everything is sold at retail. You find everything necessary in utensils, clothing, and furniture, for the lower class, but nothing dainty or choice.

A new building for the offices and records, rather elegantly built, next to the court-house, which is very much disparaged by it. There may be about 400 houses, about 60 of which are of brick and newly built, the rest of "logs and mortar."

Mr. James Smith, Esq., [the "Signer"], and the families of Mr. Hartley, [Col. Thomas], a lawyer and congressman, Mr. Harris, [probably William], and General Miller, [Henry], have been most obliging, and are the best society here. Mrs. Hall, Mr. Hartley's daughter, is a beautiful woman. Two-thirds of the inhabitants are Germans and mechanics. There are 9 lawyers.

About the prices of provisions, land, lots, etc., see one of the printed papers filled in for York Town. Mr. John Forsyth, the district surveyor, can give information about the price of land, etc.

The part of Pennsylvania now forming York County was still inhabited by Indians in 1750. The first German settlers came in 1728 and settled among them, and the Indians peaceably let them cultivate the part they liked. The present land-owners, farmers, are the children of these first settlers, who, after having served 3 or 4 years for the expenses of the trip from Europe to America, settled on the land, and gradually thrived; several of their children, being now from 50 to 60 years old, own farms of 4, 5 and 800 acres.

November 11th, left Yorktown, by a good road and through a very well cultivated country; this and Mc Collister's districts are the best land in the county: it is the center; the two sides are mountainous and inferior lands.

At Wright's Ferry, 11 miles; it is here that you cross the Susquehanna, on good pontoons. Here the river is a mile and a quarter wide, swift current, wild and high shores. Paid for 4 people, the coach, and 5 horses, 9 s., or 1 dollar, 1 s., 6 p.

F. A. MICHAUX.

We shall content ourselves with closing our travellers' accounts of York county, with that of F. A. Michaux, the botanist and naturalist, of Paris, undertaken in the year 1802. His impressions are recorded in his *Travels to the West of the Alleghany Mountains*, etc., published in London (1805). Let us greet our traveller, this time a Frenchman, at Lancaster, and accompany him from there to the time he leaves York county, for he tells us of botany, industry, how the houses are built, and "Uncle Sam" calls a group of seven or eight houses, "a town."

On the 27th of June I set out from Lancaster for Shippensburgh. There were only four of us in the stage, which was fitted up to hold twelve passengers. Columbia, situated upon the Susquehannah, is the first town that we arrived at; it is composed of about fifty houses, scattered here and there, and almost all built with wood; at this place ends the turnpike road.

It is not useless to observe here, that in the United States they give often the name of town to a group of seven or eight houses, and that the mode of constructing them is not the same everywhere. At Philadelphia the houses are built with brick. In the other towns and country places that surround them, the half, and even frequently the whole, is built with wood; but at places within seventy or eighty miles of the sea, in the central and southern states, and again more particularly in those situated to the Westward of the Alleghany Mounains, one third of the inhabitants reside in "log houses." These dwellings are made with the trunks of trees, from twenty to thirty feet in length, about five inches diameter, placed one upon another, and kept up by notches cut at their extremities. The roof is formed with pieces of similar length to those that compose the body of the house, but not quite so thick, and gradually sloped on each side. Two doors, which often supply the place of windows, are made by sawing away a part of the trunks that form the body of the house; the chimney, always placed at one of the extremities, is likewise made with the trunks of trees of a suitable length; the back of the chimney is made of clay, about six inches thick, which separates the fire from the wooden walls. Notwithstanding this want of precaution, fires very seldom happen in the country places. The space between these trunks of trees is filled up with clay, but so very carelessly, that the light may be seen through in every part; in consequence of which these huts are exceedingly cold in winter, notwithstanding the amazing quantity of wood that is burnt. The doors move upon wooden hinges, and the greater part of them have no locks. In the night time they only push them to, or fasten them with a wooden peg. Four or five days are sufficient for two men to finish one of these houses, in which not a nail is used. Two great beds receive the whole family. It frequently happens that in summer the children sleep upon the ground, in a kind of rug. The floor is raised from one to two feet above the surface of the ground, and boarded. They generally make use of feather beds, or feathers alone, and not mattresses. Sheep being very scarce, the wool is very dear; at the same time they reserve it to make stockings. The clothes belonging to the family are hung up round the room, or suspended upon a long pole.

At Columbia the Susquehannah is nearly a quarter of a mile in breadth. [Evidently the English compositors in 1805 thought that the Susquehannah could not be a mile and a quarter in width, so they "cut it down" in size to something in the nature of the rivers in England.—Ed.] We crossed it in a ferry boat. At that time it had so little water in it, that we could easily see the bottom. The banks of this river were formed by lofty and majestic hills, and the bosom of it is strewed with little islands, which seem to divide it into several streams. Some of them do not extend above five or six acres at most, and still they are as lofty as the surrounding hills. Their irregularity, and the singular forms that they present, render this situation picturesque and truly remarkable, more especially at that season of the year, when the trees were in full vegetation.

About a mile from Susquehannah I observed an "annona triloba," the fruit of which is tolerably good, although insipid. When arrived at maturity it is nearly the size of a common egg. According to the testimony of Mr. Muhlenberg [of Lancaster], this shrub grows in the environs of Philadelphia.

About twelve miles from Columbia [Susquehannah] is a little town called York, the houses of which are not so straggling as many others, and are principally built with brick. The inhabitants are computed to be upward of eighteen hundred, most of them of German origin, and none speak English. About six miles from York we passed through Dover, composed of twenty or thirty log-houses, erected here and there. The stage stopped at the house of one M'Logan, who keeps a miserable inn fifteen miles from York. That day we travelled only thirty or forty miles.

Inns are very numerous in the United States, and especially in the little towns; yet almost everywhere, except in the principal towns, they are very bad, notwithstanding rum, brandy, and whiskey (they give the name of whiskey, in the United States, to a sort of brandy made with rye), are in plenty. In fact, in houses of the above description all kinds of spirits are considered the most material, as they generally meet with great consumption. Travellers wait in common till the family go to meals. At breakfast they make use of very indifferent tea, and coffee still worse, with small slices of ham fried in the stove, to which they sometimes add eggs and a broiled chicken. At dinner they give a piece of salt beef and roasted fowls, and rum and water as a beverage. In the evening, coffee, tea, and ham. There are always several beds in the rooms where you sleep: seldom do you meet with clean sheets. Fortunate is the traveller who arrives on the day they happen to be changed; although an American would be quite indifferent about it.

Early on the 28th of June we reached Carlisle, situated about fifty-four miles from Lancaster. The town consists of about two hundred houses, a few of them built with brick, but by far the greatest part with wood. Upon the whole it has a respectable appearance, from a considerable number of large shops and warehouses. These receptacles are supplied from the interior parts of the country with large quantities of jewellery, mercery, spices, &c. The persons who keep those shops purchase and also barter with the country people for the produce of their farms, which they afterwards send off to the sea-port towns for exportation.

From M'Logan's inn to Carlisle the country is barren and mountainous, in consequence of which the houses are not so numerous on the road, being at a distance of two or three miles from each other; and out of the main road they are still more straggling. * * *

THE COLONIAL COURT HOUSE.

Having made mention of the Colonial Court House, in the "Introduction," it appears fitting to supply the reader with some additional facts concerning this ancient seat of justice and law-making in momentous times. The account handed to us by a well-known York countian, follows:

Before 1849 the people of York county, the people living west of the Susquehanna river, were compelled to go to Lancaster to attend to their legal business. In 1849 York county was erected and of course it was immediately necessary to have a court house and court officers for the convenience of the county. The York county commissioners proceeded to erect the court house in Center Square.

The court house was fifty-five feet long and forty-five feet wide. It was two stories high, having but two gables, one on the east and one on the west side. The principal entrance was on the south, facing South George Street, and another entrance was on the north, facing North George Street. The first floor was devoted to the sessions of Court and the second floor was one large room reached by stairs from the east side of the court room. It was mostly on the second floor that the Continental Congress had their sessions. It became necessary to secure additional room for court records and in 1793, a two-story brick building was erected in Centre Square immediately east of the court house, just far enough away to permit a driveway. This building was known as the State House, although no one knows why, as it was paid for by the County of York. In those days all county officers were state appointments and it may have been that that gave it the name of State House. The rapid growth of the county demanded more space for court records and in 1815 the county commissioners added a gable on the north, a gable on the south and raised the bell tower. The pictures usually shown, as in Horace Bonham's picture of the adjournment of Continental Congress at the news of Burgoyne's surrender, show the building as it was finished in 1815, and while it is strictly true to say that it was the same building, the exterior did not present the same appearance as it did in 1777, when the Continental Congress met here.

In 1841 both the Court House and the State House were torn down. Unfortunately nothing much of this building was preserved. However, one of the doorways has been preserved and is in the Memorial Hall of the York Collegiate Institute, where it is always to be seen, being open each day between the hours of 9 and 4. The people of York and visitors, too, should be shown this old doorway through which so many men of world-wide reputation passed.

INDEX.

Biographical Sketches

Appendix

BIBLIOGRAPHY

For the student of history whose needs cannot ordinarily be gratified with one or two, or even half a dozen books on the history of York county, there is presented herewith a list of books comprising a fairly complete bibliography of primary, local, and miscellaneous books dealing with York county.

Compiled from the State Library, York County Historical Society, Pennsylvania German Society's Proceedings, and the Editor's personal collection.

Albright, Rev. S. C.—First Moravian Church. Story of the Moravian Congregation at York, Pa. York 1927. 12mo

Anstadt, Rev. P.—Life and Times of Rev. S. S. Schmucker.

Aurand, A. Monroe, Jr.—An Account of the 'Witch' Murder Trial, York, Pa., 1929. Harrisburg, 1929. 8vo

Aurand, A. Monroe, Jr.—The 'Pow Wow' Book. Harrisburg 1929. 8vo

Bacon, J. Barnitz—Mason & Dixon's Line.

Balch, Thos.—Letters and Papers, etc. Phila. 1855.

Baptisms in Bleymeyer Church, Hopewell Twp., York county. Revs. George Bager and William Otterbein, comps. (See Penna. German Soc. Proc., Vol. 8)

Bittinger, Lucy Forney.—The Forney Family of Hanover, Pa.; 1690-1893. Pittsburgh 1893. 4to

Carter, W. C., (and A. J. Glossbrenner.)—History of York County from its Erection to the Present Time [1834]. York 1834. 16mo

Same—reprinted, enlarged. The Aurand Press, Harrisburg, Pa., 1930. 8vo.

Cassel, Daniel K.—History of the Mennonites. Phila. 1888

Cazenove Journal: 1794. Translated from the French. Haverford 1922. 8vo

Church Records of York and York county.

Colonial Records (Minutes of Provincial Council) 16 vols.

Cumberland and Adams Counties; History of. Chicago 1887.

Day, Sherman.—Historical Collections of the State of Penna. Phila. 1843. 8vo

Egle, William Henry.—Notes and Queries; Historical and Genealogical. (Reprint series, Harrisburg 1895-1900.) 12 vols. 4to

Egle, William Henry.—An Illustrated History of the Commonwealth of Penna. Harrisburg 1876, etc. 8vo
Fisher, H. L., Esq.—Kurzweil un' Zeitfortreib, ruhrende un' launige Gedichte in Pennsylvania-Deutscher Mundart. York, Pa., 1896. 1882.
Fisher, H. L.—Olden Times; or Penna. Rural Life, some Fifty Years Ago; and other poems. York 1888. Tall 8vo
Fisher, H. L.—'S Alt Marik Haus Mittes in d'r Schtadt, un Die Alte Zeite; en Centennial Poem in Pennsylfawnish Deutsch; in Zwe Dhel. York 1879 8vo
Flickinger Families in the U. S. of A. Rev. Robert Elliott Flickinger, et al. Des Moines 1927. Tall 8vo
Fogel, Ed. M.—Beliefs and Superstitions of the Penna.-Germans. Phila. 1915. 8vo
Gamble, A. D.—St. Patrick's Parish. Notes on the history of Catholics in York county, etc. York 1927. 8vo
Gazetteer of Penna. Thomas F. Gordon. Phila. 1832
Gibbons, Phebe Earle.—'Pennsylvania Dutch' and other Essays. Phila. 1882. 12mo
Gibson, John; Editor.—History of York County, Pa., from the earliest period to the present time, divided into general, special, township and borough histories, with a biographical department appended. Chicago 1886. 4to
Hallesche Nachrichten.—The Planting of the Lutheran Chr. in America.
Hanover; Memorial Volume of the Sesqui-Centennial Services in St. Matthew's Evan. Lutheran Church; 1743-1893.
History of Penna. Robert Proud, Phila. 1797. 2 vols. 8vo
History of Pennsylvania. Thomas F. Gordon. 1829.
Jenkins, H. M.—Pennsylvania: Colonial and Federal. 3 vol.
Jordan, John C.—An Historical Citizen. Career of Phineas Davis, noted inventor. York 1904. 15 pp
Jordan, John C.—York in its Relation to the Revolution. (A lecture delivered before the York County Historical Society, May 21, 1903.)
Kerr, Albert Boardman.—The Long Crooked River. N. Y. '29
Kuhns, Oscar.—The German and Swiss Settlements of Colonial Pennsylvania. New York 1901. 12mo
Landmark History of the United Brethren Church, in Cumberland, Lancaster, York and Lebanon counties. Reading, 1911. 8vo
Life of Chief Justice Ellis Lewis; 1798-1871. Burton Alva Konkle. Phila. 1907. 8vo
Lutheran Quarterly; Church Review; Observer; etc.
Memorial Souvenir Commemorating the 150th Anniversary of York as the Capital of the U. S. of A., 1777-1778. Pub. by the Conservation Society of York. York 1927.
McClune, H. H.—Miscellanea. Addresses, etc. York, Pa. 12mo

McSherry, James.—History of Maryland. Baltimore 1849.
Mittelberger, Gottlieb.—Travels through Penna. in 1750. Phila. (Translated from the German.)
Myers, Albert Cook.—The Immigration of the Irish Quakers into Pennsylvania; 1682-1750. Swarthmore 1902. 8vo
Newspapers of the various cities and towns of Lancaster, York, Adams and Cumberland counties, as well as of Philadelphia (old and new.)
Original documents of all sorts and descriptions available in the following libraries, etc.: Historical Society of Penna., York County Historical Society, Historical Society of Maryland, Penna. State Library, Penna. Dept. of Internal Affairs.
Penn, William. Various works of.
Penna.: Heads of Families and Census for 1790.
Pennsylvania Archives (Seven series) 104 volumes, plus.
Pennsylvania German Magazine; Quarterly and Monthly—(1900-1914.)
Pennsylvania German Society Proceedings. Various numbers.
Pennsylvania Magazine of Biography and History.
Prowell, George R.—Brief History of York County. York 1906. 8vo
Prowell, George R.—Continental Congress at York, Pa., and York County in the Revolution. 1914.
Prowell, George R.—Frederick Valentine Melsheimer; a Pioneer Entomologist and a noted Clergyman and Author. (Paper read before the Hist. Soc. of York Co., April 8, 1897.)
Prowell, George R.—History of York County, Pa.; Historical and Biographical. Chicago 1907. 2 vols. 4to
Reiley, John T.—Conewago: A collection of Catholic Local History. Martinsburg, W. Va., 1885.
Report of the Secretary of Internal Affairs; Boundaries. Harrisburg 1887. 8vo. Text and section of maps.
Report on the Re-Survey of the Maryland-Pennsylvania Boundary; part of the Mason & Dixon Line. Harrisburg 1909. 8vo (Has an extensive bibliography and primary source material list.)
Roe, F. B.—Atlas of the City of York. Phila. 1903. Folio.
Rupp, I. Daniel.—30,000 Names of Immigrants. Phila.
Rupp, I. Daniel.—Geographical Catechism of Penna., and the Western States. Harrisburg 1836. 12mo
Rupp, I. Daniel, comp.—History of Lancaster and York Counties; to which is prefixed a brief sketch of the early history of Penna., from A. D. 1681 to the year 1710. Lancaster 1845. 8vo (Two separate histories bound in one volume; two title pages; also published singly, though scarce for York County alone.)

St. Matthew's Lutheran Church, York; Baron Stiegel Pilgrim Meeting; Sunday, Aug. 31, 1913.
Sachse, Julius Friedrich.—German Pietists; German Sectarians (2 vols.); The Fatherland; etc. etc.
Scharf, J. Thomas.—History of Baltimore. Phila. 1881. 4to
Schmauk, Theodore E.—An Account of the Manners of the German Inhabitants of Penna., by Benj. Rush;—A History of the Lutheran Church in Penna. (In Penna. German Soc. Proc.)
Small, Samuel, Jr.—Genealogical records of George Small, Philip Albright, Johann Dan. Dunckel, Wm. Gettes Latimer, Thomas Bartow, John Reid, Daniel Benezet, Jean Crommelin, Joel Richardson. Phila. 1905. 4to
Smith, M. O.—History of York County (Hanover "Herald," 9 January to 25 December, 1875.)
Spangler, Edward Webster.—The Annals of the Families of Caspar, Henry, Baltzer, and George Spengler, who settled in York county respectively in 1729, 1732, 1732 and 1751. York 1896. 4to
Spencer, Mrs. Lilian White.—The York Pageant, etc. York 1927.
Stapleton, Rev. A.—Flashlights of Evangelical History.
Stapleton, Rev. A.—Memorials to the Huguenots in America. Carlisle, 1901. 8vo
Stuck, Edward; comp.—Historical Sketch and Account of the Centennial Celebration at York, Pa., July 4, 1876. York 1876. 8vo
Swank, James M.—Progressive Pennsylvania. Phila. 1908 8vo
Wanner, Atreus.—Relics of an Indian Hunting Ground, in York County, Pa. (In Smithsonian Institution; Annual Report 1892; Washington 1893 (p. 555-570). 8vo
Wayland, John Walter.—The German Element of the Shenandoah Valley of Virginia. Charlottesville, Va. 1907. 8vo
Weekly Register of Penna. Hazard. 1828-1836 (16 vols.)
Wentz, Abdel Ross.—The Beginnings of the German Element in York County, Pa. Lancaster 1916 (Also in Penna.-German Soc. Proc., vol. 24.)
Weygandt, Cornelius.—The Red Hills. Phila. 1930. 8vo
Wiley, Samuel T.; editor.—Biographical and Portrait Cyclopedia of the 19th [now 20th] Congressional District, of Penna. Pub. 1897. 4to
William Penn Senior High school "Tatler."
York and Lancaster counties—Court records, deeds, wills, &c.
York—Directories. Various.
York—Sons of Temperance.
York—City Council; Manual. Various.
York; Art Work of. Chicago 1893. Folio.
York County Almanac, 1876.

York and York County; 1749-1899. A Sesqui-Centennial Momento. By Charles A. Hawkins and Houston E. Landis. York, Pa., 1901. 16mo

York County; Atlas of. Beach Nichols. Phila. 1876. Illus. in colors. Folio.

York's Centenary Memorial; comprising a detailed description of the Centennial—Sept. 23-24, 1887. Compiled by the Centennial Committee. York 1887. 8vo

CPSIA information can be obtained
at www.ICGtesting.com
Printed in the USA
BVHW081504310321
603806BV00002B/187

9 781596 411791